Grid and Cloud Computing

S.K.B. Rathika

S.K.B. Sangeetha

K. Aravindhan

Published by

Grid and Cloud Computing

ISBN 978-93-87862-06-7

Authors

S.K.B. Rathika

S.K.B. Sangeetha

K. Aravindhan

Bonfring

309, 2nd Floor,

5th Street Extension, Gandhipuram, Coimbatore-641 012.

Tamilnadu, India.

E-mail: info@bonfring.org

Website: www.bonfring.org

Phone: 0422 4213231

About the Authors

S.K.B. Rathika completed her master degree in Computer Science and Engineering. Currently she holds a position of Assistant Professor in the Department of Computer Science & Engineering, SASURIE Academy of Engineering, Coimbatore. She received her B.E degree in Computer Science and Engineering from Anna University, Chennai in 2010 and the M.E degree in Computer Science and Engineering from Anna University, Chennai in 2012.She has three years of teaching experience. She has also published 16 International and National conferences. Her area of interest is computer networks, mobile computing.

S.K.B. Sangeetha is currently working as an Senior assistant professor in Rajalakshmi Engineering College, Chennai. She is pursuing her PhD from Anna University, Chennai. She accomplished her Master's Degree from Dr.Mahalingam College of Engineering and Technology, Coimbatore and the Bachelor's Degree from Christian College of Engineering and Technology, Dindigul, both graduated from anna university.

She has 10 years of Teaching and Research experience which has helped her to gain immense knowledge in myriad fields of Computer Science and Engineering. She is a life member of Indian Society for Technical Education, The Indian Institute of Engineers. Apart from being an educator, She also encompasses herself in many co-curricular activities and take up responsibilities only to complete them with complete appreciation. She has written three books for engineering curriculam.

She has organized and attended many seminars, faculty development programs, workshops and conferences of both National and International level. She has published around 41 research papers in several international and national forums which include various ISI, Scopus, IEEE indexed international conferences as well. She is also being an editor and reviewer for some international journals as well.

K. Aravindhan B.E., M.E., (Ph.D.,) was born in Coimbatore, Tamil Nadu and India. He currently was pursuing his Ph.D., in Information and Communication Engineering in the area of Vehicular Ad Hoc Networks from St. Peter's Institute of Higher Education and Research, Chennai. And he completed M.E., in Computer Science and Engineering from Kumaraguru College of Technology, Coimbatore and B.E., in Computer Science and Engineering from Sri Ramakrishna Institute Of Technology, Coimbatore. He is having 10 years of teaching experience in an engineering colleges and currently working as Assistant Professor in the Department of Computer Science and Engineering at SNS College of Engineering, Affiliated to Anna University, Chennai. He is a Life Member of Indian Society for Technical Education (ISTE), Life Member of Society for Engineering Education Enrichment (SEEE) and Life Member in Society for Professional Engineers (SPE) and Member in International Association of Engineers (IAENG). His research interest includes Internet of Things (IoT) and Vehicular Ad Hoc Networks. For his credentials he published more than 15 papers in refereed international journals which were indexed in Scopus and Google Scholar and 20 papers in national and international conferences. He received "Innovative Professional Award" from Society of Professional Engineers (SPE) India, Engineering Today, Chennai and "Dr. A.P.J Abdul Kalam Award for Innovative Research" from Society for Engineering Education Enrichment (SEEE), India.

CS6703   GRID AND CLOUD COMPUTING   L T P C

Objectives

The Student Should Be Made To:

1. Understand how Grid computing helps in solving large scale scientific problems.
2. Gain knowledge on the concept of virtualization that is fundamental to cloud computing.
3. Learn how to program the grid and the cloud.
4. Understand the security issues in the grid and the cloud environment.

Unit I Introduction   9

Evolution of Distributed computing: Scalable computing over the Internet –Technologies for network based systems–clusters of cooperative computers-Grid computing Infrastructures–cloud computing-service oriented architecture–Introduction to Grid Architecture and standards–Elements of Grid–Overview of Grid Architecture.

Unit II Grid Services   9

Introduction to Open Grid Services Architecture (OGSA)–Motivation–Functionality Requirements – Practical & Detailed view of OGSA/OGSI – Data intensive grid service models – OGSA services.

Unit III Virtualization   9

Cloud deployment models: public, private, hybrid, community–Categories of cloud computing: Everything as a service: Infrastructure, platform, software-Pros and Cons of cloud computing – Implementation levels of virtualization–virtualization structure–virtualization of CPU, Memory and I/O devices–virtual clusters and Resource Management–Virtualization for data center automation.

Unit IV Programming Model   9

Open source grid middleware packages–Globus Toolkit (GT4) Architecture, Configuration–Usage of Globus–Main components and Programming model-Introduction to Hadoop Framework-Mapreduce, Input splitting, map and reduce functions, specifying input and output parameters, configuring and running a job–Design of Hadoop file system, HDFS concepts, command line and java interface, dataflow of File read & File write.

Unit V Security 9

Trust models for Grid security environment–Authentication and Authorization methods–Grid security infrastructure–Cloud Infrastructure security: network, host and application level–aspects of data security, provider data and its security, Identity and access management architecture, IAM practices in the cloud, SaaS, PaaS, IaaS availability in the cloud, Key privacy issues in the cloud.

Total: 45 Periods

Outcomes

At the End of the Course, the Student Should Be Able To:

- Apply grid computing techniques to solve large scale scientific problems.
- Apply the concept of virtualization.
- Use the grid and cloud tool kits.
- Apply the security models in the grid and the cloud environment.

Text Book

1. Kai Hwang, Geoffery C. Fox and Jack J. Dongarra, "Distributed and Cloud Computing: Clusters, Grids, Clouds and the Future of Internet", First Edition, Morgan Kaufman Publisher, an Imprint of Elsevier, 2012.

References

1. Jason Venner, "Pro Hadoop- Build Scalable, Distributed Applications in the Cloud", A Press, 2009.
2. Tom White, "Hadoop the Definitive Guide", First Edition. O'Reilly, 2009.
3. Bart Jacob (Editor), "Introduction to Grid Computing", IBM Red Books, Vervante, 2005.
4. Ian Foster, Carl Kesselman, "The Grid: Blueprint for a New Computing Infrastructure", 2nd Edition.
5. Morgan Kaufmann.
6. Frederic Magoules and Jie Pan, "Introduction to Grid Computing" CRC Press, 2009.
7. Daniel Minoli, "A Networking Approach to Grid Computing", John Wiley Publication, 2005.
8. Barry Wilkinson, "Grid Computing: Techniques and Applications", Chapman and Hall, CRC, Taylor and Francis Group, 2010.

<table>
<tr><th>UNIT</th><th>CONTENTS</th><th>PAGE NO</th></tr>
</table>

UNIT I

Introduction

1.1. Scalable Computing Over the Internet

Over the past 60 years, computing technology has undergone a series of platform and environment changes. In this section, we assess evolutionary changes in machine architecture, operating system platform, network connectivity, and application workload. Instead of using a centralized computer to solve computational problems, a parallel and distributed computing system uses multiple computers to solve large-scale problems over the Internet. Thus, distributed computing becomes data-intensive and network-centric. This section identifies the applications of modern computer systems that practice parallel and distributed computing. These large-scale Internet applications have significantly enhanced the quality of life and information services in society today.

1.2. The Age of Internet Computing

Billions of people use the Internet every day. As a result, supercomputer sites and large data centers must provide high-performance computing services to huge numbers of Internet users concurrently. Because of this high demand, the Linpack Benchmark for high-performance computing (HPC) applications is no longer optimal for measuring system performance. The emergence of computing clouds instead demands high-throughput computing (HTC) systems built with parallel and distributed computing technologies . We have to upgrade data centers using fast servers, storage systems, and high-bandwidth networks. The purpose is to advance network-based computing and web services with the emerging new technologies.

1.2.1. The Platform Evolution

Computer technology has gone through five generations of development, with each generation lasting from 10 to 20 years. Successive generations are overlapped in about 10 years. For instance, from 1950 to 1970, a handful of mainframes, including the IBM 360 and CDC 6400, were built to satisfy the demands of large businesses and government organizations. From 1960 to 1980, lower-cost minicomputers such as the DEC PDP 11 and VAX Series became popular among small businesses and on college campuses. From 1970 to 1990, we saw widespread use of personal computers built with VLSI microprocessors. From 1980 to

2000, massive numbers of portable computers and pervasive devices appeared in both wired and wireless applications.

Since 1990, the use of both HPC and HTC systems hidden in clusters, grids, or Internet clouds has proliferated. These systems are employed by both consumers and high-end web-scale computing and information service. The general computing trend is to leverage shared web resources and massive amounts of data over the Internet. The evolution of HPC and HTC systems. On the HPC side, supercomputers (massively parallel processors or MPPs) are gradually replaced by clusters of cooperative computers out of a desire to share computing resources. The cluster is often a collection of homogeneous compute nodes that are physically connected in close range to one another.

On the HTC side, peer-to-peer (P2P) networks are formed for distributed file sharing and content delivery applications. A P2P system is built over many client machines. Peer machines are globally distributed in nature. P2P, cloud computing, and web service platforms are more focused on HTC applications than on HPC applications. Clustering and P2P technologies lead to the development of computational grids or data grids.

1.2.2. High-Performance Computing

For many years, HPC systems emphasize the raw speed performance. The speed of HPC systems has increased from Gflops in the early 1990s to now Pflops in 2010. This improvement was driven mainly by the demands from scientific, engineering, and manufacturing communities. For example, the Top 500 most powerful computer systems in the world are measured by floating-point speed in Linpack benchmark results. However, the number of supercomputer users is limited to less than 10% of all computer users. Today, the majority of computer users are using desktop computers or large servers when they conduct Internet searches and market-driven computing tasks.

1.2.3. High-Throughput Computing

The development of market-oriented high-end computing systems is undergoing a strategic change from an HPC paradigm to an HTC paradigm. This HTC paradigm pays more attention to high-flux computing. The main application for high-flux computing is in Internet searches and web services by millions or more users simultaneously. The performance goal thus shifts to measure high throughput or the number of tasks completed per unit of time. HTC technology needs to not only improve in terms of batch processing speed, but also address the acute problems of cost, energy savings, security, and reliability at many data and enterprise computing centers.

1.2.4. *Three New Computing Paradigms*

Advances in virtualization make it possible to see the growth of Internet clouds as a new computing paradigm. The maturity of radio-frequency identification (RFID), Global Positioning System (GPS), and sensor technologies has triggered the development of the Internet of Things (IoT). These new paradigms are only briefly introduced here. When the Internet was introduced in 1969, Leonard Klienrock of UCLA declared: —As of now, computer networks are still in their infancy, but as they grow up and become sophisticated, we will probably see the spread of computer utilities, which like present electric and telephone utilities, will service individual homes and offices across the country.‖ Many people have redefined the term —computer‖ since that time. In 1984, John Gage of Sun Microsystems created the slogan, —The network is the computer.‖ In 2008, David Patterson of UC Berkeley said, —The data center is the computer. There are dramatic differences between developing software for millions to use as a service versus distributing software to run on their PCs.‖ Recently, Rajkumar Buyya of Melbourne University simply said: —The cloud is the computer.‖

In fact, the differences among clusters, grids, P2P systems, and clouds may blur in the future. Some people view clouds as grids or clusters with modest changes through virtualization. Others feel the changes could be major, since clouds are anticipated to process huge data sets generated by the traditional Internet, social networks, and the future IoT. In subsequent chapters, the distinctions and dependencies among all distributed and cloud systems models will become clearer and more transparent.

1.2.5. *Computing Paradigm Distinctions*

The high-technology community has argued for many years about the precise definitions of centralized computing, parallel computing, distributed computing, and cloud computing. In general, distributed computing is the opposite of centralized computing. The field of parallel computing overlaps with distributed computing to a great extent, and cloud computing overlaps with distributed, centralized, and parallel computing.

Centralized computing This is a computing paradigm by which all computer resources are centralized in one physical system. All resources (processors, memory, and storage) are fully shared and tightly coupled within one integrated OS. Many data centers and supercomputers are centralized systems, but they are used in parallel, distributed, and cloud computing applications.

Parallel computing In parallel computing, all processors are either tightly coupled with centralized shared memory or loosely coupled with distributed memory. Some authors refer to this discipline as parallel processing. Inter processor communication is accomplished through shared memory or via message passing. A computer system capable of parallel computing is commonly known as a parallel computer. Programs running in a parallel computer are called parallel programs. The process of writing parallel programs is often referred to as parallel programming.

Distributed computing this is a field of computer science/engineering that studies distributed systems. A distributed system consists of multiple autonomous computers, each having its own private memory, communicating through a computer network. Information exchange in a distributed system is accomplished through message passing. A computer program that runs in a distributed system is known as a distributed program. The process of writing distributed programs is referred to as distributed programming.

Cloud computing An Internet cloud of resources can be either a centralized or a distributed computing system. The cloud applies parallel or distributed computing, or both. Clouds can be built with physical or virtualized resources over large data centers that are centralized or distributed. Some authors consider cloud computing to be a form of utility computing or service computing.

As an alternative to the preceding terms, some in the high-tech community prefer the term concurrent computing or concurrent programming. These terms typically refer to the union of parallel computing and distributing computing, although biased practitioners may interpret them differently. Ubiquitous computing refers to computing with pervasive devices at any place and time using wired or wireless communication. The Internet of Things (IoT) is a networked connection of everyday objects including computers, sensors, humans, etc. The IoT is supported by Internet clouds to achieve ubiquitous computing with any object at any place and time. Finally, the term Internet computing is even broader and covers all computing paradigms over the Internet.

1.2.6. *Distributed System Families*

Since the mid-1990s, technologies for building P2P networks and networks of clusters have been consolidated into many national projects designed to establish wide area computing infrastructures, known as computational grids or data grids. Recently, we have witnessed a surge in interest in exploring Internet cloud resources for data-intensive applications. Internet clouds are the result of moving desktop computing to service-oriented computing using server clusters and huge databases at data centers. Grids and clouds are disparity systems that place great emphasis on resource sharing in hardware, software, and data sets.

Design theory, enabling technologies, and case studies of these massively distributed systems are also covered in this book. Massively distributed systems are intended to exploit a high degree of parallelism or concurrency among many machines. In October 2010, the highest performing cluster machine was built in China with 86016 CPU processor cores and 3,211,264 GPU cores in a Tianhe-1A system. The largest computational grid connects up to hundreds of server clusters. A typical P2P network may involve millions of client machines working simultaneously. Experimental cloud computing clusters have been built with thousands of processing nodes. In the future, both HPC and HTC systems will demand multi core or many-core processors that can handle large numbers of computing threads per core. Both HPC and HTC systems emphasize parallelism and distributed computing. Future HPC and HTC systems must be able to satisfy this huge demand in computing power in terms of throughput, efficiency, scalability, and reliability. The system efficiency is decided by speed, programming, and energy factors (i.e., throughput per watt of energy consumed).

Meeting these goals requires to yield the following design objectives:

1. Efficiency measures the utilization rate of resources in an execution model by exploiting massive parallelism in HPC. For HTC, efficiency is more closely related to job throughput, data access, storage, and power efficiency.

2. Dependability measures the reliability and self-management from the chip to the system and application levels. The purpose is to provide high-throughput service with Quality of Service (QoS) assurance, even under failure conditions.

3. Adaptation in the programming model measures the ability to support billions of job requests over massive data sets and virtualized cloud resources under various workload and service models.

4. Flexibility in application deployment measures the ability of distributed systems to run well in both HPC (science and engineering) and HTC (business) applications.

1.3.   Scalable Computing Trends and New Paradigms

Several predictable trends in technology are known to drive computing applications. In fact, designers and programmers want to predict the technological capabilities of future systems. For instance, Jim Gray's paper, ―Rules of Thumb in Data Engineering,‖ is an excellent example of how technology affects applications and vice versa. In addition, Moore's law indicates that processor speed doubles every 18 months. Although Moore's law has been proven valid over the last 30 years, it is difficult to say whether it will continue to be true in the future.

Gilder's law indicates that network bandwidth has doubled each year in the past. Will that trend continue in the future? The tremendous price/performance ratio of commodity hardware was driven by the desktop, notebook, and tablet computing markets. This has also driven the adoption and use of commodity technologies in large-scale computing.

For now, it's important to understand how distributed systems emphasize both resource distribution and concurrency or high degree of parallelism (DoP). Let's review the degrees of parallelism before we discuss the special requirements for distributed computing.

1.3.1. Degrees of Parallelism

Fifty years ago, when hardware was bulky and expensive, most computers were designed in a bit-serial fashion. In this scenario, bit-level parallelism (BLP) converts bit-serial processing to word-level processing gradually. Over the years, users graduated from 4-bit microprocessors to 8-, 16-, 32-, and 64-bit CPUs. This led us to the next wave of improvement, known as instruction-level parallelism (ILP), in which the processor executes multiple instructions simultaneously rather than only one instruction at a time. For the past 30 years, we have practiced ILP through pipelining, superscalar computing, VLIW (very long instruction word) architectures, and multithreading. ILP requires branch prediction, dynamic scheduling, speculation, and compiler support to work efficiently.

Data-level parallelism (DLP) was made popular through SIMD (single instruction, multiple data) and vector machines using vector or array types of instructions. DLP requires even more hardware support and compiler assistance to work properly. Ever since the introduction of multicore processors and chip multiprocessors (CMPs), we have been exploring task-level parallelism (TLP). A modern processor explores all of the aforementioned parallelism types. In fact, BLP, ILP, and DLP are well supported by advances in hardware and compilers. However, TLP is far from being very successful due to difficulty in programming and compilation of code for efficient execution on multicore CMPs. As we move from parallel processing to distributed processing, we will see an increase in computing granularity to job-level parallelism (JLP). It is fair to say that coarse-grain parallelism is built on top of fine-grain parallelism.

1.3.2. Innovative Applications

Both HPC and HTC systems desire transparency in many application aspects. For example, data access, resource allocation, process location, concurrency in execution, job replication, and failure recovery should be made transparent to both users and system management. It highlights a few key applications that have driven the development of parallel and distributed systems over the years.

These applications spread across many important domains in science, engineering, business, education, health care, traffic control, Internet and web services, military, and government applications.

Applications of High-Performance and High-Throughput Systems Almost all applications demand computing economics, web-scale data collection, system reliability, and scalable performance. For example, distributed transaction processing is often practiced in the banking and finance industry. Transactions represent 90 percent of the existing market for reliable banking systems. Users must deal with multiple database servers in distributed transactions. Maintaining the consistency of replicated transaction records is crucial in real-time banking services. Other complications include lack of software support, network saturation, and security threats in these applications.

1.3.3. *The Trend toward Utility Computing*

It identifies major computing paradigms to facilitate the study of distributed systems and their applications. These paradigms share some common characteristics. First, they are all ubiquitous in daily life. Reliability and scalability are two major design objectives in these computing models. Second, they are aimed at autonomic operations that can be self-organized to support dynamic discovery. Finally, these paradigms are composable with QoS and SLAs (service-level agreements). These paradigms and their attributes realize the computer utility vision.

Utility computing focuses on a business model in which customers receive computing resources from a paid service provider. All grid/cloud platforms are regarded as utility service providers. However, cloud computing offers a broader concept than utility computing. Distributed cloud applications run on any available servers in some edge networks. Major technological challenges include all aspects of computer science and engineering. For example, users demand new network-efficient processors, scalable memory and storage schemes, distributed OSes, middleware for machine virtualization, new programming models, effective resource management, and application program development. These hardware and software supports are necessary to build distributed systems that explore massive parallelism at all processing levels.

1.3.4. *The Hype Cycle of New Technologies*

Any new and emerging computing and information technology may go through a hype cycle. This cycle shows the expectations for the technology at five different stages. The expectations rise sharply from the trigger period to a high peak of inflated expectations.

Through a short period of disillusionment, the expectation may drop to a valley and then increase steadily over a long enlightenment period to a plateau of productivity. The number of years for an emerging technology to reach a certain stage is marked by special symbols. The hollow circles indicate technologies that will reach mainstream adoption in two years. The gray circles represent technologies that will reach mainstream adoption in two to five years. The solid circles represent those that require five to 10 years to reach mainstream adoption, and the triangles denote those that require more than 10 years. The crossed circles represent technologies that will become obsolete before they reach the plateau.

Hype Cycles are graphical representations of the relative maturity of technologies, IT methodologies and management disciplines. They are intended solely as a research tool, and not as a specific guide to action. Gartner disclaims all warranties, express or implied, with respect to this research, including any warranties of merchantability or fitness for a particular purpose.

This Hype Cycle graphic was published by Gartner, Inc. as part of a larger research note and should be evaluated in the context of the entire report.

1.4. The Internet of Things and Cyber-Physical Systems

In this section, we will discuss two Internet development trends: the Internet of Things and cyber-physical systems. These evolutionary trends emphasize the extension of the Internet to everyday objects. We will only cover the basics of these concepts here.

1.4.1. *The Internet of Things*

The traditional Internet connects machines to machines or web pages to web pages. The concept of the IoT was introduced in 1999 at MIT.

The IoT refers to the networked interconnection of everyday objects, tools, devices, or computers. One can view the IoT as a wireless network of sensors that interconnect all things in our daily life. These things can be large or small and they vary with respect to time and place. The idea is to tag every object using RFID or a related sensor or electronic technology such as GPS.

With the introduction of the IPv6 protocol, 2^{128} IP addresses are available to distinguish all the objects on Earth, including all computers and pervasive devices. The IoT researchers have estimated that every human being will be surrounded by 1,000 to 5,000 objects. The IoT needs to be designed to track 100 trillion static or moving objects simultaneously. The IoT demands universal addressability of all of the objects or things.

To reduce the complexity of identification, search, and storage, one can set the threshold to filter out fine-grain objects. The IoT obviously extends the Internet and is more heavily developed in Asia and European countries. In the IoT era, all objects and devices are instrumented, interconnected, and interacted with each other intelligently. This communication can be made between people and things or among the things themselves. Three communication patterns co-exist: namely H2H (human-to-human), H2T (human-to-thing), and T2T (thing-to-thing). Here things include machines such as PCs and mobile phones. The idea here is to connect things (including human and machine objects) at any time and any place intelligently with low cost. Any place connections include at the PC, indoor (away from PC), outdoors, and on the move. Any time connections include daytime, night, outdoors and indoors, and on the move as well.

The dynamic connections will grow exponentially into a new dynamic network of networks, called the Internet of Things (IoT). The IoT is still in its infancy stage of development.

Many prototype IoTs with restricted areas of coverage are under experimentation at the time of this writing. Cloud computing researchers expect to use the cloud and future Internet technologies to support fast, efficient, and intelligent interactions among humans, machines, and any objects on Earth. A smart Earth should have intelligent cities, clean water, efficient power, convenient transportation, good food supplies, responsible banks, fast telecommunications, green IT, better schools, good health care, abundant resources, and so on. This dream living environment may take some time to reach fruition at different parts of the world.

1.4.2. *Cyber-Physical Systems*

A cyber-physical system (CPS) is the result of interaction between computational processes and the physical world. A CPS integrates —cyber‖ (heterogeneous, asynchronous) with —physical‖ (concurrent and information-dense) objects. A CPS merges the —3C‖ technologies of computation, communication, and control into an intelligent closed feedback system between the physical world and the information world, a concept which is actively explored in the United States.

The IoT emphasizes various networking connections among physical objects, while the CPS emphasizes exploration of virtual reality (VR) applications in the physical world. We may transform how we interact with the physical world just like the Internet transformed how we interact with the virtual world.

1.5.   Technologies for Network-based Systems

With the concept of scalable computing under our belt, it's time to explore hardware, software, and network technologies for distributed computing system design and applications. In particular, we will focus on viable approaches to building distributed operating systems for handling massive parallelism in a distributed environment.

Multi Core CPUs and Multithreading Technologies

Consider the growth of component and network technologies over the past 30 years. They are crucial to the development of HPC and HTC systems. Processor speed is measured in millions of instructions per second (MIPS) and network bandwidth is measured in megabits per second (Mbps) or gigabits per second (Gbps). The unit GE refers to 1 Gbps Ethernet bandwidth.

Advances in CPU Processors

Today, advanced CPUs or microprocessor chips assume a multi core architecture with dual, quad, six, or more processing cores. These processors exploit parallelism at ILP and TLP levels. Processor speed growth is plotted in the upper curve across generations of microprocessors or CMPs. We see growth from 1 MIPS for the VAX 780 in 1978 to 1,800 MIPS for the Intel Pentium 4 in 2002, up to a 22,000 MIPS peak for the Sun Niagara 2 in 2008. As the figure shows, Moore's law has proven to be pretty accurate in this case. The clock rate for these processors increased from 10 MHz for the Intel 286 to 4GHz for the Pentium 4 in 30 years.

However, the clock rate reached its limit on CMOS-based chips due to power limitations.

At the time of this writing, very few CPU chips run with a clock rate exceeding 5 GHz.

In other words, clock rate will not continue to improve unless chip technology matures. This limitation is attributed primarily to excessive heat generation with high frequency or high voltages. The ILP is highly exploited in modern CPU processors. ILP mechanisms include multiple-issue superscalar architecture, dynamic branch prediction, and speculative execution, among others. These ILP techniques demand hardware and compiler support. In addition, DLP and TLP are highly explored in graphics processing units (GPUs) that adopt a many-core architecture with hundreds to thousands of simple cores. Both multi-core CPU and many-core GPU processors can handle multiple instruction threads at different magnitudes today. The architecture of a typical multi core processor. Each core is essentially a processor with its own private cache (L1 cache). Multiple cores are housed in the same chip with an L2 cache that is shared by all cores. In the future, multiple CMPs could be built on the same CPU chip with even the L3 cache on the chip. Multicore and multithreaded CPUs are equipped with many high-end processors, including the Intel i7, Xeon, AMD Opteron, Sun Niagara, IBM Power 6, and X cell processors. Each core could be also multithreaded. For example, the Niagara II is built with eight cores with eight threads handled by each core. This implies that the maximum ILP and TLP that can be exploited in Niagara is 64 (8 × 8 = 64). In 2011, the Intel Core i7 990x has reported 159,000 MIPS execution rate as shown in the upper- most square.

Schematic of a modern multi core CPU chip using a hierarchy of caches, where L1 cache is private to each core, on-chip L2 cache is shared and L3 cache or DRAM Is off the chip.

Multicore CPU and Many-Core GPU Architectures

Multicore CPUs may increase from the tens of cores to hundreds or more in the future. But the CPU has reached its limit in terms of exploiting massive DLP due to the aforementioned memory wall problem. This has triggered the development of many-core GPUs with hundreds or more thin cores. Both IA-32 and IA-64 instruction set architectures are built into commercial CPUs. Now, x-86 processors have been extended to serve HPC and HTC systems in some high-end server processors. Many RISC processors have been replaced with multicore x-86 processors and many-core GPUs in the Top 500 systems. This trend indicates that x-86 upgrades will dominate in data centers and supercomputers. The GPU also has been applied in large clusters to build supercomputers in MPPs. In the future, the processor industry is also keen to develop asymmetric or heterogeneous chip multiprocessors that can house both fat CPU cores and thin GPU cores on the same chip.

Multithreading Technology

Consider the dispatch of five independent threads of instructions to four pipelined data paths (functional units) in each of the following five processor categories, from left to right: a four-issue superscalar processor, a fine-grain multithreaded processor, a coarse-grain multithreaded processor, a two-core CMP, and a simultaneous multithreaded (SMT) processor. The superscalar processor is single-threaded with four functional units. Each of the three multithreaded processors is four-way multithreaded over four functional data paths. In the dual-core processor, assume two processing cores, each a single-threaded two-way superscalar processor.

Five micro-architectures in modern CPU processors, that exploit ILP and TLP supported by multicore and multithreading technologies. Instructions from different threads are distinguished by specific shading patterns for instructions from five independent threads.

Typical instruction scheduling patterns are shown here. Only instructions from the same thread are executed in a superscalar processor. Fine-grain multithreading switches the execution of instructions from different threads per cycle. Course-grain multithreading executes many instructions from the same thread for quite a few cycles before switching to another thread. The multicore CMP executes instructions from different threads completely. The SMT allows simultaneous scheduling of instructions from different threads in the same cycle.

2GPU Computing to Exascale and Beyond

A GPU is a graphics coprocessor or accelerator mounted on a computer's graphics card or video card. A GPU offloads the CPU from tedious graphics tasks in video editing applications. The world's first GPU, the GeForce 256, was marketed by NVIDIA in 1999. These GPU chips can process a minimum of 10 million polygons per second, and are used in nearly every computer on the market today.

Some GPU features were also integrated into certain CPUs. Traditional CPUs are structured with only a few cores. For example, the Xeon X5670 CPU has six cores. However, a modern GPU chip can be built with hundreds of processing cores. Unlike CPUs, GPUs have a throughput architecture that exploits massive parallelism by executing many concurrent threads slowly, instead of executing a single long thread in a conventional microprocessor very quickly. Lately, parallel GPUs or GPU clusters have been garnering a lot of attention against the use of CPUs with limited parallelism. General-purpose computing on GPUs, known as GPGPUs, have appeared in the HPC field.

How GPUs Work

Early GPUs functioned as coprocessors attached to the CPU. Today, the NVIDIA GPU has been upgraded to 128 cores on a single chip. Furthermore, each core on a GPU can handle eight threads of instructions. This translates to having up to 1,024 threads executed concurrently on a single GPU. This is true massive parallelism, compared to only a few threads that can be handled by a conventional CPU.

The CPU is optimized for latency caches, while the GPU is optimized to deliver much higher throughput with explicit management of on-chip memory.

Modern GPUs are not restricted to accelerated graphics or video coding. They are used in HPC systems to power supercomputers with massive parallelism at multicore and multithreading levels.

GPUs are designed to handle large numbers of floating-point operations in parallel. In a way, the GPU offloads the CPU from all data-intensive calculations, not just those that are related to video processing. Conventional GPUs are widely used in mobile phones, game consoles, embedded systems, PCs, and servers. The NVIDIA CUDA Tesla or Fermi is used in GPU clusters or in HPC systems for parallel processing of massive floating-pointing data.

GPU Programming Model

The interaction between a CPU and GPU in performing parallel execution of floating-point operations concurrently. The CPU is the conventional multicore processor with limited parallelism to exploit. The GPU has a many-core architecture that has hundreds of simple processing cores organized as multiprocessors. Each core can have one or more threads. Essentially, the CPU's floating-point kernel computation role is largely offloaded to the many-core GPU. The CPU instructs the GPU to perform massive data processing. The bandwidth must be matched between the on-board main memory and the on-chip GPU memory. This process is carried out in NVIDIA's CUDA programming using the GeForce 8800 or Tesla and Fermi GPUs.

The use of a GPU along with a CPU for massively parallel execution in hundreds or thousands of processing cores.

Virtual Machines and Virtualization Middleware

A conventional computer has a single OS image. This offers a rigid architecture that tightly couples application software to a specific hardware platform. Some software running well on one machine may not be executable on another platform with a different instruction set under a fixed OS. Virtual machines (VMs) offer novel solutions to underutilized resources, application inflexibility, software manageability, and security concerns in existing physical machines.

Today, to build large clusters, grids, and clouds, we need to access large amounts of computing, storage, and networking resources in a virtualized manner. We need to aggregate those resources, and hopefully, offer a single system image. In particular, a cloud of provisioned resources must rely on virtualization of processors, memory, and I/O facilities dynamically.

Virtual Machines

The host machine is equipped with the physical hardware. An example is an x-86 architecture desktop running its installed Windows OS. The VM can be provisioned for any hardware system. The VM is built with virtual resources managed by a guest OS to run a specific application. Between the VMs and the host platform, one needs to deploy a middleware layer called a virtual machine monitor (VMM). A native VM installed with the use of a VMM called a hypervisor in privileged mode. For example, the hardware has x-86 architecture running the Windows system.

The guest OS could be a Linux system and the hypervisor is the XEN system developed at Cambridge University. This hypervisor approach is also called bare-metal VM, because the hypervisor handles the bare hardware (CPU, memory, and I/O) directly. Another architecture is the host VM here the VMM runs in non-privileged mode. The host OS need not be modified. The VM can also be implemented with a dual mode. Part of the VMM runs at the user level and another part runs at the supervisor level. In this case, the host OS may have to be modified to some extent. Multiple VMs can be ported to a given hardware system to support the virtualization process. The VM approach offers hardware independence of the OS and applications. The user application running on its dedicated OS could be bundled together as a virtual appliance that can be ported to any hardware platform. The VM could run on an OS different from that of the host computer.

VM Primitive Operations

The VMM provides the VM abstraction to the guest OS. With full virtualization, the VMM exports a VM abstraction identical to the physical machine so that a standard OS such as Windows 2000 or Linux can run just as it would on the physical hardware. Low-level VMM operations are indicated by Mendel Rosenblum.

VM multiplexing, suspension, provision, and migration in a distributed computing environment.

1. First, the VMs can be multiplexed between hardware machines.
2. Second, a VM can be suspended and stored in stable storage.
3. Third, a suspended VM can be resumed or provisioned to a new hardware platform.
4. Finally, a VM can be migrated from one hardware platform to another.

These VM operations enable a VM to be provisioned to any available hardware platform. They also enable flexibility in porting distributed application executions. Furthermore, the VM approach will significantly enhance the utilization of server resources. Multiple server functions can be consolidated on the same hardware platform to achieve higher system efficiency.

This will eliminate server sprawl via deployment of systems as VMs, which move transparency to the shared hardware. With this approach, VMware claimed that server utilization could be increased from its current 5–15 percent to 60–80 percent.

Virtual Infrastructures

Physical resources for compute, storage, and networking at the bottom are mapped to the needy applications embedded in various VMs at the top. Hardware and software are then separated. Virtual infrastructure is what connects resources to distributed applications. It is a dynamic mapping of system resources to specific applications. The result is decreased costs and increased efficiency and responsiveness. Virtualization for server consolidation and containment is a good example of this.

1.6. Clusters of Cooperative Computers

A computing cluster consists of interconnected stand-alone computers which work cooperatively as a single integrated computing resource. In the past, clustered computer systems have demonstrated impressive results in handling heavy workloads with large data sets.

Cluster Architecture

The architecture of a typical server cluster built around a low-latency, high-bandwidth interconnection network. This network can be as simple as a SAN (e.g., Myrinet) or a LAN (e.g., Ethernet). To build a larger cluster with more nodes, the interconnection network can be built with multiple levels of Gigabit Ethernet, Myrinet, or InfiniBand switches. Through hierarchical construction using a SAN, LAN, or WAN, one can build scalable clusters with an increasing number of nodes. The cluster is connected to the Internet via a virtual private network (VPN) gateway. The gateway IP address locates the cluster. The system image of a computer is decided by the way the OS manages the shared cluster resources. Most clusters have loosely coupled node computers. All resources of a server node are managed by their own OS. Thus, most clusters have multiple system images as a result of having many autonomous nodes under different OS control.

Single-System Image

Greg Pfister has indicated that an ideal cluster should merge multiple system images into a single-system image (SSI). Cluster designers desire a cluster operating system or some middleware to support SSI at various levels, including the sharing of CPUs, memory, and I/O across all cluster nodes. An SSI is an illusion created by software or hardware that presents a collection of resources as one integrated, powerful resource. SSI makes the cluster appear like a single machine to the user. A cluster with multiple system images is nothing but a collection of independent computers.

Hardware, Software, and Middleware Support

Clusters exploring massive parallelism are commonly known as MPPs. Almost all HPC clusters in the Top 500 list are also MPPs. The building blocks are computer nodes (PCs, workstations, servers, or SMP), special communication software such as PVM or MPI, and a network interface card in each computer node. Most clusters run under the Linux OS. The computer nodes are interconnected by a high-bandwidth network (such as Gigabit Ethernet, Myrinet, InfiniBand, etc.).

Special cluster middleware supports are needed to create SSI or high availability (HA). Both sequential and parallel applications can run on the cluster, and special parallel environments are needed to facilitate use of the cluster resources. For example, distributed memory has multiple images. Users may want all distributed memory to be shared by all servers by forming distributed shared memory (DSM). Many SSI features are expensive or difficult to achieve at various cluster operational levels. Instead of achieving SSI, many clusters are loosely coupled machines. Using virtualization, one can build many virtual clusters dynamically, upon user demand.

Major Cluster Design Issues

Unfortunately, a cluster-wide OS for complete resource sharing is not available yet. Middleware or OS extensions were developed at the user space to achieve SSI at selected functional levels. Without this middleware, cluster nodes cannot work together effectively to achieve cooperative computing. The software environments and applications must rely on the middleware to achieve high performance. The cluster benefits come from scalable performance, efficient message passing, high system availability, seamless fault tolerance, and cluster-wide job management.

1.7.   Grid Computing Infrastructures

In the past 30 years, users have experienced a natural growth path from Internet to web and grid computing services. Internet services such as the Telnet command enables a local computer to connect to a remote computer. A web service such as HTTP enables remote access of remote web pages. Grid computing is envisioned to allow close interaction among applications running on distant computers simultaneously. Forbes Magazine has projected the global growth of the IT-based economy from $1 trillion in 2001 to $20 trillion by 2015. The evolution from Internet to web and grid services is certainly playing a major role in this growth.

Computational Grids

Like an electric utility power grid, a computing grid offers an infrastructure that couples computers, software/middleware, special instruments, and people and sensors together. The grid is often constructed across LAN, WAN, or Internet backbone networks at a regional, national, or global scale. Enterprises or organizations present grids as integrated computing resources. They can also be viewed as virtual platforms to support virtual organizations. The computers used in a grid are primarily workstations, servers, clusters, and supercomputers. Personal computers, laptops, and PDAs can be used as access devices to a grid system.

The resource sites offer complementary computing resources, including workstations, large servers, a mesh of processors, and Linux clusters to satisfy a chain of computational needs. The grid is built across various IP broadband networks including LANs and WANs already used by enterprises or organizations over the Internet. The grid is presented to users as an integrated resource pool.

Computational grid or data grid providing computing utility, data, and information services through resource sharing and cooperation among participating organizations. Courtesy of Z. Xu, Chinese Academy of Science, 2004.

Special instruments may be involved such as using the radio telescope in SETI@Home search of life in the galaxy and the austrophysics@Swineburne for pulsars. At the server end, the grid is a network. At the client end, we see wired or wireless terminal devices. The grid integrates the computing, communication, contents, and transactions as rented services. Enterprises and consumers form the user base, which then defines the usage trends and service characteristics. Many national and international grids will be reported, the NSF TeraGrid in US, EGEE in Europe, and ChinaGrid in China for various distributed scientific grid applications.

Grid Families

Grid technology demands new distributed computing models, software/middleware support, network protocols, and hardware infrastructures. National grid projects are followed by industrial grid platform development by IBM, Microsoft, Sun, HP, Dell,Cisco, EMC, Platform Computing, and others.

New grid service providers (GSPs) and new grid applications have emerged rapidly, similar to the growth of Internet and web services in the past two decades. In grid systems are classified in essentially two categories: computational or data grids and P2P grids. Computing or data grids are built primarily at the national level.

Peer-to-Peer Network Families

An example of a well-established distributed system is the client-server architecture. In this scenario, client machines (PCs and workstations) are connected to a central server for compute, e-mail, file access, and database applications. The P2P architecture offers a distributed model of networked systems. First, a P2P network is client-oriented instead of server-oriented. In this section, P2P systems are introduced at the physical level and overlay networks at the logical level.

P2P Systems

In a P2P system, every node acts as both a client and a server, providing part of the system resources. Peer machines are simply client computers connected to the Internet. All client machines act autonomously to join or leave the system freely. This implies that no master-slave relationship exists among the peers. No central coordination or central database is needed. In other words, no peer machine has a global view of the entire P2P system. The system is self-organizing with distributed control. The architecture of a P2P network at two abstraction levels. Initially, the peers are totally unrelated. Each peer machine joins or leaves the P2P network voluntarily. Only the participating peers form the physical network at any time. Unlike the cluster or grid, a P2P network does not use a dedicated interconnection network. The physical network is simply an ad hoc network formed at various Internet domains randomly using the TCP/IP and NAI protocols. Thus, the physical network varies in size and topology dynamically due to the free membership in the P2P network.

1.8.   Cloud Computing Over the Internet

Gordon Bell, Jim Gray, and Alex Szalay have advocated: —Computational science is changing to be data-intensive. Supercomputers must be balanced systems, not just CPU farms but also petascale I/O and networking arrays.‖ In the future, working with large data sets will typically mean sending the computations (programs) to the data, rather than copying the data to the workstations. This reflects the trend in IT of moving computing and data from desktops to large data centers, where there is on-demand provision of software, hardware, and data as a service. This data explosion has promoted the idea of cloud computing.

Cloud computing has been defined differently by many users and designers. For example, IBM, a major player in cloud computing, has defined it as follows: —A cloud is a pool of virtualized computer resources. A cloud can host a variety of different workloads, including batch-style backend jobs and interactive and user-facing applications.‖ Based on this definition, a cloud allows workloads to be deployed and scaled out quickly through rapid provisioning of virtual or physical machines. The cloud supports redundant, self-recovering, highly scalable programming models that allow workloads to recover from many unavoidable hardware/software failures. Finally, the cloud system should be able to monitor resource use in real time to enable rebalancing of allocations when needed.

Internet Clouds

Cloud computing applies a virtualized platform with elastic resources on demand by provisioning hardware, software, and data sets dynamically. The idea is to move desktop computing to a service-oriented platform using server clusters and huge databases at data centers. Cloud computing leverages its low cost and simplicity to benefit both users and providers. Machine virtualization has enabled such cost-effectiveness. Cloud computing intends to satisfy many user applications simultaneously. The cloud ecosystem must be designed to be secure, trustworthy, and dependable. Some computer users think of the cloud as a centralized resource pool.

Others consider the cloud to be a server cluster which practices distributed computing over all the servers used.

Virtualized resources from data centers to form an Internet cloud, provisioned with hardware, software, storage, network, and services for paid users to run their applications.

The Cloud Landscape

Traditionally, a distributed computing system tends to be owned and operated by an autonomous administrative domain (e.g., a research laboratory or company) for on-premises computing needs. However, these traditional systems have encountered several performance bottlenecks: constant system maintenance, poor utilization, and increasing costs associated with hardware/software upgrades. Cloud computing as an on-demand computing paradigm resolves or relieves us from these problems. It depicts the cloud landscape and major cloud players, based on three cloud service models.

Three cloud service models in a cloud landscape of major providers. Courtesy of Dennis Gannon, keynote address at Cloudcom2010.

1. Infrastructure as a Service (IaaS) This model puts together infrastructures demanded by users— namely servers, storage, networks, and the data center fabric. The user can deploy and run on multiple VMs running guest OSes on specific applications. Theuser does not manage or control the underlying cloud infrastructure, but can specify when to request and release the needed resources.

2. Platform as a Service (PaaS) This model enables the user to deploy user-built applications onto a virtualized cloud platform. PaaS includes middleware, databases, development tools, and some runtime support such as Web 2.0 and Java. The platform includes both hardware and software integrated with specific programming interfaces. The provider supplies the API and software tools (e.g., Java, Python, Web 2.0, .NET). The user is freed from managing the cloud infrastructure.

3. Software as a Service (SaaS) This refers to browser-initiated application software over thousands of paid cloud customers. The SaaS model applies to business processes, industry applications, consumer relationship management (CRM), enterprise resources planning (ERP), human resources (HR), and collaborative applications. On the customer side, there is no upfront investment in servers or software licensing. On the provider side, costs are rather low, compared with conventional hosting of user applications.

Internet clouds offer four deployment modes: private, public, managed, and hybrid .These modes demand different levels of security implications.

The different SLAs imply that the security responsibility is shared among all the cloud providers, the cloud resource consumers, and the third-party cloud-enabled software providers.

Advantages of cloud computing have been advocated by many IT experts, industry leaders, and computer science researchers.

The following list highlights eight reasons to adapt the cloud for upgraded Internet applications and web services:

1. Desired location in areas with protected space and higher energy efficiency.

2. Sharing of peak-load capacity among a large pool of users, improving overall utilization.

3. Separation of infrastructure maintenance duties from domain-specific application development.

4. Significant reduction in cloud computing cost, compared with traditional computing paradigms.

5. Cloud computing programming and application development.

6. Service and data discovery and content/service distribution.

7. Privacy, security, copyright, and reliability issues.

8. Service agreements, business models, and pricing policies.

1.9.   Service-Oriented Architecture (SOA)

In grids/web services, Java, and CORBA, an entity is, respectively, a service, a Java object, and a CORBA distributed object in a variety of languages. These architectures build on the traditional seven Open Systems Interconnection (OSI) layers that provide the base networking abstractions. On top of this we have a base software environment, which would be .NET or Apache Axis for web services, the Java Virtual Machine for Java, and a broker network for CORBA. On top of this base environment one would build a higher level environment reflecting the special features of the distributed computing environment. This starts with entity interfaces and inter-entity communication, which rebuild the top four OSI layers but at the entity and not the bit level.

Layered Architecture for Web Services and Grids

The entity interfaces correspond to the Web Services Description Language (WSDL), Java method, and CORBA interface definition language (IDL) specifications in these example distributed systems. These interfaces are linked with customized, high-level communication systems: SOAP, RMI, and IIOP in the three examples. These communication systems support features including particular message patterns (such as Remote Procedure Call or RPC), fault recovery, and specialized routing. Often, these communication systems are built on message-oriented middleware (enterprise bus) infrastructure such as WebSphere MQ or Java Message Service (JMS) which provide rich functionality and support virtualization of routing, senders, and recipients.

In the case of fault tolerance, the features in the Web Services Reliable Messaging (WSRM) framework mimic the OSI layer capability (as in TCP fault tolerance) modified to match the different abstractions (such as messages versus packets, virtualized addressing) at the entity levels. Security is a critical capability that either uses or reimplements the capabilities seen in concepts such as Internet Protocol Security (IPsec) and secure sockets in the OSI layers. Entity communication is supported by higher level services for registries, metadata, and management of the entities.

Here, one might get several models with, for example, JNDI (Jini and Java Naming and Directory Interface) illustrating different approaches within the Java distributed object model. The CORBA Trading Service, UDDI (Universal Description, Discovery, and Integration), LDAP (Lightweight Directory Access Protocol), and ebXML (Electronic Business using eXtensible Markup Language) are other examples of discovery and information services. Management services include service state and lifetime support; examples include the CORBA Life Cycle and Persistent states, the different Enterprise JavaBeans models, Jini's lifetime model, and a suite of web services specifications in Chapter 5. The above language or interface terms form a collection of entity-level capabilities.

The latter can have performance advantages and offers a —shared memory‖ model allowing more convenient exchange of information. However, the distributed model has two critical advantages: namely, higher performance (from multiple CPUs when communication is unimportant) and a cleaner separation of software functions with clear software reuse and maintenance advantages. The distributed model is expected to gain popularity as the default approach to software systems. In the earlier years, CORBA and Java approaches were used in distributed systems rather than today's SOAP, XML, or REST (Representational State Transfer).

The Evolution of SOA

Service-oriented architecture (SOA) has evolved over the years. SOA applies to building grids, clouds, grids of clouds, clouds of grids, clouds of clouds (also known as interclouds), and systems of systems in general. A large number of sensors provide data-collection services, denoted as SS (sensor service). A sensor can be a ZigBee device, a Bluetooth device, a WiFi access point, a personal computer, a GPA, or a wireless phone, among other things. Raw data is collected by sensor services. All the SS devices interact with large or small computers, many forms of grids, databases, the compute cloud, the storage cloud, the filter cloud, the discovery cloud, and so on.

Filter services (fs in the figure) are used to eliminate unwanted raw data, in order to respond to specific requests from the web, the grid, or web services. The evolution of SOA: grids of clouds and grids, where —SS‖ refers to a sensor service and —fs‖ to a filter or transforming service. A collection of filter services forms a filter cloud.

Processing this data will generate useful information, and subsequently, the knowledge for our daily use. In fact, wisdom or intelligence is sorted out of large knowledge bases. Finally, we make intelligent decisions based on both biological and machine wisdom. Most distributed systems require a web interface or portal. For raw data collected by a large number of sensors to be transformed into useful information or knowledge, the data stream may go through a sequence of compute, storage, filter, and discovery clouds.

Finally, the inter-service messages converge at the portal, which is accessed by all users. Two example portals, OGFCE and HUBzero, are described using both web service (portlet) and Web 2.0 (gadget) technologies. Many distributed programming models are also built on top of these basic constructs.

Grids Versus Clouds

The boundary between grids and clouds are getting blurred in recent years. For web services, workflow technologies are used to coordinate or orchestrate services with certain specifications used to define critical business process models such as two-phase transactions. Service standard, and several important workflow approaches including Pegasus, Taverna, Kepler, Trident, and Swift. In all approaches, one is building a collection of services which together tackle all or part of a distributed computing problem. In general, a grid system applies static resources, while a cloud emphasizes elastic resources. For some researchers, the differences between grids and clouds are limited only in dynamic resource allocation based on virtualization and autonomic computing.

One can build a grid out of multiple clouds. This type of grid can do a better job than a pure cloud, because it can explicitly support negotiated resource allocation. Thus one may end up building with a system of systems: such as a cloud of clouds, a grid of clouds, or a cloud of grids, or inter-clouds as a basic SOA architecture.

Unit II

Grid Services

2.1. Grid Architecture and Service Modeling

The grid is a meta computing infrastructure that brings together computers (PCs, workstations, server clusters, supercomputers, laptops, notebooks, mobile computers, PDAs, etc.) to form a large collection of compute, storage, and network resources to solve large-scale computation problems or to enable fast information retrieval by registered users or user groups. The coupling between hardware and software with special user applications is achieved by leasing the hardware, software, middleware, databases, instruments, and networks as computing utilities. Good examples include the renting of expensive special-purpose application software on demand and transparent access to human genome databases.

The goal of grid computing is to explore fast solutions for large-scale computing problems. This objective is shared by computer clusters and massively parallel processor (MPP) systems. However, grid computing takes advantage of the existing computing resources scattered in a nation or internationally around the globe. In grids, resources owned by different organizations are aggregated together and shared by many users in collective applications. Grids rely heavy use of LAN/WAN resources across enterprises, organizations, and governments. The virtual organizations or virtual supercomputers are new concept derived from grid or cloud computing. These are virtual resources dynamically configured and are not under the full control of any single user or local administrator.

2.2. Grid History and Service Families

Network-based distributed computing becomes more and more popular among the Internet users. Recall that the Internet was developed in the 1980s to provide computer-to-computer connections using the telnet:// protocol. The web service was developed in the 1990s to establish direct linkage between web pages using the http:// protocol. Ever since the 1990s, grids became gradually available to establish large pools of shared resources. The approach is to link many Internet applications across machine platforms directly in order to eliminate isolated resource islands. We may invent upgraded protocols in the future like —grid://‖ and —cloud://‖ to realize this dream of a socialized cyberspace with greater resource sharing. The idea of the grid was pioneered by Ian Foster, Carl Kesselman and Steve Tuecke in a 2001 paper. With is ground work, they are often recognized as the fathers of the grids. The Globus Project supported by DARPA has promoted the maturity of grid technology with a rich collection of software and middleware tools for grid computing. In 2007, the concept of cloud computing was thrown out, which in many ways was extending grid computing through virtualized data centers. In this beginning section, we introduce major grid families and review the grid service evolution over the past 15 years.

Grids differ from conventional HPC clusters. Cluster nodes are more homogeneous machines that are better coordinated to work collectively and cooperatively. The grid nodes are heterogeneous computers that are more loosely coupled together over geographically dispersed sites. In 2001, Forbes Magazine advocated the emergence of the great global grid (GGG) as a new global infrastructure. This GGG evolved from the World Wide Web (WWW) technology we have enjoyed for many years.

Four Grid Service Families

Most of today's grid systems are called computational grids or data grids. Good examples are the NSF TeraGrid installed in the United States and the DataGrid built in the European Union. Information or knowledge grids post another grid class dedicated to knowledge management and distributed ontology processing. The Semantic web, also known as semantic grids, belongs to this faimly. Ontology platform falls into information or knowledge grids. Other information/knowledge grids include the Berkeley BOINC and NASA's Information Power Grid. In the business world, we see a family, called business grids, built for business data/information processing. These are represented by the HP eSpeak, IBM WebSphere, Microsoft .NET, and Sun One systems. Some business grids are being transformed into Internet clouds. The last grid class includes several grid extensions such as P2P grids and parasitic grids. This will concentrate mainly in computational or data grids. Business grids are only briefly introduced.

Grid Service Protocol Stack

To put together the resources needed in a grid platform, a layered grid architecture . The top layer corresponds to user applications to run on the grid system. The user applications demand collective services including collective computing and communications. The next layer is formed by the hardware and software resources aggregated to run the user applications under the collective operations. The connectivity layer provides the interconnection among drafted resources. This connectivity could be established directly on physical networks or it could be built with virtual networking technology. The layered grid service protocols and their relationship with the Internet service protocols. Courtesy of Foster, Kesselman, and Tuecke .The connectivity must support the grid fabric, including the network inks and virtual private channels. The fabric layer includes all computational resources, storage systems, catalogs, network resources, sensors, and their network connections. The connectivity layer enables the exchange of data between fabric layer resources. The five-layer grid architecture is closely related to the layered Internet protocol stack . The fabric layer corresponds to the link layer in the Internet stack. The connectivity layer is supported by the network and transport layers of the Internet stack. The Internet application layer supports the top three layers.

Grid Resources

It summarizes typical resources that are required to perform grid computing. Many existing protocols (IP, TCP, HTTP, FTP, and DNS) or some new communication protocols can be used to route and transfer data. The resource layer is responsible for sharing single resources. An interface is needed to claim the static structure and dynamic status of local resources. The grid should be able to accept resource requests, negotiate the Quality of Service (QoS), and perform the operations specified in user applications.

The collective layer handles the interactions among a collection of resources. This layer implements functions such as resource discovery, co-allocation, scheduling, brokering, monitoring, and diagnostics. Other desired features include replication, grid-enabled programming, workload management, collaboration, software discovery, access authorization, and community accounting and payment. The application layer comprises mainly user applications. The applications interact with components in other layers by using well-defined APIs (application programming interfaces) and SDKs (software development kits).

2.3.   CPU Scavenging and Virtual Super Computers

The process of grid resource aggregation from local and remote sources. Then we link the grid to the concept of virtual organizations in a dynamic sense. In fact, the distinction between grids and clouds becomes blurred in recent years. Traditionally, grids were formed with allocated resources statically, while clouds were formed with provisioned resources dynamically. As virtualization is applicable to grid components, some grids involving data centers become more like clouds.

Foster, et al. [15] have compared the grid problem with the anatomy problem in biology. The application users expect grids to be designed as flexible, secure, and coordinated resources shared by individuals, institutions, and virtual organizations. The grid resources could come from two possible sources. On the one hand, large-scale HPC grids can be formed with computers from resource-rich supercomputer centers owned by government agencies and research institutions. Alternatively, one could form —virtual‖ grids, casually, out of a large number of small commodity computers owned by ordinary citizens, who volunteer to share their free cycles with other users for a noble cause.

CPU Scavenging and Virtual Super Computers

Both public and virtual grids can be built over large or small machines, that are loosely coupled together to satisfy the application need. Grids differ from the conventional supercomputers in many ways in the context of distributed computing. Supercomputers like MPPs in the Top-500 list are more homogeneously structured with tightly coupled operations, while the grids are built with heterogeneous nodes running non-interactive workloads. These grid workloads may involve a large number of files and individual users. The geographically dispersed grids are more scalable and fault-tolerant with significantly lower operational costs than the supercomputers. The concept of creating a —grid‖ from the unused resources in a network of computers is known as CPU scavenging. In reality, virtual grids are built over large number of desktop computers by using their free cycles at night or during inactive usage periods. The donors are ordinary citizens on a voluntary participation basis. In practice, these client hosts also donate some disk space, RAM, and network bandwidth in addition to the raw CPU cycles. At present, many volunteer computing grids are built using the CPU scavenging model. The most famous example is the SETI@Home, which applied over 3 million computers to achieve 23.37 TFlpos as of Sept. 2001. More recent examples include the BOINC and Folding@Home, etc. In practice, these virtual grids can be viewed as virtual supercomputers.

2.4.   Grid Resource Aggregation

During the resource aggregation process for grids or clouds, several assumptions are made. First, the compute nodes and other necessary resources for grids do not join or leave the system incidentally, except when some serious faults occur in the grid. Second, cloud resources are mostly provisioned from large data centers.

Since security and reliability are very tight in these data centers, resource behavior is not predictable. Third, although resources in P2P systems are casually allocated, we can build P2P grids for distributed file sharing, content delivery, gaming, and entertainment applications. The joining or leaving of some peers has little impact on the needed functions of a P2P grid system.

We envision the grid resource aggregation process in a global setting. Hardware, software, database, and network resources are denoted by R's and are scattered all over the world. The availability and specification of these open resources is provided by Grid Information Service (GIS) agencies. The grid resource brokers assist users with fees to allocate available resources. Multiple brokers could compete to serve users. Also, multiple GISes may overlap in their resource coverage. New grid applications are enabled after the coupling of computer databases, instruments, and human operators needed in their specific applications. It should be noted that today's grid computing applications are no longer restricted to using HPC systems. HTC systems, like clouds, are even more in demand in business services.

2.5.   Virtual Organization

The grid is a distributed system integrated from shared resources to form a virtual organization (VO). The VO offers dynamic cooperation built over multiple physical organizations. The virtual resources contributed by these real organizations are managed autonomously. The grid must deal with the trust relationship in a VO. The applications in a grid vary in terms of workload and resource demand. A flexible grid system should be designed to adapt to varying workloads. In reality, physical organizations include a real company, a university, or a branch of government. These real organizations often share some common objectives.

For example, several research institutes and hospitals may undertake some joint research challenges together to explore a new cancer drug. Another concrete example is the joint venture among IBM, Apple, and Motorola to develop PowerPC processors and their supporting software in the past. The joint venture was based on the VO model. Grids definitely can promote the concept of VOs. Still, joint ventures demand resources and labor from all participants. The following example shows how two VOs or grid configurations can be formed out of three physical organizations.

Open Grid Services Architecture (OGSA)

The OGSA is an open source grid service standard jointly developed by academia and the IT industry under coordination of a working group in the Global Grid Forum (GGF). The standard was specifically developed for the emerging grid and cloud service communities. The OGSA is extended from web service concepts and technologies. The standard defines a common framework that allows businesses to build grid platforms across enterprises and business partners. The intent is to define the standards required for both open source and commercial software to support a global grid infrastructure.

2.6.   OGSA Framework

The OGSA was built on two basic software technologies: the Globus Toolkit widely adopted as a grid technology solution for scientific and technical computing, and web services (WS 2.0) as a popular standards-based framework for business and network applications. The OGSA is intended to support the creation, termination, management, and invocation of stateful, transient grid services via standard interfaces and conventions. The OGSA framework specifies the physical environment, security, infrastructure profile, resource provisioning, virtual domains, and execution environment for various grid services and API access tools.

A service is an entity that provides some capability to its client by exchanging messages. We feel that greater flexibility is needed in grid service discovery and management. The service-oriented architecture (SOA) presented serves as the foundation of grid computing services. The individual and collective states of resources are specified in this service standard. The standard also specifies interactions between these services within the particular SOA for grids. An important point is that the architecture is not layered, where the implementation of one service is built upon modules that are logically dependent. One may classify this framework as object-oriented. Many web service standards, semantics, and extensions are applied or modified in the OGSA.

OGSA Interfaces

The OGSA is centered on grid services. These services demand special well-defined application interfaces. These interfaces provide resource discovery, dynamic service creation, lifetime management, notification, and manageability. The conventions must address naming and upgradeability. The interfaces proposed by the OGSA working group. While the OGSA defines a variety of behaviors and associated interfaces, all but one of these interfaces (the grid service) is optional. Two key properties of a grid service are transience and statefulness. These properties have significant implications regarding how a grid service is named, discovered, and managed. Being transient means the service can be created and destroyed dynamically; statefulness refers to the fact that one can distinguish one service instance from another.

OGSA Grid Service Interfaces Developed by the OGSA Working Group.

Grid Service Handle

A GSH is a globally unique name that distinguishes a specific grid service instance from all others. The status of a grid service instance could be that it exists now or that it will exist in the future. These instances carry no protocol or instance-specific addresses or supported protocol bindings. Instead, these information items are encapsulated along with all other instance-specific information. In order to interact with a specific service instance, a single abstraction is defined as a GSR. Unlike a GSH, which is time-invariant, the GSR for an instance can change over the lifetime of the service. The OGSA employs a—handle-resolution‖ mechanism for mapping from a GSH to a GSR. The GSH must be globally defined for a particular instance.

However, the GSH may not always refer to the same network address. A service instance may be implemented in its own way, as long as it obeys the associated semantics. For example, the port type on which the service instance was implemented decides which operation to perform.

Grid Service Migration

This is a mechanism for creating new services and specifying assertions regarding the lifetime of a service. The OGSA model defines a standard interface, known as a factor, to implement this reference. Any service that is created must address the former services as the reference of later services.

The factory interface is labeled as a Create Service operation. This creates a requested grid service with a specified interface and returns the GSH and initial GSR for the new service instance. It should also register the new service instance with a handle resolution service. Each dynamically created grid service instance is associated with a specified lifetime.

Grid Service Migration Using GSH and GSR shows how a service instance may migrate from one location to another during execution. A GSH resolves to a different GSR for a migrated service instance before (on the left) and after (on the right) the migration at time T. The handle resolver simply returns different GSRs before and after the migration. The initial lifetime can be extended by a specified time period by explicitly requesting the client or another grid service acting on the client's behalf.

A GSH resolving to a different GSR for a migrated service instance before (shown on the left) and after (on the right) the migration at time T. If the time period expires without having received a reaffirmed interest from a client, the service instance can be terminated on its own and release the associated resources accordingly. The lifetime management enables robust termination and failure detection.

This is done by clearly defining the lifetime semantics of a service instance. Similarly, a hosting environment is guaranteed to consume bounded resources under some system failures. If the termination time of a service is reached, the hosting environment can reclaim all resources allocated.

OGSA Security Models

The OGSA supports security enforcement at various levels. The grid works in a heterogeneous distributed environment, which is essentially open to the general public. We must be able to detect intrusions or stop viruses from spreading by implementing secure conversations, single logon, access control, and auditing for non repudiation. At the security policy and user levels, we want to apply a service or endpoint policy, resource mapping rules, authorized access of critical resources, and privacy protection. At the Public Key Infrastructure (PKI) service level, the OGSA demands security binding with the security protocol stack and bridging of certificate authorities (CAs), use of multiple trusted intermediaries, and so on. Trust models and secure logging are often practiced in grid platforms.

The OGSA security model implemented at various protection levels. Courtesy of I. Foster, et al., http://www.ogf.org/documents/GFD.80.pdf

2.7.   Data-Intensive Grid Service Models

Applications in the grid are normally grouped into two categories: computation-intensive and data-intensive. For data-intensive applications, we may have to deal with massive amounts of data. For example, the data produced annually by a Large Hadron Collider may exceed several petabytes (1015 bytes). The grid system must be specially designed to discover, transfer, and manipulate these massive data sets. Transferring massive data sets is a time-consuming task. Efficient data management demands low-cost storage and high-speed data movement. Listed in the following paragraphs are several common methods for solving data movement problems.

Data Replication and Unified Namespace

This data access method is also known as caching, which is often applied to enhance data efficiency in a grid environment. By replicating the same data blocks and scattering them in multiple regions of a grid, users can access the same data with locality of references.

Furthermore, the replicas of the same data set can be a backup for one another. Some key data will not be lost in case of failures. However, data replication may demand periodic consistency checks. The increase in storage requirements and network bandwidth may cause additional problems. Replication strategies determine when and where to create a replica of the data. The factors to consider include data demand, network conditions, and transfer cost. The strategies of replication can be classified into method types: dynamic and static. For the static method, the locations and number of replicas are determined in advance and will not be modified. Although replication operations require little overhead, static strategies cannot adapt to changes in demand, bandwidth, and storage vailability. Dynamic strategies can adjust locations and number of data replicas according to changes in conditions (e.g., user behavior). However, frequent data-moving operations can result in much more overhead than in static strategies. The replication strategy must be optimized with respect to the status of data replicas. For static replication, optimization is required to determine the location and number of data replicas. For dynamic replication, optimization may be determined based on whether the data replica is being created, deleted, or moved. The most common replication strategies include preserving locality, minimizing update costs, and maximizing profits.

Grid Data Access Models

Multiple participants may want to share the same data collection. To retrieve any piece of data, we need a grid with a unique global namespace. Similarly, we desire to have unique file names. To achieve these, we have to resolve inconsistencies among multiple data objects bearing the same name. Access restrictions may be imposed to avoid confusion. Also, data needs to be protected to avoid leakage and damage. Users who want to access data have to be authenticated first and then authorized for access. In general, there are four access models for organizing a data grid, as listed here and shown in Figure 7.5.

Four architectural models for building a data grid.

Monadic model: This is a centralized data repository model. All the data is saved in a central data repository. When users want to access some data they have to submit requests directly to the central repository. No data is replicated for preserving data locality. This model is the simplest to implement for a small grid. For a large grid, this model is not efficient in terms of performance and reliability. Data replication is permitted in this model only when fault tolerance is demanded.

Hierarchical model: The hierarchical model, is suitable for building a large data grid which has only one large data access directory. The data may be transferred from the source to a second-level center.

Then some data in the regional center is transferred to the third-level center. After being forwarded several times, specific data objects are accessed directly by users. Generally speaking, a higher-level data center has a wider coverage area. It provides higher bandwidth for access than a lower-level data center. PKI security services are easier to implement in this hierarchical data access model. The European Data Grid (EDG) adopts this data access model.

Federation model: This data access model is better suited for designing a data grid with multiple sources of data supplies. Sometimes this model is also known as a mesh model. The data sources are distributed to many different locations. Although the data is shared, the data items are still owned and controlled by their original owners. According to predefined access policies, only authenticated users are authorized to request data from any data source. This mesh model may cost the most when the number of grid institutions becomes very large.

Hybrid model: This is data access model. The model combines the best features of the hierarchical and mesh models. Traditional data transfer technology, such as FTP, applies for networks with lower bandwidth. Network links in a data grid often have fairly high bandwidth, and other data transfer models are exploited by high-speed data transfer tools such as GridFTP developed with the Globus library. The cost of the hybrid model can be traded off between the two extreme models for hierarchical and mesh-connected grids.

Overview of Grid'5000 located at nine resource sites in France.

Parallel Versus Striped Data Transfers

Compared with traditional FTP data transfer, parallel data transfer opens multiple data streams for passing subdivided segments of a file simultaneously. Although the speed of each stream is the same as in sequential streaming, the total time to move data in all streams can be significantly reduced compared to FTP transfer.

In striped data transfer, a data object is partitioned into a number of sections, and each section is placed in an individual site in a data grid. When a user requests this piece of data, a data stream is created for each site, and all the sections of data objects are transferred simultaneously.

Striped data transfer can utilize the bandwidths of multiple sites more efficiently to speed up data transfer.

Grid Projects and Grid Systems Built

Grid computing provides promising solutions to contemporary users who want to effectively share and collaborate with one another in distributed and self-governing environments.

Apart from volunteer grids, most large-scale grids are national or international projects funded by public agencies. This section reviews the major grid systems developed in recent years. In particular, we describe three national grid projects that have been installed in the U.S., EU, and China.

National Grids and International Projects

Like supercomputers, national grids are mainly funded through government sources. These national grids are developed to promote research discovery, middleware products, and utility computing in grid-enabled applications.

National Grid Project

Over the past decade, many data, information, or computational grids were built in various parts of the world. It summarizes five representative grid computing systems built in the United States, European Union, United Kingdom, France, and China. We call these national grids, because they are essentially government-funded projects pushing for grand challenge applications that demand high-performance computing and high-bandwidth communication networks. Here treat the EU countries as a single entity.

Most national grids are built by linking supercomputer centers and major computer ensembles together with Internet backbones and high-bandwidth WANs or LANs. More details can be found in the cited subsequent sections.

International Grid Projects

Grid applications cannot be restricted to geographical boundaries. As summarized , several global-scale grid projects were launched or are still active in use today. These projects promote volunteer computing, utility computing, and specific software applications that utilizes grid infrastructure. International grids involve both government and industrial funding. The European Union has been a major player in grid computing. The most famous EU grid projects are the EGEE, DataGrid, and BEinGrid. In the industrial sector, we have seen grid providers including Sun Microsystems, IBM, HP, etc. International grids are built with fix-term projects. Some of them are no longer active to provide public services at the end of funding.

Unit III

Virtualization

3.1. Cloud Computing and Service Models

Over the past two decades, the world economy has rapidly moved from manufacturing to more service-oriented. In 2010, 80 percent of the U.S. economy was driven by the service industry, leaving only 15 percent in manufacturing and 5 percent in agriculture and other areas. Cloud computing benefits the service industry most and advances business computing with a new paradigm. In 2009, the global cloud service marketplace reached $17.4 billion. IDC predicted in 2010 that the cloud-based economy may increase to $44.2 billion by 2013. Developers of innovative cloud applications no longer acquire large capital equipment in advance. They just rent the resources from some large data centers that have been automated for this purpose. Users can access and deploy cloud applications from anywhere in the world at very competitive costs. Virtualized cloud platforms are often built on top of large data centers. With that in mind, we examine first the server cluster in a data center and its interconnection issues. In other words, clouds aim to power the next generation of data centers by architecting them as virtual resources over automated hardware, databases, user interfaces, and application environments. In this sense, clouds grow out of the desire to build better data centers through automated resource provisioning.

Public, Private, and Hybrid Clouds

The concept of cloud computing has evolved from cluster, grid, and utility computing. Cluster and grid computing leverage the use of many computers in parallel to solve problems of any size. Utility and Software as a Service (SaaS) provide computing resources as a service with the notion of pay per use. Cloud computing leverages dynamic resources to deliver large numbers of services to end users. Cloud computing is a high-throughput computing (HTC) paradigm whereby the infrastructure provides the services through a large data center or server farms. The cloud computing model enables users to share access to resources from anywhere at any time through their connected devices.

In this scenario, the computations (programs) are sent to where the data is located, rather than copying the data to millions of desktops as in the traditional approach. Cloud computing avoids large data movement, resulting in much better network bandwidth utilization. Furthermore, machine virtualization has enhanced resource utilization, increased application flexibility, and reduced the total cost of using virtualized data-center resources. The cloud offers significant benefit to IT companies by freeing them from the low-level task of setting up the hardware (servers) and managing the system software. Cloud computing applies a virtual platform with elastic resources put together by on-demand provisioning of hardware, software, and data sets, dynamically. The main idea is to move desktop computing to a service-oriented platform using server clusters and huge databases at data centers. Cloud computing leverages its low cost and simplicity to both providers and users. According to Ian Foster, cloud computing intends to leverage multitasking to achieve higher throughput by serving many heterogeneous applications, large or small, simultaneously.

Public Clouds

A public cloud is built over the Internet and can be accessed by any user who has paid for the service. Public clouds are owned by service providers and are accessible through a subscription. The callout box in top of the architecture of a typical public cloud. Many public clouds are available, including Google App Engine (GAE), Amazon Web Services (AWS), Microsoft Azure, IBM Blue Cloud, and Salesforce.com's Force.com. The providers of the aforementioned clouds are commercial providers that offer a publicly accessible remote interface for creating and managing VM instances within their proprietary infrastructure. A public cloud delivers a selected set of business processes. The application and infrastructure services are offered on a flexible price-per-use basis.

Private Clouds

A private cloud is built within the domain of an intranet owned by a single organization. Therefore, it is client owned and managed, and its access is limited to the owning clients and their partners. Its deployment was not meant to sell capacity over the Internet through publicly accessible interfaces. Private clouds give local users a flexible and agile private infrastructure to run service workloads within their administrative domains. A private cloud is supposed to deliver more efficient and convenient cloud services. It may impact the cloud standardization, while retaining greater customization and organizational control.

Hybrid Clouds

A hybrid cloud is built with both public and private clouds, Private clouds can also support a hybrid cloud model by supplementing local infrastructure with computing capacity from an external public cloud. For example, the Research Compute Cloud (RC2) is a private cloud, built by IBM, that interconnects the computing and IT resources at eight IBM Research Centers scattered throughout the United States, Europe, and Asia. A hybrid cloud provides access to clients, the partner network, and third parties. In summary, public clouds promote standardization, preserve capital investment, and offer application flexibility. Private clouds attempt to achieve customization and offer higher efficiency, resiliency, security, and privacy. Hybrid clouds operate in the middle, with many compromises in terms of resource sharing.

Infrastructure-as-a-Service (IaaS)

Cloud computing delivers infrastructure, platform, and software (application) as services, which are made available as subscription-based services in a pay-as-you-go model to consumers. The services provided over the cloud can be generally categorized into three different service models: namely IaaS, Platform as a Service (PaaS), and Software as a Service (SaaS). These form the three pillars on top of which cloud computing solutions are delivered to end users. All three models allow users to access services over the Internet, relying entirely on the infrastructures of cloud service providers.

These models are offered based on various SLAs between providers and users. In a broad sense, the SLA for cloud computing is addressed in terms of service availability, performance, and data protection and security.

The three cloud models at different service levels of the cloud. SaaS is applied at the application end using special interfaces by users or clients. At the PaaS layer, the cloud platform must perform billing services and handle job queuing, launching, and monitoring services. At the bottom layer of the IaaS services, databases, compute instances, the file system, and storage must be provisioned to satisfy user demands. The IaaS, PaaS, and SaaS cloud service models at different service levels.

Infrastructure as a Service

This model allows users to use virtualized IT resources for computing, storage, and networking. In short, the service is performed by rented cloud infrastructure. The user can deploy and run his applications over his chosen OS environment. The user does not manage or control the underlying cloud infrastructure, but has control over the OS, storage, deployed applications, and possibly select networking components.

This IaaS model encompasses storage as a service, compute instances as a service, and communication as a service. The Virtual Private Cloud (VPC) in Example 4.1 shows how to provide Amazon EC2 clusters and S3 storage to multiple users. Many startup cloud providers have appeared in recent years. GoGrid, FlexiScale, and Aneka are good examples. It summarizes the IaaS offerings by five public cloud providers. Interested readers can visit the companies' web sites for updated information.

Platform-as-a-Service (PaaS) and Software-as-a-Service (SaaS)

In this section, we will introduce the PaaS and SaaS models for cloud computing. SaaS is often built on top of the PaaS, which is in turn built on top of the IaaS.

Platform as a Service (PaaS)

To be able to develop, deploy, and manage the execution of applications using provisioned resources demands a cloud platform with the proper software environment. Such a platform includes operating system and runtime library support. This has triggered the creation of the PaaS model to enable users to develop and deploy their user applications. It highlights cloud platform services offered by five PaaS services.

Software as a Service (SaaS)

This refers to browser-initiated application software over thousands of cloud customers. Services and tools offered by PaaS are utilized in construction of applications and management of their deployment on resources offered by IaaS providers. The SaaS model provides software applications as a service. As a result, on the customer side, there is no upfront investment in servers or software licensing. On the provider side, costs are kept rather low, compared with conventional hosting of user applications. Customer data is stored in the cloud that is either vendor proprietary or publicly hosted to support PaaS and IaaS.The best examples of SaaS services include Google Gmail and docs, Microsoft SharePoint, and the CRM software from Salesforce.com.

They are all very successful in promoting their own business or are used by thousands of small businesses in their day-to-day operations.

Providers such as Google and Microsoft offer integrated IaaS and PaaS services, whereas others such as Amazon and GoGrid offer pure IaaS services and expect third-party PaaS providers such as Manjrasoft to offer application development and deployment services on top of their infrastructure services. To identify important cloud applications in enterprises, the success stories of three real-life cloud applications for HTC, news media, and business transactions. The benefits of using cloud services are evident in these SaaS applications.

3.2.   Implementation Levels of Virtualization

Virtualization is a computer architecture technology by which multiple virtual machines (VMs) are multiplexed in the same hardware machine. The idea of VMs can be dated back to the 1960s.

- The purpose of a VM is to enhance resource sharing by many users and improve computer performance in terms of resource utilization and application flexibility. Hardware resources (CPU, memory, I/O devices, etc.) or software resources (operating system and software libraries) can be virtualized in various functional layers. This virtualization technology has been revitalized as the demand for distributed and cloud computing increased sharply in recent years .

The idea is to separate the hardware from the software to yield better system efficiency. For example, computer users gained access to much enlarged memory space when the concept of virtual memory was introduced. Similarly, virtualization techniques can be applied to enhance the use of compute engines, networks, and storage. According to a 2009 Gartner Report, virtualization was the top strategic technology poised to change the computer industry.

With sufficient storage, any computer platform can be installed in another host computer, even if they use processors with different instruction sets and run with distinct operating systems on the same hardware.

Levels of Virtualization Implementation

A traditional computer runs with a host operating system specially tailored for its hardware architecture. After virtualization, different user applications managed by their own operating systems (guest OS) can run on the same hardware, independent of the host OS. This is often done by adding additional software, called a virtualization layer. This virtualization layer is known as hypervisor or virtual machine monitor (VMM).

The VMs are shown in the upper boxes, where applications run with their own guest OS over the virtualized CPU, memory, and I/O resources. The architecture of a computer system before and after virtualization, where VMM stands for virtual machine monitor.

The main function of the software layer for virtualization is to virtualize the physical hardware of a host machine into virtual resources to be used by the VMs, exclusively. This can be implemented at various operational levels, as we will discuss shortly. The virtualization software creates the abstraction of VMs by interposing a virtualization layer at various levels of a computer system.

Common virtualization layers include the instruction set architecture (ISA) level, hardware level, operating system level, library support level, and application level. Virtualization ranging from hardware to applications in five abstraction levels.

Instruction Set Architecture Level

At the ISA level, virtualization is performed by emulating a given ISA by the ISA of the host machine. For example, MIPS binary code can run on an x86-based host machine with the help of ISA emulation. With this approach, it is possible to run a large amount of legacy binary code written for various processors on any given new hardware host machine. Instruction set emulation leads to virtual ISAs created on any hardware machine. The basic emulation method is through code interpretation. An interpreter program interprets the source instructions to target instructions one by one.

One source instruction may require tens or hundreds of native target instructions to perform its function. Obviously, this process is relatively slow. For better performance, dynamic binary translation is desired. This approach translates basic blocks of dynamic source instructions to target instructions. The basic blocks can also be extended to program traces or super blocks to increase translation efficiency. Instruction set emulation requires binary translation and optimization. A virtual instruction set architecture (V-ISA) thus requires adding a processor-specific software translation layer to the compiler.

Hardware Abstraction Level

Hardware-level virtualization is performed right on top of the bare hardware. On the one hand, this approach generates a virtual hardware environment for a VM. On the other hand, the process manages the underlying hardware through virtualization. The idea is to virtualize a computer's resources, such as its processors, memory, and I/O devices. The intention is to upgrade the hardware utilization rate by multiple users concurrently. The idea was implemented in the IBM VM/370 in the 1960s. More recently, the Xen hypervisor has been applied to virtualize x86-based machines to run Linux or other guest OS applications.

Operating System Level

This refers to an abstraction layer between traditional OS and user applications. OS-level virtualization creates isolated containers on a single physical server and the OS instances to utilize the hardware and software in data centers.

The containers behave like real servers. OS-level virtualization is commonly used in creating virtual hosting environments to allocate hardware resources among a large number of mutually distrusting users. It is also used, to a lesser extent, in consolidating server hardware by moving services on separate hosts into containers or VMs on one server. OS-level virtualization is depicted.

Library Support Level

Most applications use APIs exported by user-level libraries rather than using lengthy system calls by the OS. Since most systems provide well-documented APIs, such an interface becomes another candidate for virtualization. Virtualization with library interfaces is possible by controlling the communication link between applications and the rest of a system through API hooks. The software tool WINE has implemented this approach to support Windows applications on top of UNIX hosts. Another example is the vCUDA which allows applications executing within VMs to leverage GPU hardware acceleration. This approach is detailed.

User-Application Level

Virtualization at the application level virtualizes an application as a VM. On a traditional OS, an application often runs as a process. Therefore, application-level virtualization is also known as process-level virtualization. The most popular approach is to deploy high level language (HLL) VMs. In this scenario, the virtualization layer sits as an application program on top of the operating system, and the layer exports an abstraction of a VM that can run programs written and compiled to a particular abstract machine definition. Any program written in the HLL and compiled for this VM will be able to run on it. The Microsoft .NET CLR and Java Virtual Machine (JVM) are two good examples of this class of VM.

Other forms of application-level virtualization are known as application isolation, application sandboxing, or application streaming. The process involves wrapping the application in a layer that is isolated from the host OS and other applications. The result is an application that is much easier to distribute and remove from user workstations. An example is the LANDesk application virtualization platform which deploys software applications as self-contained, executable files in an isolated environment without requiring installation, system modifications, or elevated security privileges.

Relative Merits of Different Approaches

Compares the relative merits of implementing virtualization at various levels. The column headings correspond to four technical merits. ―Higher Performance‖ and ―Application Flexibility‖ are self-explanatory. ―Implementation Complexity‖ implies the cost to implement that particular virtualization level. ―Application Isolation‖ refers to the effort required to isolate resources committed to different VMs. Each row corresponds to a particular level of virtualization. Relative Merits of Virtualization at Various Levels (More ―X‖'s Means Higher Merit, with a Maximum of 5 X's).

The number of X's in the table cells reflects the advantage points of each implementation level. Five X's implies the best case and one X implies the worst case. Overall, hardware and OS support will yield the highest performance. However, the hardware and application levels are also the most expensive to implement. User isolation is the most difficult to achieve. ISA implementation offers the best application flexibility.

VMM Design Requirements and Providers

As mentioned earlier, hardware-level virtualization inserts a layer between real hardware and traditional operating systems. This layer is commonly called the Virtual Machine Monitor (VMM) and it manages the hardware resources of a computing system. Each time programs access the hardware the VMM captures the process. In this sense, the VMM acts as a traditional OS. One hardware component, such as the CPU, can be virtualized as several virtual copies. Therefore, several traditional operating systems which are the same or different can sit on the same set of hardware simultaneously.

There are three requirements for a VMM. First, a VMM should provide an environment for programs which is essentially identical to the original machine. Second, programs run in this environment should show, at worst, only minor decreases in speed. Third, a VMM should be in complete control of the system resources. Any program run under a VMM should exhibit a function identical to that which it runs on the original machine directly. Two possible exceptions in terms of differences are permitted with this requirement: differences caused by the availability of system resources and differences caused by timing dependencies. The former arises when more than one VM is running on the same machine.

The hardware resource requirements, such as memory, of each VM are reduced, but the sum of them is greater than that of the real machine installed. The latter qualification is required because of the intervening level of software and the effect of any other VMs concurrently existing on the same hardware. Obviously, these two differences pertain to performance, while the function a VMM provides stays the same as that of a real machine. However, the identical environment requirement excludes the behavior of the usual time-sharing operating system from being classed as a VMM.

A VMM should demonstrate efficiency in using the VMs. Compared with a physical machine, no one prefers a VMM if its efficiency is too low. Traditional emulators and complete software interpreters (simulators) emulate each instruction by means of functions or macros. Such a method provides the most flexible solutions for VMMs.

However, emulators or simulators are too slow to be used as real machines. To guarantee the efficiency of a VMM, a statistically dominant subset of the virtual processor's instructions needs to be executed directly by the real processor, with no software intervention by the VMM , compares four hypervisors and VMMs that are in use today.

Comparison of Four VMM and Hypervisor Software Packages Complete control of these resources by a VMM includes the following aspects:

- The VMM is responsible for allocating hardware resources for programs.
    - It is not possible for a program to access any resource not explicitly allocated to it; and
    - It is possible under certain circumstances for a VMM to regain control of resources already allocated. Not all processors satisfy these requirements for a VMM. A VMM is tightly related to the architectures of processors. It is difficult to implement a VMM for some types of processors, such as the x86. Specific limitations include the inability to trap on some privileged instructions. If a processor is not designed to support virtualization primarily, it is necessary to modify the hardware to satisfy the three requirements for a VMM. This is known as hardware-assisted virtualization.

Virtualization Support at the OS Level

With the help of VM technology, a new computing mode known as cloud computing is emerging. Cloud computing is transforming the computing landscape by shifting the hardware and staffing costs of managing a computational center to third parties, just like banks. However, cloud computing has at least two challenges. The first is the ability to use a variable number of physical machines and VM instances depending on the needs of a problem. For example, a task may need only a single CPU during some phases of execution but may need hundreds of CPUs at other times. The second challenge concerns the slow operation of instantiating new VMs. Currently, new VMs originate either as fresh boots or as replicates of a template VM, unaware of the current application state. Therefore, to better support cloud computing, a large amount of research and development should be done.

Why OS-Level Virtualization?

As mentioned earlier, it is slow to initialize a hardware-level VM because each VM creates its own image from scratch. In a cloud computing environment, perhaps thousands of VMs need to be initialized simultaneously. Besides slow operation, storing the VM images also becomes an issue. As a matter of fact, there is considerable repeated content among VM images. Moreover, full virtualization at the hardware level also has the disadvantages of slow performance and low density, and the need for para-virtualization to modify the guest OS. To reduce the performance overhead of hardware-level virtualization, even hardware modification is needed. OS-level virtualization provides a feasible solution for these hardware-level virtualization issues. Operating system virtualization inserts a virtualization layer inside an operating system to partition a machine's physical resources. It enables multiple isolated VMs within a single operating system kernel. This kind of VM is often called a virtual execution environment (VE), Virtual Private System (VPS), or simply container. From the user's point of view, VEs look like real servers. This means a VE has its own set of processes, file system, user accounts, network interfaces with IP addresses, routing tables, firewall rules, and other personal settings. Although VEs can be customized for different people, they share the same operating system kernel. Therefore, OS-level virtualization is also called single-OS image virtualization which illustrates operating system virtualization from the point of view of a machine stack.

The OpenVZ virtualization layer inside the host OS, which provides some OS images to create VMs quickly. Courtesy of OpenVZ User's Guide

Advantages of OS Extensions

Compared to hardware-level virtualization, the benefits of OS extensions are twofold:

1. VMs at the operating system level have minimal startup/shutdown costs, low resource requirements, and high scalability.

(a) For an OS-level VM, it is possible for a VM and its host environment to synchronize state changes when necessary. These benefits can be achieved via two mechanisms of OS-level virtualization.

   - All OS-level VMs on the same physical machine share a single operating system kernel; and the virtualization layer can be designed in a way that allows processes in VMs to access as many resources of the host machine as possible, but never to modify them. In cloud computing, the first and second benefits can be used to overcome the defects of slow initialization of VMs at the hardware level, and being unaware of the current application state, respectively.

Disadvantages of OS Extensions

The main disadvantage of OS extensions is that all the VMs at operating system level on a single container must have the same kind of guest operating system. That is, although different OS-level VMs may have different operating system distributions, they must pertain to the same operating system family. For example, a Windows distribution such as Windows XP cannot run on a Linux-based container. However, users of cloud computing have various preferences. Some prefer Windows and others prefer Linux or other operating systems. Therefore, there is a challenge for OS-level virtualization in such cases illustrates the concept of OS-level virtualization. The virtualization layer is inserted inside the OS to partition the hardware resources for multiple VMs to run their applications in multiple virtual environments. To implement OS-level virtualization, isolated execution environments (VMs) should be created based on a single OS kernel. Furthermore, the access requests from a VM need to be redirected to the VM's local resource partition on the physical machine. For example, the chroot command in a UNIX system can create several virtual root directories within a host OS. These virtual root directories are the root directories of all VMs created.

There are two ways to implement virtual root directories: duplicating common resources to each VM partition; or sharing most resources with the host environment and only creating private resource copies on the VM on demand. The first way incurs significant resource costs and overhead on a physical machine. This issue neutralizes the benefits of OS-level virtualization, compared with hardware-assisted virtualization.

Therefore, OS-level virtualization is often a second choice.

Virtualization on Linux or Windows Platforms

By far, most reported OS-level virtualization systems are Linux-based. Virtualization support on the Windows-based platform is still in the research stage. The Linux kernel offers an abstraction layer to allow software processes to work with and operate on resources without knowing the hardware details. New hardware may need a new Linux kernel to support. Therefore, different Linux platforms use patched kernels to provide special support for extended functionality.

However, most Linux platforms are not tied to a special kernel. In such a case, a host can run several VMs simultaneously on the same hardware, summarizes several examples of OS-level virtualization tools that have been developed in recent years. Two OS tools (Linux vServer and OpenVZ) support Linux platforms to run other platform-based applications through virtualization.

These two OS-level tools are illustrated in the third tool, FVM, is an attempt specifically developed for virtualization on the Windows NT platform. Virtualization Support for Linux and Windows NT Platforms Uses system call interfaces to create VMs at the NY kernel space; multiple VMs are supported by virtualized namespace and copy-on-write.

Middleware Support for Virtualization

Library-level virtualization is also known as user-level Application Binary Interface (ABI) or API emulation. This type of virtualization can create execution environments for running alien programs on a platform rather than creating a VM to run the entire operating system. API call interception and remapping are the key functions performed. This section provides an overview of several library-level virtualization systems: namely the Windows Application Binary Interface (WABI), lxrun, WINE, Visual MainWin, and vCUDA.

3.3. Virtualization Structures/Tools and Mechanisms

In general, there are three typical classes of VM architecture showed the architectures of a machine before and after virtualization. Before virtualization, the operating system manages the hardware. After virtualization, a virtualization layer is inserted between the hardware and the operating system. In such a case, the virtualization layer is responsible for converting portions of the real hardware into virtual hardware. Therefore, different operating systems such as Linux and Windows can run on the same physical machine, simultaneously. Depending on the position of the virtualization layer, there are several classes of VM architectures, namely the hypervisor architecture, para-virtualization, and host-based virtualization. The hypervisor is also known as the VMM (Virtual Machine Monitor). They both perform the same virtualization operations.

Hypervisor and Xen Architecture

The hypervisor supports hardware-level virtualization on bare metal devices like CPU, memory, disk and network interfaces. The hypervisor software sits directly between the physical hardware and its OS. This virtualization layer is referred to as either the VMM or the hypervisor. The hypervisor provides hypercalls for the guest OSes and applications. Depending on the functionality, a hypervisor can assume a micro-kernel architecture like the Microsoft Hyper-V. Or it can assume a monolithic hypervisor architecture like the VMware ESX for server virtualization.

A micro-kernel hypervisor includes only the basic and unchanging functions (such as physical memory management and processor scheduling). The device drivers and other changeable components are outside the hypervisor. A monolithic hypervisor implements all the aforementioned functions, including those of the device drivers. Therefore, the size of the hypervisor code of a micro-kernel hypervisor is smaller than that of a monolithic hypervisor. Essentially, a hypervisor must be able to convert physical devices into virtual resources dedicated for the deployed VM to use.

The Xen Architecture

Xen is an open source hypervisor program developed by Cambridge University. Xen is a micro-kernel hypervisor, which separates the policy from the mechanism. The Xen hypervisor implements all the mechanisms, leaving the policy to be handled by Domain 0. Xen does not include any device drivers natively . It just provides a mechanism by which a guest OS can have direct access to the physical devices. As a result, the size of the Xen hypervisor is kept rather small. Xen provides a virtual environment located between the hardware and the OS. A number of vendors are in the process of developing commercial Xen hypervisors, among them are Citrix XenServer and Oracle VM.

The core components of a Xen system are the hypervisor, kernel, and applications. The organization of the three components is important. Like other virtualization systems, many guest OSes can run on top of the hypervisor. However, not all guest OSes are created equal, and one in particular controls the others. The guest OS, which has control ability, is called Domain 0, and the others are called Domain U. Domain 0 is a privileged guest OS of Xen. It is first loaded when Xen boots without any file system drivers being available. Domain 0 is designed to access hardware directly and manage devices.

Therefore, one of the responsibilities of Domain 0 is to allocate and map hardware resources for the guest domains (the Domain U domains).

For example, Xen is based on Linux and its security level is C2. Its management VM is named Domain 0, which has the privilege to manage other VMs implemented on the same host. If Domain 0 is compromised, the hacker can control the entire system. So, in the VM system, security policies are needed to improve the security of Domain 0. Domain 0, behaving as a VMM, allows users to create, copy, save, read, modify, share, migrate, and roll back VMs as easily as manipulating a file, which flexibly provides tremendous benefits for users. Unfortunately, it also brings a series of security problems during the software life cycle and data lifetime. Traditionally, a machine's lifetime can be envisioned as a straight line where the current state of the machine is a point that progresses monotonically as the software executes. During this time, configuration changes are made, software is installed, and patches are applied. In such an environment, the VM state is akin to a tree: At any point, execution can go into N different branches where multiple instances of a VM can exist at any point in this tree at any given time. VMs are allowed to roll back to previous states in their execution (e.g., to fix configuration errors) or rerun from the same point many times (e.g., as a means of distributing dynamic content or circulating a —live‖ system image).

Binary Translation with Full Virtualization

Depending on implementation technologies, hardware virtualization can be classified into two categories: full virtualization and host-based virtualization. Full virtualization does not need to modify the host OS. It relies on binary translation to trap and to virtualize the execution of certain sensitive, nonvirtualizable instructions. The guest OSes and their applications consist of noncritical and critical instructions. In a host-based system, both a host OS and a guest OS are used. A virtualization software layer is built between the host OS and guest OS. These two classes of VM architecture are introduced next.

Full Virtualization

With full virtualization, noncritical instructions run on the hardware directly while critical instructions are discovered and replaced with traps into the VMM to be emulated by software. Both the hypervisor and VMM approaches are considered full virtualization. Why are only critical instructions trapped into the VMM? This is because binary translation can incur a large performance overhead. Noncritical instructions do not control hardware or threaten the security of the system, but critical instructions do. Therefore, running noncritical instructions on hardware not only can promote efficiency, but also can ensure system security.

Binary Translation of Guest OS Requests Using a VMM

This approach was implemented by VMware and many other software companies. VMware puts the VMM at Ring 0 and the guest OS at Ring 1. The VMM scans the instruction stream and identifies the privileged, control- and behavior-sensitive instructions. When these instructions are identified, they are trapped into the VMM, which emulates the behavior of these instructions. The method used in this emulation is called binary translation. Therefore, full virtualization combines binary translation and direct execution. The guest OS is completely decoupled from the underlying hardware. Consequently, the guest OS is unaware that it is being virtualized. Indirect execution of complex instructions via binary translation of guest OS requests using the VMM plus direct execution of simple instructions on the same host.

Courtesy of VM Ware The performance of full virtualization may not be ideal, because it involves binary translation which is rather time-consuming. In particular, the full virtualization of I/O-intensive applications is a really a big challenge. Binary translation employs a code cache to store translated hot instructions to improve performance, but it increases the cost of memory usage. At the time of this writing, the performance of full virtualization on the x86 architecture is typically 80 percent to 97 percent that of the host machine.

Host-Based Virtualization

An alternative VM architecture is to install a virtualization layer on top of the host OS. This host OS is still responsible for managing the hardware. The guest OSes are installed and run on top of the virtualization layer. Dedicated applications may run on the VMs. Certainly, some other applications can also run with the host OS directly. This host-based architecture has some distinct advantages, as enumerated next. First, the user can install this VM architecture without modifying the host OS. The virtualizing software can rely on the host OS to provide device drivers and other low-level services. This will simplify the VM design and ease its deployment. Second, the host-based approach appeals to many host machine configurations. Compared to the hypervisor/VMM architecture, the performance of the host-based architecture may also be low. When an application requests hardware access, it involves four layers of mapping which downgrades performance significantly. When the ISA of a guest OS is different from the ISA of the underlying hardware, binary translation must be adopted. Although the host-based architecture has flexibility, the performance is too low to be useful in practice.

Para-Virtualization with Compiler Support

Para-virtualization needs to modify the guest operating systems. A para-virtualized VM provides special APIs requiring substantial OS modifications in user applications. Performance degradation is a critical issue of a virtualized system. No one wants to use a VM if it is much slower than using a physical machine. The virtualization layer can be inserted at different positions in a machine software stack. However, para-virtualization attempts to reduce the virtualization overhead, and thus improve performance by modifying only the guest OS kernel, illustrates the concept of a para-virtualized VM architecture. The guest operating systems are para-virtualized. They are assisted by an intelligent compiler to replace the nonvirtualizable OS instructions by hypercalls. The traditional x86 processor offers four instruction execution rings: Rings 0, 1, 2, and 3.

The lower the ring number, the higher the privilege of instruction being executed. The OS is responsible for managing the hardware and the privileged instructions to execute at Ring 0, while user-level applications run at Ring 3. The best example of para-virtualization is the KVM to be described below.

Para-virtualized VM architecture, which involves modifying the guest OS kernel to replace nonvirtualizable instructions with hypercalls for the hypervisor or the VMM to carry out the virtualization process.

The use of a para-virtualized guest OS assisted by an intelligent compiler to replace nonvirtualizable OS instructions by hypercalls. Courtesy of VMW are:

Para-Virtualization Architecture

When the x86 processor is virtualized, a virtualization layer is inserted between the hardware and the OS. According to the x86 ring definition, the virtualization layer should also be installed at Ring 0. Different instructions at Ring 0 may cause some problems. Para-virtualization replaces nonvirtualizable instructions with hypercalls that communicate directly with the hypervisor or VMM. However, when the guest OS kernel is modified for virtualization, it can no longer run on the hardware directly.

Although para-virtualization reduces the overhead, it has incurred other problems. First, its compatibility and portability may be in doubt, because it must support the unmodified OS as well. Second, the cost of maintaining para-virtualized OSes is high, because they may require deep OS kernel modifications. Finally, the performance advantage of para-virtualization varies greatly due to workload variations. Compared with full virtualization, para-virtualization is relatively easy and more practical. The main problem in full virtualization is its low performance in binary translation. To speed up binary translation is difficult. Therefore, many virtualization products employ the para-virtualization architecture. The popular Xen, KVM, and VMware ESX are good examples.

KVM (Kernel-Based VM)

This is a Linux para-virtualization system—a part of the Linux version 2.6.20 kernel. Memory management and scheduling activities are carried out by the existing Linux kernel. The KVM does the rest, which makes it simpler than the hypervisor that controls the entire machine. KVM is a hardware-assisted para-virtualization tool, which improves performance and supports unmodified guest OSes such as Windows, Linux, Solaris, and other UNIX variants.

Para-Virtualization with Compiler Support

Unlike the full virtualization architecture which intercepts and emulates privileged and sensitive instructions at runtime, para-virtualization handles these instructions at compile time. The guest OS kernel is modified to replace the privileged and sensitive instructions with hypercalls to the hypervisor or VMM. Xen assumes such a para-virtualization architecture. The guest OS running in a guest domain may run at Ring 1 instead of at Ring 0. This implies that the guest OS may not be able to execute some privileged and sensitive instructions. The privileged instructions are implemented by hypercalls to the hypervisor. After replacing the instructions with hypercalls, the modified guest OS emulates the behavior of the original guest OS. On an UNIX system, a system call involves an interrupt or service routine. The hypercalls apply a dedicated service routine in Xen.

3.4. Virtualization of CPU, Memory, and I/O Devices

To support virtualization, processors such as the x86 employ a special running mode and instructions, known as hardware-assisted virtualization. In this way, the VMM and guest OS run in different modes and all sensitive instructions of the guest OS and its applications are trapped in the VMM. To save processor states, mode switching is completed by hardware. For the x86 architecture, Intel and AMD have proprietary technologies for hardware-assisted virtualization.

Hardware Support for Virtualization

Modern operating systems and processors permit multiple processes to run simultaneously.

If there is no protection mechanism in a processor, all instructions from different processes will access the hardware directly and cause a system crash. Therefore, all processors have at least two modes, user mode and supervisor mode, to ensure controlled access of critical hardware. Instructions running in supervisor mode are called privileged instructions. Other instructions are unprivileged instructions. In a virtualized environment, it is more difficult to make OSes and applications run correctly because there are more layers in the machine stack. Intel's hardware support approach.

At the time of this writing, many hardware virtualization products were available. The VMware Workstation is a VM software suite for x86 and x86-64 computers. This software suite allows users to set up multiple x86 and x86-64 virtual computers and to use one or more of these VMs simultaneously with the host operating system. The VMware Workstation assumes the host-based virtualization. Xen is a hypervisor for use in IA-32, x86-64, Itanium, and PowerPC 970 hosts.

Actually, Xen modifies Linux as the lowest and most privileged layer, or a hypervisor. One or more guest OS can run on top of the hypervisor. KVM (Kernel-based Virtual Machine) is a Linux kernel virtualization infrastructure. KVM can support hardware-assisted virtualization and para virtualization by using the Intel VT-x or AMD-v and VirtIO framework, respectively. The VirtIO framework includes a para virtual Ethernet card, a disk I/O controller, a balloon device for adjusting guest memory usage, and a VGA graphics interface using VMware drivers.

CPU Virtualization

A VM is a duplicate of an existing computer system in which a majority of the VM instructions are executed on the host processor in native mode. Thus, unprivileged instructions of VMs run directly on the host machine for higher efficiency. Other critical instructions should be handled carefully for correctness and stability. The critical instructions are divided into three categories: privileged instructions, control-sensitive instructions, and behavior-sensitive instructions. Privileged instructions execute in a privileged mode and will be trapped if executed outside this mode. Control-sensitive instructions attempt to change the configuration of resources used. Behavior-sensitive instructions have different behaviors depending on the configuration of resources, including the load and store operations over the virtual memory. A CPU architecture is virtualizable if it supports the ability to run the VM's privileged and unprivileged instructions in the CPU's user mode while the VMM runs in supervisor mode. When the privileged instructions including control- and behavior-sensitive instructions of a VM are executed, they are trapped in the VMM. In this case, the VMM acts as a unified mediator for hardware access from different VMs to guarantee the correctness and stability of the whole system. However, not all CPU architectures are virtualizable. RISC CPU architectures can be naturally virtualized because all control-and behavior-sensitive instructions are privileged instructions. On the contrary, x86 CPU architectures are not primarily designed to support virtualization. This is because about 10 sensitive instructions, such as SGDT and SMSW, are not privileged instructions. When these instructions execute in virtualization, they cannot be trapped in the VMM. On a native UNIX-like system, a system call triggers the 80h interrupt and passes control to the OS kernel. The interrupt handler in the kernel is then invoked to process the system call.

On a para virtualization system such as Xen, a system call in the guest OS first triggers the 80h interrupt normally. Almost at the same time, the 82h interrupt in the hypervisor is triggered. Incidentally, control is passed on to the hypervisor as well. When the hypervisor completes its task for the guest OS system call, it passes control back to the guest OS kernel. Certainly, the guest OS kernel may also invoke the hyper call while it's running. Although para virtualization of a CPU lets unmodified applications run in the VM, it causes a small performance penalty.

Hardware-Assisted CPU Virtualization

This technique attempts to simplify virtualization because full or paravirtualization is complicated. Intel and AMD add an additional mode called privilege mode level (some people call it Ring-1) to x86 processors. Therefore, operating systems can still run at Ring 0 and the hypervisor can run at Ring -1. All the privileged and sensitive instructions are trapped in the hypervisor automatically. This technique removes the difficulty of implementing binary translation of full virtualization. It also lets the operating system run in VMs without modification.

Memory Virtualization

Virtual memory virtualization is similar to the virtual memory support provided by modern operating systems. In a traditional execution environment, the operating system maintains mappings of virtual memory to machine memory using page tables, which is a one-stage mapping from virtual memory to machine memory. All modern x86 CPUs include a memory management unit (MMU) and a translation look aside buffer (TLB) to optimize virtual memory performance. However, in a virtual execution environment, virtual memory virtualization involves sharing the physical system memory in RAM and dynamically allocating it to the physical memory of the VMs. That means a two-stage mapping process should be maintained by the guest OS and the VMM, respectively: virtual memory to physical memory and physical memory to machine memory. Furthermore, MMU virtualization should be supported, which is transparent to the guest OS. The guest OS continues to control the mapping of virtual addresses to the physical memory addresses of VMs. But the guest OS cannot directly access the actual machine memory.

The VMM is responsible for mapping the guest physical memory to the actual machine memory, shows the two-level memory mapping procedure. Two-level memory mapping procedure. Courtesy of R. Rblig, et al. Since each page table of the guest OSes has a separate page table in the VMM corresponding to it, the VMM page table is called the shadow page table. Nested page tables add another layer of indirection to virtual memory. The MMU already handles virtual-to-physical translations as defined by the OS. Then the physical memory addresses are translated to machine addresses using another set of page tables defined by the hypervisor. Since modern operating systems maintain a set of page tables for every process, the shadow page tables will get flooded. Consequently, the performance overhead and cost of memory will be very high.

VMware uses shadow page tables to perform virtual-memory-to-machine-memory address translation. Processors use TLB hardware to map the virtual memory directly to the machine memory to avoid the two levels of translation on every access. When the guest OS changes the virtual memory to a physical memory mapping, the VMM updates the shadow page tables to enable a direct lookup. The AMD Barcelona processor has featured hardware-assisted memory virtualization since 2007. It provides hardware assistance to the two-stage address translation in a virtual execution environment by using a technology called nested paging.

I/O Virtualization

I/O virtualization involves managing the routing of I/O requests between virtual devices and the shared physical hardware. At the time of this writing, there are three ways to implement I/O virtualization: full device emulation, para-virtualization, and direct I/O. Full device emulation is the first approach for I/O virtualization. Generally, this approach emulates well-known, real-world devices. All the functions of a device or bus infrastructure, such as device enumeration, identification, interrupts, and DMA, are replicated in software. This software is located in the VMM and acts as a virtual device. The I/O access requests of the guest OS are trapped in the VMM which interacts with the I/O devices. Device emulation for I/O virtualization implemented inside the middle layer that maps real I/O devices into the virtual devices for the guest device driver to use. Courtesy of V. Chadha, et al. and Y. Dong, et al. A single hardware device can be shared by multiple VMs that run concurrently. However, software emulation runs much slower than the hardware it emulates.

The para-virtualization method of I/O virtualization is typically used in Xen. It is also known as the split driver model consisting of a frontend driver and a backend driver. The frontend driver is running in Domain U and the backend driver is running in Domain 0. They interact with each other via a block of shared memory. The frontend driver manages the I/O requests of the guest OSes and the backend driver is responsible for managing the real I/O devices and multiplexing the I/O data of different VMs. Although para-I/O-virtualization achieves better device performance than full device emulation, it comes with a higher CPU overhead.

Direct I/O virtualization lets the VM access devices directly. It can achieve close-to-native performance without high CPU costs. However, current direct I/O virtualization implementations focus on networking for mainframes. There are a lot of challenges for commodity hardware devices.

For example, when a physical device is reclaimed (required by workload migration) for later reassignment, it may have been set to an arbitrary state (e.g., DMA to some arbitrary memory locations) that can function incorrectly or even crash the whole system. Since software-based I/O virtualization requires a very high overhead of device emulation, hardware-assisted I/O virtualization is critical. Intel VT-d supports the remapping of I/O DMA transfers and device-generated interrupts. The architecture of VT-d provides the flexibility to support multiple usage models that may run unmodified, special-purpose, or ―virtualization-aware‖ guest OSes.

Another way to help I/O virtualization is via self-virtualized I/O (SV-IO) . The key idea of SV-IO is to harness the rich resources of a multi core processor. All tasks associated with virtualizing an I/O device are encapsulated in SV-IO. It provides virtual devices and an associated access API to VMs and a management API to the VMM. SV-IO defines one virtual interface (VIF) for every kind of virtualized I/O device, such as virtual network interfaces, virtual block devices (disk), virtual camera devices, and others. The guest OS interacts with the VIFs via VIF device drivers. Each VIF consists of two message queues. One is for outgoing messages to the devices and the other is for incoming messages from the devices. In addition, each VIF has a unique ID for identifying it in SV-IO.

Virtual Clusters and Resource Management

A physical cluster is a collection of servers (physical machines) interconnected by a physical network such as a LAN. various clustering techniques on physical machines. Here, we introduce virtual clusters and study its properties as well as explore their potential applications. In this section, we will study three critical design issues of virtual clusters: live migration of VMs, memory and file migrations, and dynamic deployment of virtual clusters. When a traditional VM is initialized, the administrator needs to manually write configuration information or specify the configuration sources. When more VMs join a network, an inefficient configuration always causes problems with overloading or underutilization. Amazon's Elastic Compute Cloud (EC2) is a good example of a web service that provides elastic computing power in a cloud. EC2 permits customers to create VMs and to manage user accounts over the time of their use. Most virtualization platforms, including XenServer and VMware ESX Server, support a bridging mode which allows all domains to appear on the network as individual hosts. By using this mode, VMs can communicate with one another freely through the virtual network interface card and configure the network automatically.

Physical Versus Virtual Clusters

Virtual clusters are built with VMs installed at distributed servers from one or more physical clusters. The VMs in a virtual cluster are interconnected logically by a virtual network across several physical networks. Figure 3.18 illustrates the concepts of virtual clusters and physical clusters. Each virtual cluster is formed with physical machines or a VM hosted by multiple physical clusters. The virtual cluster boundaries are shown as distinct boundaries. A cloud platform with four virtual clusters over three physical clusters shaded differently. Courtesy of Fan Zhang, Tsinghua University.

The provisioning of VMs to a virtual cluster is done dynamically to have the following interesting properties:

- The virtual cluster nodes can be either physical or virtual machines. Multiple VMs running with different OSes can be deployed on the same physical node.
- A VM runs with a guest OS, which is often different from the host OS, that manages the resources in the physical machine, where the VM is implemented.
- The purpose of using VMs is to consolidate multiple functionalities on the same server. This will greatly enhance server utilization and application flexibility.
- VMs can be colonized (replicated) in multiple servers for the purpose of promoting distributed parallelism, fault tolerance, and disaster recovery.
- The size (number of nodes) of a virtual cluster can grow or shrink dynamically, similar to the way an overlay network varies in size in a peer-to-peer (P2P) network.
- The failure of any physical nodes may disable some VMs installed on the failing nodes. But the failure of VMs will not pull down the host system.

Since system virtualization has been widely used, it is necessary to effectively manage VMs running on a mass of physical computing nodes (also called virtual clusters) and consequently build a high-performance virtualized computing environment. This involves virtual cluster deployment, monitoring and management over large-scale clusters, as well as resource scheduling, load balancing, server consolidation, fault tolerance, and other techniques. The different node colors refer to different virtual clusters. In a virtual cluster system, it is quite important to store the large number of VM images efficiently. The concept of a virtual cluster based on application partitioning or customization. The different colors in the figure represent the nodes in different virtual clusters. As a large number of VM images might be present, the most important thing is to determine how to store those images in the system efficiently. There are common installations for most users or applications, such as operating systems or user-level programming libraries. These software packages can be preinstalled as templates (called template VMs). With these templates, users can build their own software stacks. New OS instances can be copied from the template VM. User-specific components such as programming libraries and applications can be installed to those instances. The concept of a virtual cluster based on application partitioning. Courtesy of Kang Chen, Tsinghua University 2008.

Three physical clusters and Four virtual clusters are created on the right, over the physical clusters. The physical machines are also called host systems. In contrast, the VMs are guest systems. The host and guest systems may run with different operating systems. Each VM can be installed on a remote server or replicated on multiple servers belonging to the same or different physical clusters. The boundary of a virtual cluster can change as VM nodes are added, removed, or migrated dynamically over time.

Fast Deployment and Effective Scheduling

The system should have the capability of fast deployment. Here, deployment means two things: to construct and distribute software stacks (OS, libraries, applications) to a physical node inside clusters as fast as possible, and to quickly switch runtime environments from one user's virtual cluster to another user's virtual cluster. If one user finishes using his system, the corresponding virtual cluster should shut down or suspend quickly to save the resources to run other VMs for other users.

The concept of —green computing‖ has attracted much attention recently. However, previous approaches have focused on saving the energy cost of components in a single workstation without a global vision. Consequently, they do not necessarily reduce the power consumption of the whole cluster. Other cluster-wide energy-efficient techniques can only be applied to homogeneous workstations and specific applications. The live migration of VMs allows workloads of one node to transfer to another node. However, it does not guarantee that VMs can randomly migrate among themselves. In fact, the potential overhead caused by live migrations of VMs cannot be ignored.

The overhead may have serious negative effects on cluster utilization, throughput, and QoS issues. Therefore, the challenge is to determine how to design migration strategies to implement green computing without influencing the performance of clusters. Another advantage of virtualization is load balancing of applications in a virtual cluster. Load balancing can be achieved using the load index and frequency of user logins. The automatic scale-up and scale-down mechanism of a virtual cluster can be implemented based on this model. Consequently, we can increase the resource utilization of nodes and shorten the response time of systems. Mapping VMs onto the most appropriate physical node should promote performance. Dynamically adjusting loads among nodes by live migration of VMs is desired, when the loads on cluster nodes become quite unbalanced.

High-Performance Virtual Storage

The template VM can be distributed to several physical hosts in the cluster to customize the VMs. In addition, existing software packages reduce the time for customization as well as switching virtual environments. It is important to efficiently manage the disk spaces occupied by template software packages. Some storage architecture design can be applied to reduce duplicated blocks in a distributed file system of virtual clusters. Hash values are used to compare the contents of data blocks. Users have their own profiles which store the identification of the data blocks for corresponding VMs in a user-specific virtual cluster. New blocks are created when users modify the corresponding data. Newly created blocks are identified in the users' profiles. Basically, there are four steps to deploy a group of VMs onto a target cluster: preparing the disk image, configuring the VMs, choosing the destination nodes, and executing the VM deployment command on every host. Many systems use templates to simplify the disk image preparation process. A template is a disk image that includes a preinstalled operating system with or without certain application software. Users choose a proper template according to their requirements and make a duplicate of it as their own disk image. Templates could implement the COW (Copy on Write) format. A new COW backup file is very small and easy to create and transfer. Therefore, it definitely reduces disk space consumption. In addition, VM deployment time is much shorter than that of copying the whole raw image file. Every VM is configured with a name, disk image, network setting, and allocated CPU and memory. One needs to record each VM configuration into a file. However, this method is inefficient when managing a large group of VMs. VMs with the same configurations could use preedited profiles to simplify the process. In this scenario, the system configures the VMs according to the chosen profile. Most configuration items use the same settings, while some of them, such as UUID, VM name, and IP address, are assigned with automatically calculated values. Normally, users do not care which host is running their VM. A strategy to choose the proper destination host for any VM is needed. The deployment principle is to fulfill the VM requirement and to balance workloads among the whole host network.

Live VM Migration Steps and Performance Effects

In a cluster built with mixed nodes of host and guest systems, the normal method of operation is to run everything on the physical machine. When a VM fails, its role could be replaced by another VM on a different node, as long as they both run with the same guest OS. In other words, a physical node can fail over to a VM on another host. This is different from physical-to-physical failover in a traditional physical cluster. The advantage is enhanced failover flexibility. The potential drawback is that a VM must stop playing its role if its residing host node fails. However, this problem can be mitigated with VM life migration. Figure 3.20 shows the process of life migration of a VM from host A to host B. The migration copies the VM state file from the storage area to the host machine. Live migration process of a VM from one host to another. Courtesy of C. Clark, et al. are four ways to manage a virtual cluster. First, you can use a guest-based manager, by which the cluster manager resides on a guest system. In this case, multiple VMs form a virtual cluster. For example, openMosix is an open source Linux cluster running different guest systems on top of the Xen hypervisor. Another example is Sun's cluster Oasis, an experimental Solaris cluster of VMs supported by a VMware VMM.

Second, you can build a cluster manager on the host systems. The host-based manager supervises the guest systems and can restart the guest system on another physical machine. A good example is the VMware HA system that can restart a guest system after failure.

These two cluster management systems are either guest-only or host-only, but they do not mix. A third way to manage a virtual cluster is to use an independent cluster manager on both the host and guest systems. This will make infrastructure management more complex, however. Finally, you can use an integrated cluster on the guest and host systems. This means the manager must be designed to distinguish between virtualized resources and physical resources. Various cluster management schemes can be greatly enhanced when VM life migration is enabled with minimal overhead.

VMs can be live-migrated from one physical machine to another; in case of failure, one VM can be replaced by another VM. Virtual clusters can be applied in computational grids, cloud platforms, and high-performance computing (HPC) systems. The major attraction of this scenario is that virtual clustering provides dynamic resources that can be quickly put together upon user demand or after a node failure. In particular, virtual clustering plays a key role in cloud computing. When a VM runs a live service, it is necessary to make a trade-off to ensure that the migration occurs in a manner that minimizes all three metrics. The motivation is to design a live VM migration scheme with negligible downtime, the lowest network bandwidth consumption possible, and a reasonable total migration time.

Furthermore, we should ensure that the migration will not disrupt other active services residing in the same host through resource contention (e.g., CPU, network bandwidth). A VM can be in one of the following four states. An inactive state is defined by the virtualization platform, under which the VM is not enabled. An active state refers to a VM that has been instantiated at the virtualization platform to perform a real task. A paused state corresponds to a VM that has been instantiated but disabled to process a task or paused in a waiting state. A VM enters the suspended state if its machine file and virtual resources are stored back to the disk, live migration of a VM consists of the following six steps:

Steps 0 and 1: Start migration. This step makes preparations for the migration, including determining the migrating VM and the destination host. Although users could manually make a

VM migrate to an appointed host, in most circumstances, the migration is automatically started by strategies such as load balancing and server consolidation.

Steps 2: Transfer memory. Since the whole execution state of the VM is stored in memory, sending the VM's memory to the destination node ensures continuity of the service provided by the VM. All of the memory data is transferred in the first round, and then the migration controller recopies the memory data which is changed in the last round. These steps keep iterating until the dirty portion of the memory is small enough to handle the final copy. Although pre-copying memory is performed iteratively, the execution of programs is not obviously interrupted.

Step 3: Suspend the VM and copy the last portion of the data. The migrating VM's execution is suspended when the last round's memory data is transferred. Other non memory data such as CPU and network states should be sent as well. During this step, the VM is stopped and its applications will no longer run. This —service unavailable‖ time is called the —downtime‖ of migration, which should be as short as possible so that it can be negligible to users.

Steps 4 and 5: Commit and activate the new host. After all the needed data is copied, on the destination host, the VM reloads the states and recovers the execution of programs in it, and the service provided by this VM continues. Then the network connection is redirected to the new VM and the dependency to the source host is cleared. The whole migration process finishes by removing the original VM from the source host.

The effect on the data transmission rate (Mbit/second) of live migration of a VM from one host to another. Before copying the VM with 512 KB files for 100 clients, the data throughput was 870 MB/second. The first pre-copy takes 63 seconds, during which the rate is reduced to 765 MB/second. Then the data rate reduces to 694 MB/second in 9.8 seconds for more iterations of the copying process. The system experiences only 165 ms of downtime, before the VM is restored at the destination host. This experimental result shows a very small migration overhead in live transfer of a VM between host nodes. This is critical to achieve dynamic cluster reconfiguration and disaster recovery as needed in cloud computing.

Effect on data transmission rate of a VM migrated from one failing web server to another. Courtesy of C. Clark, et al. With the emergence of widespread cluster computing more than a decade ago, many cluster configuration and management systems have been developed to achieve a range of goals. These goals naturally influence individual approaches to cluster management. VM technology has become a popular method for simplifying management and sharing of physical computing resources. Platforms such as VMware and Xen allow multiple

VMs with different operating systems and configurations to coexist on the same physical host in mutual isolation. Clustering inexpensive computers is an effective way to obtain reliable, scalable computing power for network services and compute-intensive applications

Migration of Memory, Files, and Network Resources

Since clusters have a high initial cost of ownership, including space, power conditioning, and cooling equipment, leasing or sharing access to a common cluster is an attractive solution when demands vary over time. Shared clusters offer economies of scale and more effective utilization of resources by multiplexing. Early configuration and management systems focus on expressive and scalable mechanisms for defining clusters for specific types of service, and physically partition cluster nodes among those types. When one system migrates to another physical node, we should consider the following issues.

Memory Migration

This is one of the most important aspects of VM migration. Moving the memory instance of a VM from one physical host to another can be approached in any number of ways. But traditionally, the concepts behind the techniques tend to share common implementation paradigms.

The techniques employed for this purpose depend upon the characteristics of application/workloads supported by the guest OS.

Memory migration can be in a range of hundreds of megabytes to a few gigabytes in a typical system today, and it needs to be done in an efficient manner. The Internet Suspend-Resume (ISR) technique exploits temporal locality as memory states are likely to have considerable overlap in the suspended and the resumed instances of a VM. Temporal locality refers to the fact that the memory states differ only by the amount of work done since a VM was last suspended before being initiated for migration.

To exploit temporal locality, each file in the file system is represented as a tree of small sub files. A copy of this tree exists in both the suspended and resumed VM instances. The advantage of using a tree-based representation of files is that the caching ensures the transmission of only those files which have been changed.

The ISR technique deals with situations where the migration of live machines is not a necessity. Predictably, the downtime (the period during which the service is unavailable due to there being no currently executing instance of a VM) is high, compared to some of the other techniques.

File System Migration

To support VM migration, a system must provide each VM with a consistent, location-independent view of the file system that is available on all hosts. A simple way to achieve this is to provide each VM with its own virtual disk which the file system is mapped to and transport the contents of this virtual disk along with the other states of the VM. However, due to the current trend of high-capacity disks, migration of the contents of an entire disk over a network is not a viable solution. Another way is to have a global file system across all machines where a VM could be located. This way removes the need to copy files from one machine to another because all files are network-accessible.

A distributed file system is used in ISR serving as a transport mechanism for propagating a suspended VM state. The actual file systems themselves are not mapped onto the distributed file system. Instead, the VMM only accesses its local file system. The relevant VM files are explicitly copied into the local file system for a resume operation and taken out of the local file system for a suspend operation. This approach relieves developers from the complexities of implementing several different file system calls for different distributed file systems. It also essentially disassociates the VMM from any particular distributed file system semantics. However, this decoupling means that the VMM has to store the contents of each VM's virtual disks in its local files, which have to be moved around with the other state information of that VM.

In smart copying, the VMM exploits spatial locality. Typically, people often move between the same small number of locations, such as their home and office. In these conditions, it is possible to transmit only the difference between the two file systems at suspending and resuming locations. This technique significantly reduces the amount of actual physical data that has to be moved. In situations where there is no locality to exploit, a different approach is to synthesize much of the state at the resuming site. On many systems, user files only form a small fraction of the actual data on disk. Operating system and application software account for the majority of storage space. The proactive state transfer solution works in those cases where the resuming site can be predicted with reasonable confidence.

Network Migration

A migrating VM should maintain all open network connections without relying on forwarding mechanisms on the original host or on support from mobility or redirection mechanisms. To enable remote systems to locate and communicate with a VM, each VM must be assigned a virtual IP address known to other entities. This address can be distinct from the

IP address of the host machine where the VM is currently located. Each VM can also have its own distinct virtual MAC address. The VMM maintains a mapping of the virtual IP and MAC addresses to their corresponding VMs. In general, a migrating VM includes all the protocol states and carries its IP address with it.

If the source and destination machines of a VM migration are typically connected to a single switched LAN, an unsolicited ARP reply from the migrating host is provided advertising that the IP has moved to a new location. This solves the open network connection problem by reconfiguring all the peers to send future packets to a new location. Although a few packets that have already been transmitted might be lost, there are no other problems with this mechanism. Alternatively, on a switched network, the migrating OS can keep its original Ethernet MAC address and rely on the network switch to detect its move to a new port.

Live migration means moving a VM from one physical node to another while keeping its OS environment and applications unbroken. This capability is being increasingly utilized in today's enterprise environments to provide efficient online system maintenance, reconfiguration, load balancing, and proactive fault tolerance. It provides desirable features to satisfy requirements for computing resources in modern computing systems, including server consolidation, performance isolation, and ease of management. As a result, many implementations are available which support the feature using disparate functionalities. Traditional migration suspends VMs before the transportation and then resumes them at the end of the process. By importing the pre copy mechanism, a VM could be live-migrated without stopping the VM and keep the applications running during the migration. Live migration is a key feature of system virtualization technologies. Here, we focus on VM migration within a cluster environment where a network-accessible storage system, such as storage area network (SAN) or network attached storage (NAS), is employed. Only memory and CPU status needs to be transferred from the source node to the target node. Live migration techniques mainly use the precopy approach, which first transfers all memory pages, and then only copies modified pages during the last round iteratively. The VM service downtime is expected to be minimal by using iterative copy operations. When applications' writable working set becomes small, the VM is suspended and only the CPU state and dirty pages in the last round are sent out to the destination. In the precopy phase, although a VM service is still available, much performance degradation will occur because the migration daemon continually consumes network bandwidth to transfer dirty pages in each round. An adaptive rate limiting approach is employed to mitigate this issue, but total migration time is prolonged by nearly 10 times. Moreover, the maximum number of iterations must be set because not all applications' dirty pages are ensured to converge to a small writable working set over multiple rounds. In fact, these issues with the precopy approach are caused by the large amount of transferred data during the whole migration process. A check pointing/recovery and trace/replay approach (CR/TR-Motion) is proposed to provide fast VM migration. This approach transfers the execution trace file in iterations rather than dirty pages, which is logged by a trace daemon. Apparently, the total size of all log files is much less than that of dirty pages. So, total migration time and downtime of migration are drastically reduced. However, CR/TR-Motion is valid only when the log replay rate is larger than the log growth rate. The inequality between source and target nodes limits the application scope of live migration in clusters. Another strategy of postcopy is introduced for live migration of VMs. Here, all memory pages are transferred only once during the whole migration process and the baseline total migration time is reduced. But the downtime is much higher than that of precopy due to the latency of fetching pages from the source node before the VM can be resumed on the target. With the advent of multicore or many-core machines, abundant CPU resources are available. Even if several VMs reside on a same multi core machine, CPU resources are still rich because physical CPUs are frequently amenable to multiplexing. We can exploit these copious CPU resources to compress page frames and the amount of transferred data can be significantly reduced. Memory compression algorithms typically have little memory overhead. Decompression is simple and very fast and requires no memory for decompression.

3.5.   Virtualization for Data-Center Automation

Data centers have grown rapidly in recent years, and all major IT companies are pouring their resources into building new data centers. In addition, Google, Yahoo!, Amazon, Microsoft, HP, Apple, and IBM are all in the game. All these companies have invested billions of dollars in data-center construction and automation. Data-center automation means that huge volumes of hardware, software, and database resources in these data centers can be allocated dynamically to millions of Internet users simultaneously, with guaranteed QoS and cost-effectiveness.

This automation process is triggered by the growth of virtualization products and cloud computing services. From 2006 to 2011, according to an IDC 2007 report on the growth of virtualization and its market distribution in major IT sectors. In 2006, virtualization has a market share of $1,044 million in business and enterprise opportunities. The majority was dominated by production consolidation and software development. Virtualization is moving towards enhancing mobility, reducing planned downtime (for maintenance), and increasing the number of virtual clients.

The latest virtualization development highlights high availability (HA), backup services, workload balancing, and further increases in client bases. IDC projected that automation, service orientation, policy-based, and variable costs in the virtualization market. The total business opportunities may increase to $3.2 billion by 2011. The major market share moves to the areas of HA, utility computing, production consolidation, and client bases. In what follows, we will discuss server consolidation, virtual storage, OS support, and trust management in automated data-center designs.

Server Consolidation in Data Centers

In data centers, a large number of heterogeneous workloads can run on servers at various times.

These heterogeneous workloads can be roughly divided into two categories: chatty workloads and noninteractive workloads. Chatty workloads may burst at some point and return to a silent state at some other point. A web video service is an example of this, whereby a lot of people use it at night and few people use it during the day. Noninteractive workloads do not require people's efforts to make progress after they are submitted. High-performance computing is a typical example of this. At various stages, the requirements for resources of these workloads are dramatically different. However, to guarantee that a workload will always be able to cope with all demand levels, the workload is statically allocated enough resources so that peak demand is satisfied.

In this case, the granularity of resource optimization is focused on the CPU, memory, and network interfaces. Therefore, it is common that most servers in data centers are underutilized. A large amount of hardware, space, power, and management cost of these servers is wasted.

Server consolidation is an approach to improve the low utility ratio of hardware resources by reducing the number of physical servers. Among several server consolidation techniques such as centralized and physical consolidation, virtualization-based server consolidation is the most powerful. Data centers need to optimize their resource management. Yet these techniques are performed with the granularity of a full server machine, which makes resource management far from well optimized. Server virtualization enables smaller resource allocation than a physical machine.

In general, the use of VMs increases resource management complexity. This causes a challenge in terms of how to improve resource utilization as well as guarantee QoS in data centers. In detail, server virtualization has the following side effects:

Consolidation enhances hardware utilization. Many underutilized servers are consolidated into fewer servers to enhance resource utilization. Consolidation also facilitates backup services and disaster recovery.

1. This approach enables more agile provisioning and deployment of resources. In a virtual environment, the images of the guest OSes and their applications are readily cloned and reused.

2. The total cost of ownership is reduced. In this sense, server virtualization causes deferred purchases of new servers, a smaller data-center footprint, lower maintenance costs, and lower power, cooling, and cabling requirements.

3. This approach improves availability and business continuity. The crash of a guest OS has no effect on the host OS or any other guest OS. It becomes easier to transfer a VM from one server to another, because virtual servers are unaware of the underlying hardware.

To automate data-center operations, one must consider resource scheduling, architectural support, power management, automatic or autonomic resource management, performance of analytical models, and so on. In virtualized data centers, an efficient, on-demand, fine-grained scheduler is one of the key factors to improve resource utilization. Scheduling and reallocations can be done in a wide range of levels in a set of data centers. The levels match at least at the VM level, server level, and data-center level.

Ideally, scheduling and resource reallocations should be done at all levels. However, due to the complexity of this, current techniques only focus on a single level or, at most, two levels.

Dynamic CPU allocation is based on VM utilization and application-level QoS metrics. One method considers both CPU and memory flowing as well as automatically adjusting resource overhead based on varying workloads in hosted services. Another scheme uses a two-level resource management system to handle the complexity involved. A local controller at the VM level and a global controller at the server level are designed. They implement autonomic resource allocation via the interaction of the local and global controllers. Multicore and virtualization are two cutting techniques that can enhance each other. However, the use of CMP is far from well optimized. The memory system of CMP is a typical example. One can design a virtual hierarchy on a CMP in data centers. One can consider protocols that minimize the memory access time, inter-VM interferences, facilitating VM reassignment, and supporting inter-VM sharing. One can also consider a VM-aware power budgeting scheme using multiple managers integrated to achieve better power management. The power budgeting policies cannot ignore the heterogeneity problems. Consequently, one must address the trade-off of power saving and data-center performance.

Virtual Storage Management

The term —storage virtualization‖ was widely used before the renaissance of system virtualization. Yet the term has a different meaning in a system virtualization environment. Previously, storage virtualization was largely used to describe the aggregation and repartitioning of disks at very coarse time scales for use by physical machines. In system virtualization, virtual storage includes the storage managed by VMMs and guest OSes. Generally, the data stored in this environment can be classified into two categories: VM images and application data. The VM images are special to the virtual environment, while application data includes all other data which is the same as the data in traditional OS environments. The most important aspects of system virtualization are encapsulation and isolation.

Traditional operating systems and applications running on them can be encapsulated in VMs. Only one operating system runs in a virtualization while many applications run in the operating system. System virtualization allows multiple VMs to run on a physical machine and the VMs are completely isolated. To achieve encapsulation and isolation, both the system software and the hardware platform, such as CPUs and chipsets, are rapidly updated. However, storage is lagging. The storage systems become the main bottleneck of VM deployment.

In virtualization environments, a virtualization layer is inserted between the hardware and traditional operating systems or a traditional operating system is modified to support virtualization. This procedure complicates storage operations. On the one hand, storage management of the guest OS performs as though it is operating in a real hard disk while the guest OSes cannot access the hard disk directly. On the other hand, many guest OSes contest the hard disk when many VMs are running on a single physical machine. Therefore, storage management of the underlying VMM is much more complex than that of guest OSes (traditional OSes).

In addition, the storage primitives used by VMs are not nimble. Hence, operations such as remapping volumes across hosts and check pointing disks are frequently clumsy and esoteric, and sometimes simply unavailable. In data centers, there are often thousands of VMs, which cause the VM images to become flooded. Many researchers tried to solve these problems in virtual storage management. The main purposes of their research are to make management easy while enhancing performance and reducing the amount of storage occupied by the VM images. Parallax is a distributed storage system customized for virtualization environments.

Content Addressable Storage (CAS) is a solution to reduce the total size of VM images, and therefore supports a large set of VM-based systems in data centers.

Since traditional storage management techniques do not consider the features of storage in virtualization environments, Parallax designs a novel architecture in which storage features that have traditionally been implemented directly on high-end storage arrays and switchers are relocated into a federation of storage VMs. These storage VMs share the same physical hosts as the VMs that they serve. It provides an overview of the Parallax system architecture. It supports all popular system virtualization techniques, such as para virtualization and full virtualization. For each physical machine, Parallax customizes a special storage appliance VM. The storage appliance VM acts as a block virtualization layer between individual VMs and the physical storage device. It provides a virtual disk for each VM on the same physical machine.

UNIT IV

Programming Model

4.1. Open Source Grid Middleware Packages

As reviewed in Berman, Fox, and Hey, many software, middleware, and programming environments have been developed for grid computing over past 15 years. Below we assess their relative strength and limitations based on recently reported applications. We first introduce some grid standards and popular APIs. Then we present the desired software support and middleware developed for grid computing includes four grid middleware packages.

Grid Software Support and Middleware Packages.

BOINC Berkeley Open Infrastructure for Network Computing.

UNICORE Middleware developed by the German grid computing community.

Globus (GT4) A middleware library jointly developed by Argonne National Lab., Univ. of Chicago, and USC Information Science Institute, funded by DARPA, NSF, and NIH. CGSP in ChinaGrid

The CGSP (ChinaGrid Support Platform) is a middleware library developed by 20 top universities in China as part of the ChinaGrid Project.

Condor-G Originally developed at the Univ. of Wisconsin for general distributed computing, and later extended to Condor-G for grid job management.

Sun Grid Engine (SGE)

Developed by Sun Microsystems for business grid applications. Applied to private grids and local clusters within enterprises or campuses.

Grid Standards and APIs

Grid standards have been developed over the years. The Open Grid Forum (formally Global Grid Forum) and Object Management Group are two well-formed organizations behind those standards. We have already introduced the OGSA (Open Grid Services Architecture) in standards including the GLUE for resource representation, SAGA (Simple API for Grid Applications), GSI (Grid Security Infrastructure), OGSI (Open Grid Service Infrastructure), and WSRE (Web Service Resource Framework).

The grid standards have guided the development of several middleware libraries and API tools for grid computing. They are applied in both research grids and production grids today. Research grids tested include the EGEE, France Grilles, D-Grid (German), CNGrid (China), TeraGrid (USA), etc. Production grids built with the standards include the EGEE, INFN grid (Italian), NorduGrid, Sun Grid, Techila, and Xgrid . We review next the software environments and middleware implementations based on these standards.

Software Support and Middleware

Grid middleware is specifically designed a layer between hardware and the software. The middleware products enable the sharing of heterogeneous resources and managing virtual organizations created around the grid. Middleware glues the allocated resources with specific user applications. Popular grid middleware tools include the Globus Toolkits (USA), gLight, UNICORE (German), BOINC (Berkeley), CGSP (China), Condor-G, and Sun Grid Engine, etc. summarizes the grid software support and middleware packages developed for grid systems since 1995. In subsequent sections, we will describe the features in Condor-G, SGE, GT4, and CGSP.

4.2.   The Globus Toolkit Architecture (GT4)

The Globus Toolkit, started in 1995 with funding from DARPA, is an open middleware library for the grid computing communities.

These open source software libraries support many operational grids and their applications on an international basis. The toolkit addresses common problems and issues related to grid resource discovery, management, communication, security, fault detection, and portability. The software itself provides a variety of components and capabilities. The library includes a rich set of service implementations. The implemented software supports grid infrastructure management, provides tools for building new web services in Java, C, and Python, builds a powerful standard-based security infrastructure and client APIs (in different languages), and offers comprehensive command-line programs for accessing various grid services.

The Globus Toolkit was initially motivated by a desire to remove obstacles that prevent seamless collaboration, and thus sharing of resources and services, in scientific and engineering applications.

The shared resources can be computers, storage, data, services, networks, science instruments (e.g., sensors), and so on. The Globus library version GT4. Globus Tookit GT4 supports distributed and cluster computing services. Courtesy of I. Foster.

The GT4 Library

GT4 offers the middle-level core services in grid applications. The high-level services and tools, such as MPI, Condor-G, and Nirod/G, are developed by third parties for general-purpose distributed computing applications. The local services, such as LSF, TCP, Linux, and Condor, are at the bottom level and are fundamental tools supplied by other developers summarizes GT4's core grid services by module name. Essentially, these functional modules help users to discover available resources, move data between sites, manage user credentials, and so on. As a de facto standard in grid middleware, GT4 is based on industry-standard web service technologies.

Functional Modules in Globus GT4 Library

Service Functionality Module Name Functional Description

Global Resource Allocation Manager GRAM Grid Resource Access and Management (HTTP-based).

Communication Nexus Unicast and multicast communication.

Grid Security Infrastructure GSI Authentication and related security services.

Monitory and Discovery Service MDS Distributed access to structure and state information.

Health and Status HBM Heartbeat monitoring of system components.

Global Access of Secondary Storage GASS Grid access of data in remote secondary storage.

Grid File Transfer GridFTP Inter-node fast file transfer.

Nexus is used for collective communications and HBM for heartbeat monitoring of resource nodes. GridFTP is for speeding up internode file transfers. The module GASS is used for global access of secondary storage. More details of the functional modules of Globus GT4 and their applications are available at www.globus.org/toolkit/.

Globus Job Workflow

The typical job workflow when using the Globus tools. A typical job execution sequence proceeds as follows: The user delegates his credentials to a delegation service. The user submits a job request to GRAM with the delegation identifier as a parameter. GRAM parses the request, retrieves the user proxy certificate from the delegation service, and then acts on behalf of the user. GRAM sends a transfer request to the RFT (Reliable File Transfer), which applies GridFTP to bring in the necessary files. GRAM invokes a local scheduler via a GRAM adapter and the SEG (Scheduler Event Generator) initiates a set of user jobs. The local scheduler reports the job state to the SEG. Once the job is complete, GRAM uses RFT and GridFTP to stage out the resultant files. The grid monitors the progress of these operations and sends the user a notification when they succeed, fail, or are delayed.

Globus job workflow among interactive functional modules.

Client-Globus Interactions

GT4 service programs are designed to support user applications .There are strong interactions between provider programs and user code. GT4 makes heavy use of industry-standard web service protocols and mechanisms in service description, discovery, access, authentication, authorization, and the like. GT4 makes extensive use of Java, C, and Python to write user code. Web service mechanisms define specific interfaces for grid computing. Web services provide flexible, extensible, and widely adopted XML-based interfaces.

Client and GT4 server interactions; vertical boxes correspond to service programs and horizontal boxes represent the user codes. Courtesy of Foster and Kesselman GT4 components do not, in general, address end-user needs directly. Instead, GT4 provides a set of infrastructure services for accessing, monitoring, managing, and controlling access to infrastructure elements. The server code in the vertical boxes in corresponds to 15 grid services that are in heavy use in the GT4 library. These demand computational, communication, data, and storage resources. We must enable a range of end-user tools that provide the higher-level capabilities needed in specific user applications. Wherever possible, GT4 implements standards to facilitate construction of operable and reusable user code. Developers can use these services and libraries to build simple and complex systems quickly.

A high-security subsystem addresses message protection, authentication, delegation, and authorization. Comprising both a set of service implementations (server programs at the bottom of Figure 7.21) and associated client libraries at the top, GT4 provides both web services and non-WS applications. The horizontal boxes in the client domain denote custom applications and/or third-party tools that access GT4 services. The toolkit programs provide a set of useful infrastructure services.

Globus container serving as a runtime environment for implementing web services in a grid platform. Courtesy of Foster and Kesselman Three containers are used to host user-developed services written in Java, Python, and C, respectively. These containers provide implementations of security, management, discovery, state management, and other mechanisms frequently required when building services.

They extend open source service hosting environments with support for a range of useful web service specifications, including WSRF, WS-Notification, and WS-Security. A set of client libraries allow client programs in Java, C, and Python to invoke operations on both GT4 and user-developed services.

In many cases, multiple interfaces provide different levels of control: For example, in the case of GridFTP, there is not only a simple command-line client (globus-url-copy) but also control and data channel libraries for use in programs—and the XIO library allowing for the integration of alternative transports. The use of uniform abstractions and mechanisms means clients can interact with different services in similar ways, which facilitates construction of complex, interoperable systems and encourages code reuse Parallel Computing and Programming Paradigms

Consider a distributed computing system consisting of a set of networked nodes or workers. The system issues for running a typical parallel program in either a parallel or a distributed manner would include the following:

1) Partitioning This is applicable to both computation and data as follows:
2) Computation partitioning This splits a given job or a program into smaller tasks. Partitioning greatly depends on correctly identifying portions of the job or program that can be performed concurrently. In other words, upon identifying parallelism in the structure of the program, it can be divided into parts to be run on different workers. Different parts may process different data or a copy of the same data.
3) Data partitioning This splits the input or intermediate data into smaller pieces. Similarly, upon identification of parallelism in the input data, it can also be divided into pieces to be processed on different workers. Data pieces may be processed by different parts of a program or a copy of the same program.
4) Mapping This assigns the either smaller parts of a program or the smaller pieces of data to underlying resources. This process aims to appropriately assign such parts or pieces to be run simultaneously on different workers and is usually handled by resource allocators in the system.
5) Synchronization Because different workers may perform different tasks, synchronization and coordination among workers is necessary so that race conditions are prevented and data dependency among different workers is properly managed.
6) Multiple accesses to a shared resource by different workers may raise race conditions, whereas data dependency happens when a worker needs the processed data of other workers.

- Communication Because data dependency is one of the main reasons for communication among workers, communication is always triggered when the intermediate data is sent to workers.

- Scheduling For a job or program, when the number of computation parts (tasks) or data pieces is more than the number of available workers, a scheduler selects a sequence of tasks or data pieces to be assigned to the workers. It is worth noting that the resource allocator performs the actual mapping of the computation or data pieces to workers, while the scheduler only picks the next part from the queue of unassigned tasks based on a set of rules called the scheduling policy. For multiple jobs or programs, a scheduler selects a sequence of jobs or programs to be run on the distributed computing system. In this case, scheduling is also necessary when system resources are not sufficient to simultaneously run multiple jobs or programs.

Motivation for Programming Paradigms

Because handling the whole data flow of parallel and distributed programming is very time-consuming and requires specialized knowledge of programming, dealing with these issues may affect the productivity of the programmer and may even result in affecting the program's time to market. Furthermore, it may detract the programmer from concentrating on the logic of the program itself. Therefore, parallel and distributed programming paradigms or models are offered to abstract many parts of the data flow from users.

In other words, these models aim to provide users with an abstraction layer to hide implementation details of the data flow which users formerly ought to write codes for. Therefore, simplicity of writing parallel programs is an important metric for parallel and distributed programming paradigms.

Other motivations behind parallel and distributed programming models are (1) to improve productivity of programmers, (2) to decrease programs' time to market, (3) to leverage underlying resources more efficiently, (4) to increase system throughput, and (5) to support higher levels of abstraction.

MapReduce, Hadoop, and Dryad are three of the most recently proposed parallel and distributed programming models. They were developed for information retrieval applications but have been shown to be applicable for a variety of important applications . Further, the loose coupling of components in these paradigms makes them suitable for VM implementation and leads to much better fault tolerance and scalability for some applications than traditional parallel computing models such as MPI.

MapReduce, Twister, and Iterative MapReduce

MapReduce, is a software framework which supports parallel and distributed computing on large data sets. This software framework abstracts the data flow of running a parallel program on a distributed computing system by providing users with two interfaces in the form of two functions:

Map and Reduce. Users can override these two functions to interact with and manipulate the data flow of running their programs illustrates the logical data flow from the Map to the Reduce function in MapReduce frameworks. In this framework, the —value‖ part of the data, (key, value), is the actual data, and the —key‖ part is only used by the MapReduce controller to control the data flow.

Formal Definition of MapReduce

The MapReduce software framework provides an abstraction layer with the data flow and flow of control to users, and hides the implementation of all data flow steps such as data partitioning, mapping, synchronization, communication, and scheduling. Here, although the data flow in such frameworks is predefined, the abstraction layer provides two well-defined interfaces in the form of two functions: Map and Reduce . These two main functions can be overridden by the user to achieve specific objectives the MapReduce framework with data flow and control flow. Therefore, the user overrides the Map and Reduce functions first and then invokes the provided MapReduce (Spec, & Results) function from the library to start the flow of data. The MapReduce function, MapReduce (Spec, & Results), takes an important parameter which is a specification object, the Spec. This object is first initialized inside the user's program, and then the user writes code to fill it with the names of input and output files, as well as other optional tuning parameters. This object is also filled with the name of the Map and Reduce functions to identify these user-defined functions to the MapReduce library.

The overall structure of a user's program containing the Map, Reduce, and the Main functions is given below. The Map and Reduce are two major subroutines. They will be called to implement the desired function performed in the main program.

```
Map Function (.... )
  {
    ... ...
  }
Reduce Function (.... )
  {
```

... ...

    }

    Main Function (....)

    {

    Initialize Spec object

    ... ...

    MapReduce (Spec, & Results)

    }

MapReduce Logical Data Flow

The input data to both the Map and the Reduce functions has a particular structure. This also pertains for the output data. The input data to the Map function is in the form of a (key, value) pair. For example, the key is the line offset within the input file and the value is the content of the line. The output data from the Map function is structured as (key, value) pairs called intermediate (key, value) pairs. In other words, the user-defined Map function processes each input (key, value) pair and produces a number of (zero, one, or more) intermediate (key, value) pairs. Here, the goal is to process all input (key, value) pairs to the Map function in parallel.

MapReduce logical data flow in 5 processing stages over successive (key, value) pairs. In turn, the Reduce function receives the intermediate (key, value) pairs in the form of a group of intermediate values associated with one intermediate key, (key, [set of values]). In fact, the MapReduce framework forms these groups by first sorting the intermediate (key, value) pairs and then grouping values with the same key. It should be noted that the data is sorted to simplify the grouping process. The Reduce function processes each (key, [set of values]) group and produces a set of (key, value) pairs as output. To clarify the data flow in a sample MapReduce application, one of the well-known MapReduce problems, namely word count, to count the number of occurrences of each word in a collection of documents is presented here demonstrates the data flow of the word-count problem for a simple input file containing only two lines as follows: (1) —most people ignore most poetry‖ and (2) —most poetry ignores most people.‖ In this case, the Map function simultaneously produces a number of intermediate (key, value) pairs for each line of content so that each word is the intermediate key with 1 as its intermediate value; for example, (ignore, 1). Then the MapReduce library collects all the generated intermediate (key, value) pairs and sorts them to group the 1's for identical words; for example, (people, [1,1]). Groups are then sent to the Reduce function in parallel so that it can sum up the 1 values for each word and generate the actual number of occurrence for each word in the file; for example, (people, 2).

The data flow of a word-count problem using the MapReduce functions (Map, Sort, Group and Reduce) in a cascade operations.

Formal Notation of MapReduce Data Flow

The Map function is applied in parallel to every input (key, value) pair, and produces new set of intermediate (key, value) pairs as follows:

Then the MapReduce library collects all the produced intermediate (key, value) pairs from all input (key, value) pairs, and sorts them based on the —key‖ part. It then groups the values of all occurrences of the same key.

Finally, the Reduce function is applied in parallel to each group producing the collection of values as output as illustrated here:

Strategy to Solve MapReduce Problems

As mentioned earlier, after grouping all the intermediate data, the values of all occurrences of the same key are sorted and grouped together. As a result, after grouping, each key becomes unique in all intermediate data.

Therefore, finding unique keys is the starting point to solving a typical MapReduce problem. Then the intermediate (key, value) pairs as the output of the Map function will be automatically found. The following three examples explain how to define keys and values in such problems:

Problem 1: Counting the number of occurrences of each word in a collection of documents.

Solution: unique —key‖: each word, intermediate —value‖: number of occurrences.

Problem 2: Counting the number of occurrences of words having the same size, or the same number of letters, in a collection of documents.

Solution: unique —key‖: each word, intermediate —value‖: size of the word.

Problem 3: Counting the number of occurrences of anagrams in a collection of documents. Anagrams are words with the same set of letters but in a different order (e.g., the words —listen‖ and —silent‖).

Solution: unique —key‖: alphabetically sorted sequence of letters for each word (e.g., eilnst‖), intermediate —value‖: number of occurrences.

MapReduce Actual Data and Control Flow

The main responsibility of the MapReduce framework is to efficiently run a user's program on a distributed computing system. Therefore, the MapReduce framework meticulously handles all partitioning, mapping, synchronization, communication, and scheduling details of such data flows. We summarize this in the following distinct steps:

1. Data partitioning The MapReduce library splits the input data (files), already stored in GFS, into M pieces that also correspond to the number of map tasks.

2. Computation partitioning This is implicitly handled (in the MapReduce framework) by obliging users to write their programs in the form of the Map and Reduce functions. therefore, the MapReduce library only generates copies of a user program (e.g., by a fork system call) containing the Map and the Reduce functions, distributes them, and starts them up on a number of available computation engines.

3. Determining the master and workers The MapReduce architecture is based on a master-worker model. Therefore, one of the copies of the user program becomes the master and the rest become workers. The master picks idle workers, and assigns the map and reduce tasks to them. A map/reduce worker is typically a computation engine such as a cluster node to run map/reduce tasks by executing Map/Reduce functions. Steps 4–7 describe the map workers.

4. Reading the input data (data distribution) Each map worker reads its corresponding portion of the input data, namely the input data split, and sends it to its Map function. Although a map worker may run more than one Map function, which means it has been assigned more than one input data split, each worker is usually assigned one input split only.

5. Map function Each Map function receives the input data split as a set of (key, value) pairs to process and produce the intermediated (key, value) pairs.

6. Combiner function This is an optional local function within the map worker which applies to intermediate (key, value) pairs. The user can invoke the Combiner function inside the user program. The Combiner function runs the same code written by users for the Reduce function as its functionality is identical to it. The Combiner function merges the local data of each map worker before sending it over the network to effectively reduce its communication costs. As mentioned in our discussion of logical data flow, the MapReduce framework sorts and groups the data before it is processed by the Reduce function. Similarly, the MapReduce framework will also sort and group the local data on each map worker if the user invokes the Combiner function.

7. Partitioning function As mentioned in our discussion of the MapReduce data flow, the intermediate (key, value) pairs with identical keys are grouped together because all values inside each group should be processed by only one Reduce function to generate the final result. However, in real implementations, since there are M map and R reduce tasks, intermediate (key, value) pairs with the same key might be produced by different map tasks, although they should be grouped and processed together by one Reduce function only.

Therefore, the intermediate (key, value) pairs produced by each map worker are partitioned into R regions, equal to the number of reduce tasks, by the Partitioning function to guarantee that all (key, value) pairs with identical keys are stored in the same region. As a result, since reduce worker i reads the data of region i of all map workers, all (key, value) pairs with the same key will be gathered by reduce worker I accordingly .

To implement this technique, a Partitioning function could simply be a hash function (e.g., Hash (key) mod R) that forwards the data into particular regions. It is also worth noting that the locations of the buffered data in these R partitions are sent to the master for later forwarding of data to the reduce workers shows the data flow implementation of all data flow steps. The following are two networking steps:

8. Synchronization MapReduce applies a simple synchronization policy to coordinate map workers with reduce workers, in which the communication between them starts when all map tasks finish.

9. Communication Reduce worker i, already notified of the location of region i of all map workers, uses a remote procedure call to read the data from the respective region of all map workers. Since all reduce workers read the data from all map workers, all-to-all communication among all map and reduce workers, which incurs network congestion, occurs in the network. This issue is one of the major bottlenecks in increasing the performance of such systems . A data transfer module was proposed to schedule data transfers independently .Steps 10 and 11 correspond to the reduce worker domain:

10. Sorting and Grouping When the process of reading the input data is finalized by a reduce worker, the data is initially buffered in the local disk of the reduce worker. Then the reduce worker groups intermediate (key, value) pairs by sorting the data based on their keys, followed by grouping all occurrences of identical keys. Note that the buffered data is sorted and grouped because the number of unique keys produced

by a map worker may be more than R regions in which more than one key exists in each region of a map worker.

11. Reduce function The reduce worker iterates over the grouped (key, value) pairs, and for each unique key, it sends the key and corresponding values to the Reduce function. Then this function processes its input data and stores the output results in predetermined files in the user's program.

Use of MapReduce Partitioning Function to Link the Map and Reduce Workers

To better clarify the interrelated data control and control flow in the MapReduce framework, shows the exact order of processing control in such a system contrasting with dataflow. Data flow implementation of many functions in the Map workers and in the Reduce workers through multiple sequences of partitioning, combining, synchronization and communication, sorting and grouping, and reduce operations. Control flow implementation of the MapReduce functionalities in Map workers and Reduce workers (running user programs) from input files to the output files under the control of the master user program. Courtesy of Yahoo! Pig Tutorial

Compute-Data Affinity

The MapReduce software framework was first proposed and implemented by Google. The first implementation was coded in C. The implementation takes advantage of GFS as the underlying layer. MapReduce could perfectly adapt itself to GFS. GFS is a distributed file system where files are divided into fixed-size blocks (chunks) and blocks are distributed and stored on cluster nodes. As stated earlier, the MapReduce library splits the input data (files) into fixed-size blocks, and ideally performs the Map function in parallel on each block. In this case, as GFS has already stored files as a set of blocks, the MapReduce framework just needs to send a copy of the user's program containing the Map function to the nodes' already stored data blocks. This is the notion of sending computation toward data rather than sending data toward computation. Note that the default GFS block size is 64 MB which is identical to that of the MapReduce framework.

Twister and Iterative MapReduce

It is important to understand the performance of different runtimes and, in particular, to compare MPI and MapReduce. The two major sources of parallel overhead are load imbalance and communication (which is equivalent to synchronization overhead as communication synchronizes parallel units [threads or processes] in Categories 2 and 6). The communication overhead in MapReduce can be quite high, for two reasons:

1. MapReduce reads and writes via files, whereas MPI transfers information directly between nodes over the network.

2. MPI does not transfer all data from node to node, but just the amount needed to update information. We can call the MPI flow δ flow and the MapReduce flow full data flow.

3. The same phenomenon is seen in all classic parallel|| loosely synchronous applications which typically exhibit an iteration structure over compute phases followed by communication phases. We can address the performance issues with two important changes:

4. Stream information between steps without writing intermediate steps to disk.

5. Use long-running threads or processors to communicate the δ (between iterations) flow.

These changes will lead to major performance increases at the cost of poorer fault tolerance and ease to support dynamic changes such as the number of available nodes.

This concept has been investigated in several projects while the direct idea of using MPI for MapReduce applications is investigated in . The Twister programming paradigm and its implementation architecture at run time are illustrated whose performance results for K means are shown in Figure 6.8 [55,56], where Twister is much faster than traditional MapReduce. Twister distinguishes the static data which is never reloaded from the dynamic δ flow that is communicated.

Twister: An iterative MapReduce programming paradigm for repeated MapReduce execution.

4.3. Hadoop Library from Apache

Hadoop is an open source implementation of MapReduce coded and released in Java (rather than C) by Apache. The Hadoop implementation of MapReduce uses the Hadoop Distributed File System (HDFS) as its underlying layer rather than GFS. The Hadoop core is divided into two fundamental layers: the MapReduce engine and HDFS. The MapReduce engine is the computation engine running on top of HDFS as its data storage manager. The following two sections cover the details of these two fundamental layers.

HDFS: HDFS is a distributed file system inspired by GFS that organizes files and stores their data on a distributed computing system.

HDFS Architecture: HDFS has a master/slave architecture containing a single NameNode as the master and a number of DataNodes as workers (slaves). To store a file in this architecture, HDFS splits the file into fixed-size blocks (e.g., 64 MB) and stores them on workers (Data

Nodes). The mapping of blocks to DataNodes is determined by the NameNode. The NameNode (master) also manages the file system's metadata and namespace. In such systems, the namespace is the area maintaining the metadata, and metadata refers to all the information stored by a file system that is needed for overall management of all files. For example, NameNode in the metadata stores all information regarding the location of input splits/blocks in all DataNodes. Each DataNode, usually one per node in a cluster, manages the storage attached to the node. Each DataNode is responsible for storing and retrieving its file blocks.

HDFS Features: Distributed file systems have special requirements, such as performance, scalability, concurrency control, fault tolerance, and security requirements, to operate efficiently. However, because HDFS is not a general-purpose file system, as it only executes specific types of applications, it does not need all the requirements of a general distributed file system. For example, security has never been supported for HDFS systems. The following discussion highlights two important characteristics of HDFS to distinguish it from other generic distributed file systems. HDFS Fault Tolerance: One of the main aspects of HDFS is its fault tolerance characteristic. Since Hadoop is designed to be deployed on low-cost hardware by default, a hardware failure in this system is considered to be common rather than an exception. Therefore, Hadoop considers the following issues to fulfill reliability requirements of the file system:

1. Block replication To reliably store data in HDFS, file blocks are replicated in this system. In other words, HDFS stores a file as a set of blocks and each block is replicated and distributed across the whole cluster. The replication factor is set by the user and is three by default.

2. Replica placement The placement of replicas is another factor to fulfill the desired fault tolerance in HDFS. Although storing replicas on different nodes (DataNodes) located in different racks across the whole cluster provides more reliability, it is sometimes ignored as the cost of communication between two nodes in different racks is relatively high in comparison with that of different nodes located in the same rack. Therefore, sometimes HDFS compromises its reliability to achieve lower communication costs. For example, for the default replication factor of three, HDFS stores one replica in the same node the original data is stored, one replica on a different node but in the same rack, and one replica on a different node in a different rack to provide three copies of the data .

3. Heartbeat and Blockreport messages Heartbeats and Blockreports are periodic messages sent to the NameNode by each DataNode in a cluster. Receipt of a Heartbeat

implies that the DataNode is functioning properly, while each Blockreport contains a list of all blocks on a DataNode. The NameNode receives such messages because it is the sole decision maker of all replicas in the system.

HDFS High-Throughput Access to Large Data Sets (Files): Because HDFS is primarily designed for batch processing rather than interactive processing, data access throughput in HDFS is more important than latency. Also, because applications run on HDFS typically have large data sets, individual files are broken into large blocks (e.g., 64 MB) to allow HDFS to decrease the amount of metadata storage required per file. This provides two advantages: The list of blocks per file will shrink as the size of individual blocks increases, and by keeping large amounts of data sequentially within a block, HDFS provides fast streaming reads of data.

HDFS Operation: The control flow of HDFS operations such as write and read can properly highlight roles of the NameNode and DataNodes in the managing operations. In this section, the control flow of the main operations of HDFS on files is further described to manifest the interaction between the user, the NameNode, and the DataNodes in such systems.

4. Reading a file To read a file in HDFS, a user sends an —open‖ request to the NameNode to get the location of file blocks. For each file block, the NameNode returns the address of a set of DataNodes containing replica information for the requested file. The number of addresses depends on the number of block replicas. Upon receiving such information, the user calls the read function to connect to the closest DataNode containing the first block of the file. After the first block is streamed from the respective DataNode to the user, the established connection is terminated and the same process is repeated for all blocks of the requested file until the whole file is streamed to the user.

5. Writing to a file To write a file in HDFS, a user sends a —create‖ request to the NameNode to create a new file in the file system namespace. If the file does not exist, the NameNode notifies the user and allows him to start writing data to the file by calling the write function. The first block of the file is written to an internal queue termed the data queue while a data streamer monitors its writing into a DataNode. Since each file block needs to be replicated by a predefined factor, the data streamer first sends a request to the NameNode to get a list of suitable DataNodes to store replicas of the first block.

The steamer then stores the block in the first allocated DataNode. Afterward, the block is forwarded to the second DataNode by the first DataNode. The process continues until all allocated DataNodes receive a replica of the first block from the previous DataNode.

Once this replication process is finalized, the same process starts for the second block and continues until all blocks of the file are stored and replicated on the file system.

Architecture of MapReduce in Hadoop

The topmost layer of Hadoop is the MapReduce engine that manages the data flow and control flow of MapReduce jobs over distributed computing systems shows the MapReduce engine architecture cooperating with HDFS. Similar to HDFS, the MapReduce engine also has a master/slave architecture consisting of a single JobTracker as the master and a number of TaskTrackers as the slaves (workers). The JobTracker manages the MapReduce job over a cluster and is responsible for monitoring jobs and assigning tasks to TaskTrackers. The TaskTracker manages the execution of the map and/or reduce tasks on a single computation node in the cluster. HDFS and MapReduce architecture in Hadoop where boxes with different shadings refer to different functional nodes applied to different blocks of data.

Each TaskTracker node has a number of simultaneous execution slots, each executing either a map or a reduce task. Slots are defined as the number of simultaneous threads supported by CPUs of the TaskTracker node. For example, a TaskTracker node with N CPUs, each supporting M threads, has M * N simultaneous execution slots . It is worth noting that each data block is processed by one map task running on a single slot. Therefore, there is a one-to-one correspondence between map tasks in a TaskTracker and data blocks in the respective DataNode.

Running a Job in Hadoop

Three components contribute in running a job in this system: a user node, a JobTracker, and several TaskTrackers. The data flow starts by calling the runJob(conf) function inside a user program running on the user node, in which conf is an object containing some tuning parameters for the MapReduce framework and HDFS. The runJob(conf) function and conf are comparable to the MapReduce (Spec, &Results) function and Spec in the first implementation of MapReduce by Google, depicts the data flow of running a MapReduce job in Hadoop . Data flow in running a MapReduce job at various task trackers using the Hadoop library.

1. Job Submission Each job is submitted from a user node to the JobTracker node that might be situated in a different node within the cluster through the following procedure:
2. A user node asks for a new job ID from the JobTracker and computes input file splits.
3. The user node copies some resources, such as the job's JAR file, configuration file, and computed input splits, to the JobTracker's file system.

4. The user node submits the job to the JobTracker by calling the submitJob() function.

5. Task assignment The JobTracker creates one map task for each computed input split by the user node and assigns the map tasks to the execution slots of the TaskTrackers.

The JobTracker considers the localization of the data when assigning the map tasks to the TaskTrackers. The JobTracker also creates reduce tasks and assigns them to the TaskTrackers. The number of reduce tasks is predetermined by the user, and there is no locality consideration in assigning them.

6. Task execution the control flow to execute a task (either map or reduce) starts inside the TaskTracker by copying the job JAR file to its file system. Instructions inside the job JAR file are executed after launching a Java Virtual Machine (JVM) to run its map or reduce task.

7. Task running check A task running check is performed by receiving periodic heartbeat messages to the JobTracker from the TaskTrackers. Each heartbeat notifies the JobTracker that the sending TaskTracker is alive, and whether the sending TaskTracker is ready to run a new task.

Unit V

Security

5.1.   Trust Models for Grid Security Enforcement

Many potential security issues may occur in a grid environment if qualified security mechanisms are not in place. These issues include network sniffers, out-of-control access, faulty operation, malicious operation, integration of local security mechanisms, delegation, dynamic resources and services, attack provenance, and so on. Computational grids are motivated by the desire to share processing resources among many organizations to solve large-scale problems. Indeed, grid sites may exhibit unacceptable security conditions and system vulnerabilities.

On the one hand, a user job demands the resource site to provide security assurance by issuing a security demand (SD). On the other hand, the site needs to reveal its trustworthiness, called its trust index (TI). These two parameters must satisfy a security-assurance condition: $TI \geq SD$ during the job mapping process. When determining its security demand, users usually care about some typical attributes. These attributes and their values are dynamically changing and depend heavily on the trust model, security policy, accumulated reputation, self-defense capability, attack history, and site vulnerability. Three challenges are outlined below to establish the trust among grid sites .

The first challenge is integration with existing systems and technologies. The resources sites in a grid are usually heterogeneous and autonomous. It is unrealistic to expect that a single type of security can be compatible with and adopted by every hosting environment. At the same time, existing security infrastructure on the sites cannot be replaced overnight. Thus, to be successful, grid security architecture needs to step up to the challenge of integrating with existing security architecture and models across platforms and hosting environments.

The second challenge is interoperability with different —hosting environments.‖ Services are often invoked across multiple domains, and need to be able to interact with one another. The interoperation is demanded at the protocol, policy, and identity levels.

For all these levels, interoperation must be protected securely. The third challenge is to construct trust relationships among interacting hosting environments. Grid service requests can be handled by combining resources on multiple security domains. Trust relationships are required by these domains during the end-to-end traversals. A service needs to be open to friendly and interested entities so that they can submit requests and access securely.

Resource sharing among entities is one of the major goals of grid computing. A trust relationship must be established before the entities in the grid interoperate with one another. The entities have to choose other entities that can meet the requirements of trust to coordinate with. The entities that submit requests should believe the resource providers will try to process their requests and return the results with a specified QoS. To create the proper trust relationship between grid entities, two kinds of trust models are often used. One is the PKI-based model, which mainly exploits the PKI to authenticate and authorize entities; we will discuss this in the next section. The other is the reputation-based model.

The grid aims to construct a large-scale network computing system by integrating distributed, heterogeneous, and autonomous resources. The security challenges faced by the grid are much greater than other computing systems. Before any effective sharing and cooperation occurs, a trust relationship has to be established among participants.

Otherwise, not only will participants be reluctant to share their resources and services, but also the grid may cause a lot of damage.

A Generalized Trust Model

At the bottom, we identify three major factors which influence the trustworthiness of a resource site. An inference module is required to aggregate these factors. Followings are some existing inference or aggregation methods. An intra-site fuzzy inference procedure is called to assess defense capability and direct reputation. Defense capability is decided by the firewall, intrusion detection system (IDS), intrusion response capability, and anti-virus capacity of the individual resource site. Direct reputation is decided based on the job success rate, site utilization, job turnaround time, and job slowdown ratio measured. Recommended trust is also known as secondary trust and is obtained indirectly over the grid network.

A general trust model for grid computing. Courtesy of Song, Hwang, and Kwok, 2005

Reputation-Based Trust Model

In a reputation-based model, jobs are sent to a resource site only when the site is trustworthy to meet users' demands. The site trustworthiness is usually calculated from the following information: the defense capability, direct reputation, and recommendation trust. The defense capability refers to the site's ability to protect itself from danger. It is assessed according to such factors as intrusion detection, firewall, response capabilities, anti-virus capacity, and so on. Direct reputation is based on experiences of prior jobs previously submitted to the site. The reputation is measured by many factors such as prior job execution success rate, cumulative site utilization, job turnaround time, job slowdown ratio, and so on. A positive experience associated with a site will improve its reputation. On the contrary, a negative experience with a site will decrease its reputation.

A Fuzzy-Trust Model

In this model, the job security demand (SD) is supplied by the user programs. The trust index (TI) of a resource site is aggregated through the fuzzy-logic inference process over all related parameters. Specifically, one can use a two-level fuzzy logic to estimate the aggregation of numerous trust parameters and security attributes into scalar quantities that are easy to use in the job scheduling and resource mapping process.

The TI is normalized as a single real number with 0 representing the condition with the highest risk at a site and 1 representing the condition which is totally risk-free or fully trusted. The fuzzy inference is accomplished through four steps: fuzzification, inference, aggregation, and defuzzification. The second salient feature of the trust model is that if a site's trust index cannot match the job security demand (i.e., SD > TI), the trust model could deduce detailed security features to guide the site security upgrade as a result of tuning the fuzzy system.

Authentication and Authorization Methods

The major authentication methods in the grid include passwords, PKI, and Kerberos. The password is the simplest method to identify users, but the most vulnerable one to use.The PKI is the most popular method supported by GSI. To implement PKI, we use a trusted third party, called the certificate authority (CA). Each user applies a unique pair of public and private keys. The public keys are issued by the CA by issuing a certificate, after recognizing a legitimate user. The private key is exclusive for each user to use, and is unknown to any other users. A digital certificate in IEEE X.509 format consists of the user name, user public key, CA name, and a secrete signature of the user. The following example illustrates the use of a PKI service in a grid environment.

Authorization for Access Control

The authorization is a process to exercise access control of shared resources. Decisions can be made either at the access point of service or at a centralized place. Typically, the resource is a host that provides processors and storage for services deployed on it. Based on a set predefined policies or rules, the resource may enforce access for local services. The central authority is a special entity which is capable of issuing and revoking polices of access rights granted to remote accesses. The authority can be classified into three categories: attribute authorities, policy authorities, and identity authorities. Attribute authorities issue attribute assertions; policy authorities issue authorization policies; identity authorities issue certificates. The authorization server makes the final authorization decision.

Three Authorization Models

The subject is the user and the resource refers to the machine side. The subject-push model is shown at the top diagram. The user conducts handshake with the authority first and then with the resource site in a sequence. The resource-pulling model puts the resource in the middle. The user checks the resource first. Then the resource contacts its authority to verify the request, and the authority authorizes at step 3. Finally the resource accepts or rejects the request from the subject at step 4. The authorization agent model puts the authority in the middle. The subject check with the authority at step 1 and the authority makes decisions on the access of the requested resources. The authorization process is complete at steps 3 and 4 in the reverse direction.

5.2.   Grid Security Infrastructure (GSI)

Although the grid is increasingly deployed as a common approach to constructing dynamic, inter domain, distributed computing and data collaborations, ―lack of security/trust between different services‖ is still an important challenge of the grid. The grid requires a security infrastructure with the following properties: easy to use; conforms with the VO's security needs while working well with site policies of each resource provider site; and provides appropriate authentication and encryption of all interactions.

The GSI is an important step toward satisfying these requirements. As a well-known security solution in the grid environment, GSI is a portion of the Globus Toolkit and provides fundamental security services needed to support grids, including supporting for message protection, authentication and delegation, and authorization.

GSI enables secure authentication and communication over an open network, and permits mutual authentication across and among distributed sites with single sign-on capability. No centrally managed security system is required, and the grid maintains the integrity of its members' local policies.

GSI supports both message-level security, which supports the WS-Security standard and the WS-Secure Conversation specification to provide message protection for SOAP messages, and transport-level security, which means authentication via TLS with support for X.509 proxy certificates.

GSI Functional Layers

GT4 provides distinct WS and pre-WS authentication and authorization capabilities. Both build on the same base, namely the X.509 standard and entity certificates and proxy certificates, which are used to identify persistent entities such as users and servers and to support the temporary delegation of privileges to other entities, respectively. As shown , GSI may be thought of as being composed of four distinct functions: message protection, authentication, delegation, and authorization.

TLS (transport-level security) or WS-Security and WS-Secure Conversation (message-level) are used as message protection mechanisms in combination with SOAP. X.509 End Entity Certificates or Username and Password are used as authentication credentials.

X.509 Proxy Certificates and WS-Trust are used for delegation. An Authorization Framework allows for a variety of authorization schemes, including a ―grid-mapfile‖

ACL, an ACL defined by a service, a custom authorization handler, and access to an authorization service via the SAML protocol.

In addition, associated security tools provide for the storage of X.509 credentials (MyProxy and Delegation services), the mapping between GSI and other authentication mechanisms (e.g., KX509 and PKINIT for Kerberos, MyProxy for one-time passwords), and maintenance of information used for authorization (VOMS, GUMS, PERMIS).

The remainder of this section reviews both the GT implementations of each of these functions and the standards that are used in these implementations. The web services portions of GT4 use SOAP as their message protocol for communication. Message protection can be provided either by transport-level security, which transports SOAP messages over TLS, or by message-level security, which is signing and/or encrypting portions of the SOAP message using the WS-Security standard. Here we describe these two methods.

Transport-Level Security

Transport-level security entails SOAP messages conveyed over a network connection protected by TLS.

TLS provides for both integrity protection and privacy (via encryption). Transport-level security is normally used in conjunction with X.509 credentials for authentication, but can also be used without such credentials to provide message protection without authentication, often referred to as ―anonymous transport-level security.‖ In this mode of operation, authentication may be done by username and password in a SOAP message.

Message-Level Security

GSI also provides message-level security for message protection for SOAP messages by implementing the WS-Security standard and the WS-Secure Conversation specification.

The WS-Security standard from OASIS defines a framework for applying security to individual SOAP messages; WS-Secure Conversation is a proposed standard from IBM and Microsoft that allows for an initial exchange of messages to establish a security context which can then be used to protect subsequent messages in a manner that requires less computational overhead (i.e., it allows the trade-off of initial overhead for setting up the session for lower overhead for messages).

GSI conforms to this standard. GSI uses these mechanisms to provide security on a per-message basis, that is, to an individual message without any preexisting context between the sender and receiver (outside of sharing some set of trust roots). GSI, as described further in the subsequent section on authentication, allows for both X.509 public key credentials and the combination of username and password for authentication; however, differences still exist. With username/password, only the WS-Security standard can be used to allow for authentication; that is, a receiver can verify the identity of the communication initiator.

GSI allows three additional protection mechanisms. The first is integrity protection, by which a receiver can verify that messages were not altered in transit from the sender. The second is encryption, by which messages can be protected to provide confidentiality. The third is replay prevention, by which a receiver can verify that it has not received the same message previously. These protections are provided between WS-Security and WS-Secure Conversation. The former applies the keys associated with the sender and receiver's X.509 credentials. The X.509 credentials are used to establish a session key that is used to provide the message protection.

Authentication and Delegation

GSI has traditionally supported authentication and delegation through the use of X.509 certificates and public keys. As a new feature in GT4, GSI also supports authentication through plain usernames and passwords as a deployment option. We discuss both methods in this section. GSI uses X.509 certificates to identify persistent users and services.

As a central concept in GSI authentication, a certificate includes four primary pieces of information: (1) a subject name, which identifies the person or object that the certificate represents; (2) the public key belonging to the subject; (3) the identity of a CA that has signed the certificate to certify that the public key and the identity both belong to the subject; and (4) the digital signature of the named CA. X.509 provides each entity with a unique identifier (i.e., a distinguished name) and a method to assert that identifier to another party through the use of an asymmetric key pair bound to the identifier by the certificate.

The X.509 certificate used by GSI are conformant to the relevant standards and conventions. Grid deployments around the world have established their own CAs based on third-party software to issue the X.509 certificate for use with GSI and the Globus Toolkit. GSI also supports delegation and single sign-on through the use of standard X.509 proxy certificates. Proxy certificates allow bearers of X.509 to delegate their privileges temporarily to another entity. For the purposes of authentication and authorization, GSI treats certificates and proxy certificates equivalently. Authentication with X.509 credentials can be accomplished either via TLS, in the case of transport-level security, or via signature as specified by WS-Security, in the case of message-level security.

Trust Delegation

To reduce or even avoid the number of times the user must enter his passphrase when several grids are used or have agents (local or remote) requesting services on behalf of a user, GSI provides a delegation capability and a delegation service that provides an interface to allow clients to delegate (and renew) X.509 proxy certificates to a service. The interface to this service is based on the WS-Trust specification. A proxy consists of a new certificate and a private key. The key pair that is used for the proxy, that is, the public key embedded in the certificate and the private key, may either be regenerated for each proxy or be obtained by other means. The new certificate contains the owner's identity, modified slightly to indicate that it is a proxy. The new certificate is signed by the owner, rather than a CA.

A sequence of trust delegations in which new certificates are signed by the owners rather by the CA. The certificate also includes a time notation after which the proxy should no longer be accepted by others. Proxies have limited lifetimes. Because the proxy isn't valid for very long, it doesn't have to stay quite as secure as the owner's private key, and thus it is possible to store the proxy's private key in a local storage system without being encrypted, as long as the permissions on the file prevent anyone else from looking at them easily. Once a proxy is created and stored, the user can use the proxy certificate and private key for mutual authentication without entering a password. When proxies are used, the mutual authentication process differs slightly. The remote party receives not only the proxy's certificate (signed by the owner), but also the owner's certificate. During mutual authentication, the owner's public key (obtained from her certificate) is used to validate the signature on the proxy certificate. The CA's public key is then used to validate the signature on the owner's certificate. This establishes a chain of trust from the CA to the last proxy through the successive owners of resources. The GSI uses WS-Security with textual usernames and passwords. This mechanism supports more rudimentary web service applications. When using usernames and passwords as opposed to X.509 credentials, the GSI provides authentication, but no advanced security features such as delegation, confidentiality, integrity, and replay prevention. However, one can use usernames and passwords with anonymous transport-level security such as unauthenticated TLS to ensure privacy.

UNIT I

Introduction

Part A

1. Define cloud computing

Cloud computing is the delivery of computing as a service rather than a product, hereby shared resources, software, and information are provided to computers and other devices as a utility.

2. What is Distributed computing

This is a field of computer science/engineering that studies distributed systems. A distributed system consists of multiple autonomous computers, each having its own private memory, communicating through a computer network. Information exchange in a distributed system is accomplished through message passing. A computer program that runs in a distributed system is known as a distributed program. The process of writing distributed programs is referred to as distributed programming.

3. Difference between distributed and parallel computing.

Distributed	Parallel
Each processor has its own private memory (distributed memory). Information is exchanged by passing messages between the processors.	All processors may have access to a shared memory to exchange information between processors
It is loosely coupled	It is tightly coupled
An important goal and challenge of distributed systems is location transparency	Large problems can often be divided into smaller ones, which are then solved concurrently ("in parallel").

4. What is mean by service oriented architecture?

In grids/web services, Java, and CORBA, an entity is, respectively, a service, a Java object, and a CORBA distributed object in a variety of languages. These architectures build on the traditional seven Open Systems Interconnection (OSI) layers that provide the base networking abstractions. On top of this we have a base software environment, which would be .NET or Apache Axis for web services, the Java Virtual Machine for Java, and a broker network for CORBA.

5. What is High Performance Computing (HPC).

Supercomputer sites and large data centers must provide high-performance computing services to huge numbers of Internet users concurrently. Because of this high demand, the Linpack Benchmark for high-performance computing (HPC) applications is no longer optimal for measuring system performance. The emergence of computing clouds instead demands high-throughput computing (HTC) systems built with parallel and distributed computing technologies. We have to upgrade data centers using fast servers, storage systems, and high-bandwidth networks. The purpose is to advance network-based computing and web services with the emerging new technologies.

6. Define peer-to-peer network.

The P2P architecture offers a distributed model of networked systems. Every node acts as both a client and a server, providing part of the system resources. Peer machines are simply client computers connected to the Internet. All client machines act autonomously to join or leave the system freely. This implies that no master-slave relationship exists among the peers. No central coordination or central database is needed.

7. What are the Three New Computing Paradigms

- Radio-frequency identification (RFID).
- Global Positioning System (GPS).
- Internet of Things (IoT).

8. What is degree of parallelism and types

The degree of parallelism (DOP) is a metric which indicates how many operations can be or are being simultaneously executed by a computer. It is especially useful for describing the performance of parallel programs and multi-processor systems.

- Bit-level parallelism (BLP).
- Data-level parallelism (DLP).
- Instruction-level parallelism (ILP).
- Processors and chip.
- VLIW (very long instruction word) multiprocessors (CMPs).
- Job-level parallelism (JLP).

9. What is Cyber-Physical Systems

A cyber-physical system (CPS) is the result of interaction between computational processes and the physical world. A CPS integrates —cyber‖ (heterogeneous, asynchronous) with —physical‖ (concurrent and information-dense) objects.

10. Define multi core CPU.

Advanced CPUs or microprocessor chips assume a multi-core architecture with dual, quad, six, or more processing cores. These processors exploit parallelism at ILP and TLP levels. CPU has reached its limit in terms of exploiting massive DLP due to the aforementioned memory wall problem

11. Define GPU.

A GPU is a graphics coprocessor or accelerator on a computer's graphics card or video card. A GPU offloads the CPU from tedious graphics tasks in video editing applications. The GPU chips can process a minimum of 10 million polygons per second. GPU's have a throughput architecture that exploits massive parallelism by executing many concurrent threads.

12. Clusters of Cooperative Computers

A computing cluster consists of interconnected stand-alone computers which work cooperatively as a single integrated computing resource.

13. What is single-system image (SSI)

An ideal cluster should merge multiple system images into a single-system image (SSI). Cluster designers desire a cluster operating system or some middleware to support SSI at various levels, including the sharing of CPUs, memory, and I/O across all cluster nodes.

14. What is Grid Computing

Grid computing is the collection of computer resources from multiple locations to reach a common goal. The grid can be thought of as a distributed system with non-interactive workloads that involve a large number of files. Grid computing is distinguished from conventional high performance computing systems such as cluster computing in that grid computers have each node set to perform a different task/application.

15. What is Computational Grids

A computing grid offers an infrastructure that couples computers, software/middleware, special instruments, and people and sensors together. The grid is often constructed across LAN, WAN, or Internet backbone networks at a regional, national, or global scale. Enterprises or organizations present grids as integrated computing resources.

16. What is Overlay Networks and its types

Overlay is a virtual network formed by mapping each physical machine with its ID, logically, through a virtual mapping . When a new peer joins the system, its peer ID is added as a node in the overlay network.

Two Types of Overlay Networks

1. Unstructured.
2. Structured.

17. Write the any three Grid Applications.

- Schedulers.

- Resource Broker.

- Load Balancing.

18. Difference between grid and cloud computing

Grid computing	cloud computing
Grids enable access to shared computing power and storage capacity from your desktop	Clouds enable access to leased computing power and storage capacity from your desktop
In computing centres distributed across different sites, countries and continents	The cloud providers private data centres which are often centralised in a few locations with excellent network connections and cheap electrical power.
Grids were designed to handle large sets of limited duration jobs that produce or use large quantities of data (e.g. the LHC)	Clouds best support long term services and longer Running jobs (E.g. facebook.com)

19. What are the derivatives of grid computing?

There are 8 derivatives of grid computing. They are as follows:

a) Compute grid.

b) Data grid.

c) Science grid.

1. Access grid

2. Knowledge grid

3. Cluster grid

4. Terra grid

5. Commodity grid.

20. What is grid infrastructure?

Grid infrastructure forms the core foundation for successful grid applications. This infrastructure is a complex combination of number of capabilities and resources identified for the specific problem and environment being addressed.

21. What are the Applications of High-Performance and High-Throughput Systems

1. **Science and engineering-** Scientific simulations, genomic analysis, etc. Earthquake prediction, global warming, weather forecasting, etc.

2. **Business, education, services industry, and health care-** Telecommunication, content delivery, e-commerce, etc. Banking, stock exchanges, transaction processing, etc. Air traffic control, electric power grids, distance education, etc. Health care, hospital automation, telemedicine, etc.,

3. **Internet and web services, and government applications-** Internet search, data centers, decision-making systems, etc. Traffic monitoring, worm containment, cyber security, etc. Digital government, online tax return processing, social networking, etc.

22. What is Utility computing?

It is a service provisioning model in which a service provider makes computing resources and infrastructure management available to the customer as needed, and charges them for specific usage rather than a flat rate

23. What is SLA?

A service-level agreement (SLA) is a part of a standardized service contract where a service is formally defined. Particular aspects of the service – scope, quality, responsibilities – are agreed between the service provider and the service user. A common feature of an SLA is a contracted delivery time (of the service or performance).

Part B

1. **Describe about Evolution of Distributed computing.**

    Distributed computing is a field of computer science that studies distributed systems.

A distributed system is a model in which components located on networked computers communicate and coordinate their actions by passing messages The components interact with each other in order to achieve a **common** goal. Three significant characteristics of distributed systems are: concurrency of components, lack of a global clock, and independent failure of components. Examples of distributed systems vary from SOA-based systems to massively multiplayer online games to peer-to-peer applications.

A computer program that runs in a distributed system is called a **distributed program**, and distributed programming is the process of writing such programs. There are many alternatives for the message passing mechanism, including pure HTTP, RPC-like connectors and message queues.

History

The use of concurrent processes that communicate by message-passing has its roots in operating system architectures studied in the 1960s. The first widespread distributed systems were local-area networks such as Ethernet, which was invented in the 1970s.

ARPANET, the predecessor of the Internet, was introduced in the late 1960s, and ARPANET e-mail was invented in the early 1970s. E-mail became the most successful application of ARPANET, and it is probably the earliest example of a large-scale distributed application. In addition to ARPANET, and its successor, the Internet, other early worldwide computer networks included Usenet and FidoNet from the 1980s, both of which were used to support distributed discussion systems.

The study of distributed computing became its own branch of computer science in the late 1970s and early 1980s. The first conference in the field, Symposium on Principles of Distributed Computing (PODC), dates back to 1982, and its European counterpart International Symposium on Distributed Computing (DISC) was first held in 1985.

2. Explain in detail about Scalable computing over the Internet

A parallel and distributed computing system uses multiple computers to solve large-scale problems over the Internet. Thus, distributed computing becomes data-intensive and network-centric. Identifies the applications of modern computer systems that practice parallel and distributed computing. These large-scale Internet applications have significantly enhanced the quality of life and information services in society today.

The Age of Internet Computing

Billions of people use the Internet every day. As a result, supercomputer sites and large data centers must provide high-performance computing services to huge numbers of Internet users concurrently. Because of this high demand, the Linpack Benchmark for high-performance computing (HPC) applications is no longer optimal for measuring system performance. The emergence of computing clouds instead demands high-throughput computing (HTC) systems built with parallel and distributed computing technologies We have to upgrade data centers using fast servers, storage systems, and high-bandwidth networks. The purpose is to advance network-based computing and web services with the emerging new technologies.

The Platform Evolution

Computer technology has gone through five generations of development, with each generation lasting from 10 to 20 years. Successive generations are overlapped in about 10 years. For instance, from 1950 to 1970, a handful of mainframes, including the IBM 360 and CDC 6400, were built to satisfy the demands of large businesses and government organizations. From 1960 to 1980, lower-cost minicomputers such as the DEC PDP 11 and VAX Series became popular among small businesses and on college campuses.

- From 1970 to 1990, we saw widespread use of personal computers built with VLSI microprocessors.

- From 1980 to 2000, massive numbers of portable computers and pervasive devices appeared in both wired and wireless applications.

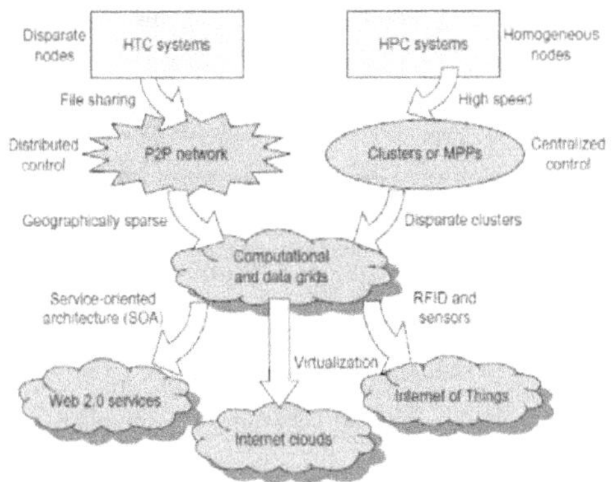

Evolutionary trend toward parallel, distributed, and cloud computing with clusters, MPPs, P2P networks, grids, clouds, web services, and the Internet of Things.

High-Performance Computing

The speed of HPC systems has increased from Gflops in the early 1990s to now Pflops in 2010. This improvement was driven mainly by the demands from scientific, engineering, and manufacturing communities.

High-Throughput Computing

The development of market-oriented high-end computing systems is undergoing a strategic change from an HPC paradigm to an HTC paradigm. This HTC paradigm pays more attention to high-flux computing. The main application for high-flux computing is in Internet searches and web services by millions or more users simultaneously. The performance goal thus shifts to measure high throughput or the number of tasks completed per unit of time.

Three New Computing Paradigms

Radio-frequency identification (RFID), Global Positioning System (GPS), and sensor technologies has triggered the development of the Internet of Things (IoT).

Computing Paradigm Distinctions

In general distributed computing is the opposite of centralized computing. The field of parallel computing overlaps with distributed computing to a great extent, and cloud computing overlaps with distributed, centralized, and parallel computing.

Centralized computing this is a computing paradigm by which all computer resources are centralized in one physical system. All resources (processors, memory, and storage) are fully shared and tightly coupled within one integrated OS. Many data centers and supercomputers are centralized systems, but they are used in parallel, distributed, and cloud computing applications

- Parallel computing in parallel computing, all processors are either tightly coupled with centralized shared memory or loosely coupled with distributed memory. Some authors refer to this discipline as parallel processing. Inter processor communication is accomplished through shared memory or via message passing. A computer system capable of parallel computing is commonly known as a parallel computer. Programs running in a parallel computer are called parallel programs. The process of writing parallel programs is often referred to as parallel programming.
- Distributed computing This is a field of computer science/engineering that studies distributed systems. A distributed system consists of multiple autonomous computers, each having its own private memory, communicating through a computer network. Information exchange in a distributed system is accomplished through message passing. A computer program that runs in a distributed system is known as a distributed program. The process of writing distributed programs is referred to as distributed programming.
- Cloud computing An Internet cloud of resources can be either a centralized or a distributed computing system. The cloud applies parallel or distributed computing, or both. Clouds can be built with physical or virtualized resources over large data centers that are centralized or distributed. Some authors consider cloud computing to be a form of utility computing or service computing.

The high-tech community prefers the term concurrent computing or concurrent programming. Parallel computing and distributing computing, although biased practitioners may interpret them differently. Ubiquitous computing refers to computing with pervasive devices at any place and time using wired or wireless communication. The Internet of Things (IoT) is a networked connection of everyday objects including computers, sensors, humans, etc.

The IoT is supported by Internet clouds to achieve ubiquitous computing with any object at any place and time. Finally, the term Internet computing is even broader and covers all computing paradigms over the Internet.

Distributed System Families

Since the mid-1990s, technologies for building P2P networks and networks of clusters have been consolidated into many national projects designed to establish wide area computing infrastructures, known as computational grids or data grids.

Meeting these Goals Requires Yielding the Following Design Objectives

Efficiency measures the utilization rate of resources in an execution model by exploiting massive parallelism in HPC. For HTC, efficiency is more closely related to job throughput, data access, storage, and power efficiency.

- **Dependability** measures the reliability and self-management from the chip to the system and application levels. The purpose is to provide high-throughput service with Quality of Service (QoS) assurance, even under failure conditions.
- **Adaptation in the programming model** measures the ability to support billions of job requests over massive data sets and virtualized cloud resources under various workload and service models.
- **Flexibility** in application deployment measures the ability of distributed systems to run well in both HPC (science and engineering) and HTC (business) applications.

Scalable Computing Trends and New Paradigms

Several predictable trends in technology are known to drive computing applications. In fact, designers and programmers want to predict the technological capabilities of future systems.

For instance, Jim Gray's paper,—Rules of Thumb in Data Engineering,‖ is an excellent example of how technology affects applications and vice versa. In addition, Moore's law indicates that processor speed doubles every 18 months. Although Moore's law has been proven valid over the last 30 years, it is difficult to say whether it will continue to be true in the future.

Degrees of Parallelism

When hardware was bulky and expensive, most computers were designed in a bit-serial fashion. In this scenario, bit-level parallelism (BLP) converts bit-serial processing to word-level processing gradually. Users graduated from 4-bit microprocessors to 8-, 16-, 32-, and 64-bit CPUs.

This led us to the next wave of improvement, known as instruction-level parallelism (ILP), in which the processor executes multiple instructions simultaneously rather than only one instruction at a time. Practiced ILP through pipelining, superscalar computing, VLIW (very long instruction word) architectures, and multithreading. ILP requires branch prediction, dynamic scheduling, speculation, and compiler support to work efficiently. Data-level parallelism (DLP) was made popular through SIMD (single instruction, multiple data) and vector machines using vector or array types of instructions.

DLP requires even more hardware support and compiler assistance to work properly. Ever since the introduction of multi core processors and chip multiprocessors (CMPs), exploring task-level parallelism (TLP).A modern processor explores all of the aforementioned parallelism types. In fact, BLP, ILP, and As we move from parallel processing to distributed processing, increase in computing granularity to job-level parallelism (JLP). It is fair to say that coarse-grain parallelism is built on top of fine-grain parallelism.

Innovative Applications

Applications of High-Performance and High-Throughput Systems

Domain	Specific Applications
Science and engineering	Scientific simulations, genomic analysis, etc.
	Earthquake prediction, global warming, weather forecasting, etc.
Business, education, services industry, and health care	Telecommunication, content delivery, e-commerce, etc.
	Banking, stock exchanges, transaction processing, etc.
	Air traffic control, electric power grids, distance education, etc.
	Health care, hospital automation, telemedicine, etc.
Internet and web services, and government applications	Internet search, data centers, decision-making systems, etc.
	Traffic monitoring, worm containment, cyber security, etc.
	Digital government, online tax return processing, social networking, etc.
Mission-critical applications	Military command and control, intelligent systems, crisis management, etc.

The Trend toward Utility Computing

All ubiquitous in daily life. Reliability and scalability are two major design objectives in these computing models.

Second, they are aimed at autonomic operations that can be self-organized to support dynamic discovery. Finally, these paradigms are composable with QoS and SLAs (service-level agreements).

These paradigms and their attributes realize the computer utility vision.

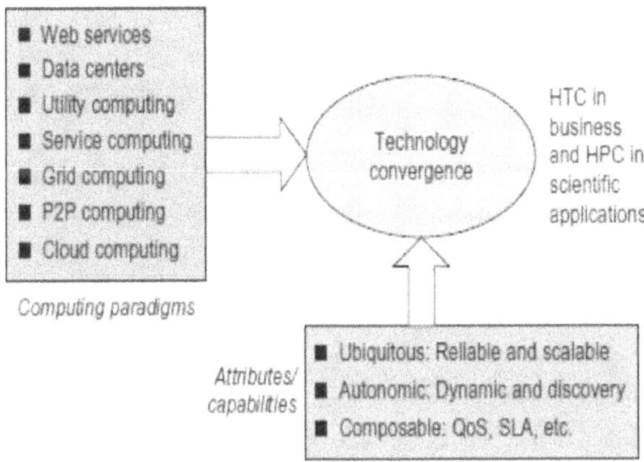

The vision of computer utilities in modern distributed computing systems.

The Hype Cycle of New Technologies

For example, at that time consumer-generated media was at the disillusionment stage, and it was predicted to take less than two years to reach its plateau of adoption. Internet micropayment systems were forecast to take two to five years to move from the enlightenment stage to maturity.

It was believed that 3D printing would take five to 10 years to move from the rising expectation stage to mainstream adoption, and mesh network sensors were expected to take more than 10 years to move from the inflated expectation stage to a plateau of mainstream adoption.

The Internet of Things and Cyber-Physical Systems the Internet of Things

The traditional Internet connects machines to machines or web pages to web pages. The concept of the IoT was introduced in 1999 at MIT. The IoT refers to the networked interconnection of everyday objects, tools, devices, or computers. One can view the IoT as a wireless network of sensors that interconnect all things in our daily life.

Cyber-Physical Systems

A cyber-physical system (CPS) is the result of interaction between computational processes and the physical world.

A CPS integrates—cyber‖ (heterogeneous, asynchronous) with—physical‖ (concurrent and information-dense) objects.

A CPS merges the—3C‖ technologies of computation, communication, and control into an intelligent closed feedback system between the physical world and the information world, a concept which is actively explored in the United States. The IoT emphasizes various networking connections among physical objects, while the CPS emphasizes exploration of virtual reality (VR) applications in the physical world.

3. Explain in detail about Multicore CPUs and Multithreading Technologies

The growth of component and network technologies over the past 30 years. They are crucial to the development of HPC and HTC systems. Processor speed is measured in millions of instructions per second (MIPS) and network bandwidth is measured in megabits per second (Mbps) or gigabits per second (Gbps). The unit GE refers to 1 Gbps Ethernet bandwidth

Advances in CPU Processors

Advanced CPUs or microprocessor chips assume a multi core architecture with dual, quad, six, or more processing cores.

These processors exploit parallelism at ILP and TLP levels. Processor speed growth is plotted in the upper curve in the diagram across generations of microprocessors or CMPs. We see growth from 1 MIPS for the VAX 780 in 1978 to 1,800 MIPS for the Intel Pentium 4 in 2002, up to a 22,000 MIPS peak for the Sun Niagara 2 in 2008. As the figure shows, Moore's law has proven to be pretty accurate in this case. The clock rate for these processors increased from 10 MHz for the Intel 286 to 4 GHz for the Pentium 4 in 30 years.

The clock rate reached its limit on CMOS-based chips due to power limitations. At the time of this writing, very few CPU chips run with a clock rate exceeding 5 GHz. In other words, clock rate will not continue to improve unless chip technology matures. This limitation is attributed primarily to excessive heat generation with high frequency or high voltages. The ILP is highly exploited in modern CPU processors.

ILP mechanisms include multiple-issue superscalar architecture, dynamic branch prediction, and speculative execution, among others. These ILP techniques demand hardware and compiler support.

In addition, DLP and TLP are highly explored in graphics processing units (GPUs) that adopt a many-core architecture with hundreds to thousands of simple cores.

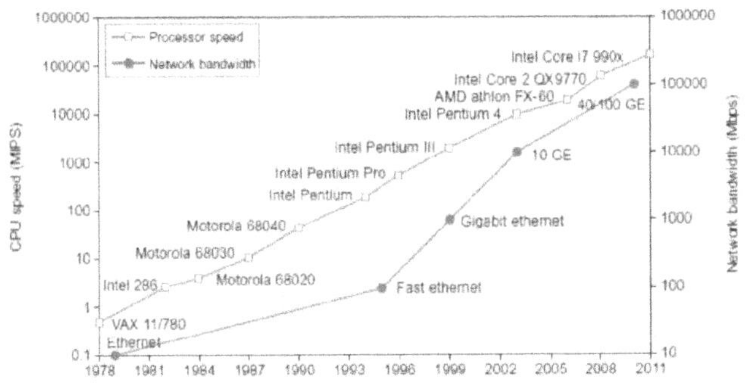

Improvement in processor and network technologies over 33 years.

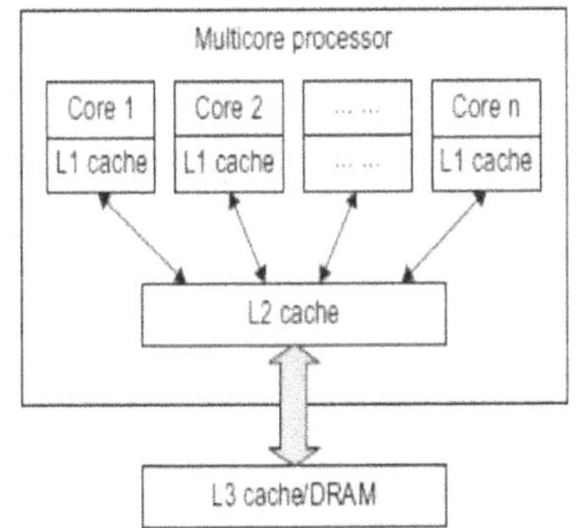

Schematic of a modern multicore CPU chip using a hierarchy of caches, where L1 cache is private to each core, on-chip L2 cache is shared and L3 cache or DRAM is off the chip.

Both multi-core CPU and many-core GPU processors can handle multiple instruction threads at different magnitudes today. The architecture of a typical multi core processor. Each core is essentially a processor with its own private cache (L1 cache). Multiple cores are housed in the same chip with an L2 cache that is shared by all cores. In the future, multiple CMPs could be built on the same CPU chip with even the L3 cache on the chip. Multicore and multithreaded CPUs are equipped with many high-end processors, including the Intel i7, Xeon, AMD Opteron, Sun Niagara, IBM Power 6, and X cell processors. Each core could be also multithreaded. For example, the Niagara II is built with eight cores with eight threads handled by each core. This implies that the maximum ILP and TLP that can be exploited in Niagara is 64 (8 × 8 = 64). In 2011, the Intel Core i7 990x has reported 159,000 MIPS execution rate as shown in the uppermost square.

Multicore CPU and Many-Core GPU Architectures

Multicore CPUs may increase from the tens of cores to hundreds or more in the future. But the CPU has reached its limit in terms of exploiting massive DLP due to the aforementioned memory wall problem. This has triggered the development of many-core GPUs with hundreds or more thin cores. Both IA-32 and IA-64 instruction set architectures are built into commercial CPUs. Now, x-86 processors have been extended to serve HPC and HTC systems in some high-end server processors.

Many RISC processors have been replaced with multicore x-86 processors and many-core GPUs in the Top 500 systems. This trend indicates that x-86 upgrades will dominate in data centers and supercomputers. The GPU also has been applied in large clusters to build supercomputers in MPPs. In the future, the processor industry is also keen to develop asymmetric or heterogeneous chip multiprocessors that can house both fat CPU cores and thin GPU cores on the same chip

Multithreading Technology

The dispatch of five independent threads of instructions to four pipelined data paths (functional units) in each of the following five processor categories from left to right: a

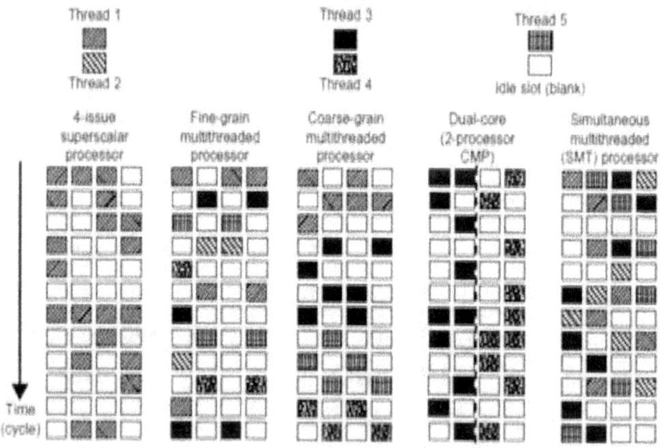

Five micro-architectures in modern CPU processors, that exploit ILP and TLP supported by multicore and multithreading technologies.

Four-issue superscalar processor, a fine-grain multithreaded processor, a coarse-grain multithreaded processor, a two-core CMP, and a simultaneous multithreaded (SMT) processor. The superscalar processor is single-threaded with four functional units. Each of the three multithreaded processors is four-way multithreaded over four functional data paths. In the dual-core processor, assume two processing cores, each a single-threaded two-way superscalar processor.

Instructions from different threads are distinguished by specific shading patterns for instructions from five independent threads. Typical instruction scheduling patterns are shown here. Only instructions from the same thread are executed in a superscalar processor. Fine-grain multithreading switches the execution of instructions from different threads per cycle. Course-grain multithreading executes many instructions from the same thread for quite a few cycles before switching to another thread. The multicore CMP executes instructions from different threads completely. The SMT allows simultaneous scheduling of instructions from different threads in the same cycle.

These execution patterns closely mimic an ordinary program. The blank squares correspond to no available instructions for an instruction data path at a particular processor cycle. More blank cells imply lower scheduling efficiency. The maximum ILP or maximum TLP is difficult to achieve at each processor cycle. The point here is to demonstrate your understanding of typical instruction scheduling patterns in these five different micro-architectures in modern processors.

4. Explain in detail about GPU Computing to Exascale and Beyond

A GPU is a graphics coprocessor or accelerator mounted on a computer's graphics card or video card. A GPU offloads the CPU from tedious graphics tasks in video editing applications. The world's first GPU, the GeForce 256, was marketed by NVIDIA in 1999. These GPU chips can process a minimum of 10 million polygons per second, and are used in nearly every computer on the market today.

Some GPU features were also integrated into certain CPUs. Traditional CPUs are structured with only a few cores. For example, the Xeon X5670 CPU has six cores. However, a modern GPU chip can be built with hundreds of processing cores.

GPUs have a throughput architecture that exploits massive parallelism by executing many concurrent threads slowly, instead of executing a single long thread in a conventional microprocessor very quickly.

Lately, parallel GPUs or GPU clusters have been garnering a lot of attention against the use of CPUs with limited parallelism. General-purpose computing on GPUs, known as GPGPUs, have appeared in the HPC field. NVIDIA's CUDA model was for HPC using GPGPUs.

How GPUs Work

Early GPUs functioned as coprocessors attached to the CPU. Today, the NVIDIA GPU has been upgraded to 128 cores on a single chip. Furthermore, each core on a GPU can handle eight threads of instructions. This translates to having up to 1,024 threads executed concurrently on a single GPU. This is true massive parallelism, compared to only a few threads that can be handled by a conventional CPU. The CPU is optimized for latency caches, while the GPU is optimized to deliver much higher throughput with explicit management of on-chip memory Modern GPUs are not restricted to accelerated graphics or video coding. They are used in HPC systems to power supercomputers with massive parallelism at multi core and multithreading levels. GPUs are designed to handle large numbers of floating-point operations in parallel. In a way, the GPU offloads the CPU from all data-intensive calculations, not just those that are related to video processing. Conventional GPUs are widely used in mobile phones, game consoles, embedded systems, PCs, and servers. The NVIDIA CUDA Tesla or Fermi is used in GPU clusters or in HPC systems for parallel processing of massive floating-pointing data.

GPU Programming Model

The interaction between a CPU and GPU in performing parallel execution of floating-point operations concurrently. The CPU is the conventional multi core processor with limited parallelism to exploit. The GPU has a many-core architecture that has hundreds of simple processing cores organized as multiprocessors. Each core can have one or more threads. Essentially, the CPU's floating-point kernel computation role is largely offloaded to the many-core GPU. The CPU instructs the GPU to perform massive data processing. The bandwidth must be matched between the on-board main memory and the on-chip GPU memory.

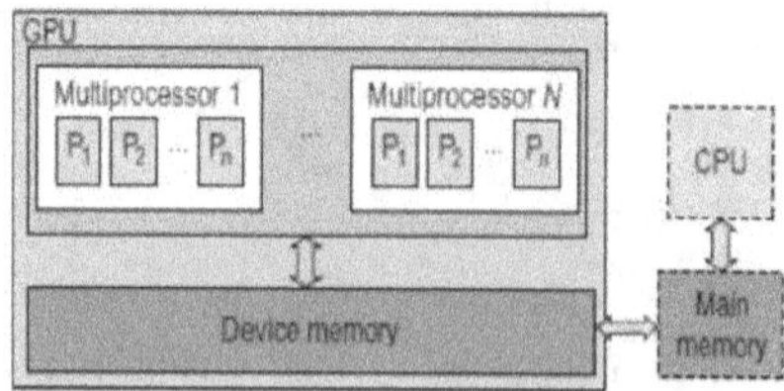

The use of a GPU along with a CPU for massively parallel execution in hundreds or thousands of processing cores.

In November 2010, three of the five fastest supercomputers in the world (the Tianhe-1a, Nebulae, and Tsubame) used large numbers of GPU chips to accelerate floating-point computations. The architecture of the Fermi GPU, a next-generation GPU from NVIDIA. This is a streaming multiprocessor (SM) module. Multiple SMs can be built on a single GPU chip. The Fermi chip has 16 SMs implemented with 3 billion transistors. Each SM comprises up to 512 streaming processors (SPs), known as CUDA cores. The Tesla GPUs used in the Tianhe-1a have a similar architecture, with 448 CUDA cores.

All functional units and CUDA cores are interconnected by an NoC (network on chip) to a large number of SRAM banks (L2 caches). Each SM has a 64 KB L1 cache. The 768 KB unified L2 cache is shared by all SMs and serves all load, store, and texture operations. Memory controllers are used to connect to 6 GB of off-chip DRAMs. The SM schedules threads in groups of 32 parallel threads called warps. In total, 256/512 FMA (fused multiply and add) operations can be done in parallel to produce 32/64-bit floating-point results. The 512 CUDA cores in an SM can work in parallel to deliver up to 515 Gflops of double-precision results, if fully utilized. With 16 SMs, a single GPU has a peak speed of 82.4 Tflops. Only 12 Fermi GPUs have the potential to reach the Pflops performance thousand-core GPUs may appear in Exascale (Eflops or 1018 flops) systems.

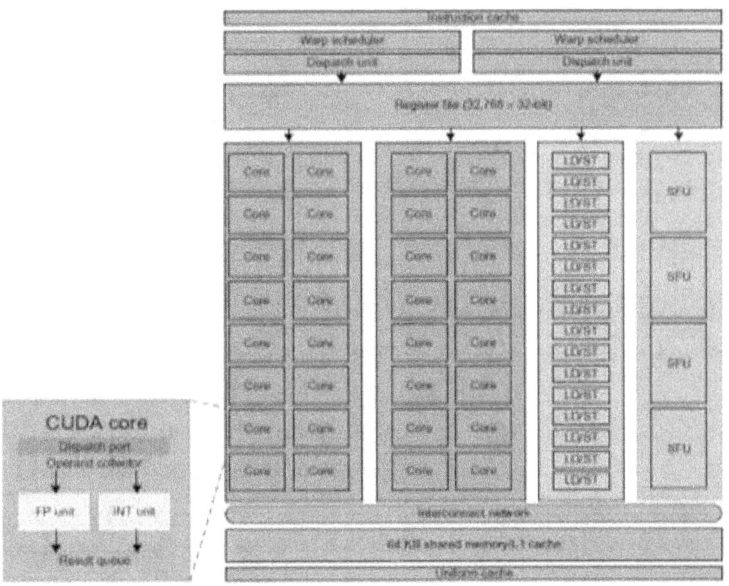

This reflects a trend toward building future MPPs with hybrid architectures of both types of processing chips. In a DARPA report published in September 2008, four challenges are identified for exascale computing: (1) energy and power, (2) memory and storage, (3) concurrency and locality, and (4) system resiliency.

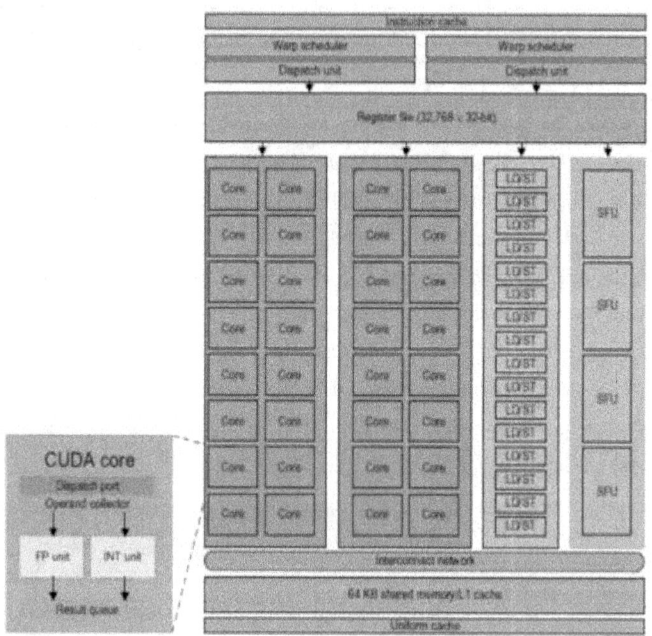

NVIDIA Fermi GPU built with 16 streaming multiprocessors (SMs) of 32 CUDA cores each; only one SM is

Power Efficiency of the GPU

Bill Dally of Stanford University considers power and massive parallelism as the major benefits of GPUs over CPUs for the future. By extrapolating current technology and computer architecture, it was estimated that 60 Gflops/watt per core is needed to run an exaflops system Power constrains what we can put in a CPU or GPU chip. Dally has estimated that the CPU chip consumes about 2 nJ/instruction, while the GPU chip requires 200 pJ/instruction, which is 1/10 less than that of the CPU. The CPU is optimized for latency in caches and memory, while the GPU is optimized for throughput with explicit management of on-chip memory.

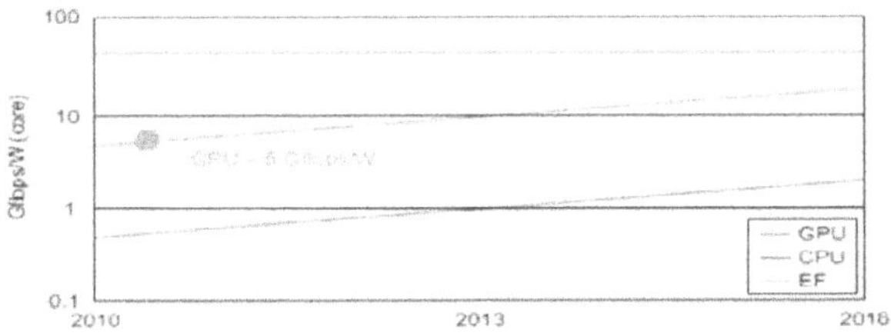

The GPU performance (middle line, measured 5 Gtlops/W/core in 2011), compared with the lower CPU performance (lower line measured 0.8 Gflops/W/core in 2011) and the estimated 60 Gflops/W/core performance in 2011 for the Exascale (EF in upper curve) in the future.

This may limit the scaling of future supercomputers. However, the GPUs may close the gap with the CPUs. Data movement dominates power consumption. One needs to optimize the storage hierarchy and tailor the memory to the applications. We need to promote self-aware OS and runtime support and build locality-aware compilers and auto-tuners for GPU based MPPs. This implies that both power and software are the real challenges in future parallel and distributed computing system

5. i) Describe about Virtual Machines and Virtualization Middleware

A conventional computer has a single OS image. This offers a rigid architecture that tightly couples application software to a specific hardware platform. Some software running well on one machine may not be executable on another platform with a different instruction set under a fixed OS. Virtual machines (VMs) offer novel solutions to underutilized resources, application inflexibility, software manageability, and security concerns in existing physical machines.

To build large clusters, grids, and clouds, we need to access large amounts of computing, storage, and networking resources in a virtualized manner.

In particular, a cloud of provisioned resources must rely on virtualization of processors, memory, and I/O facilities dynamically

Virtual Machines

The host machine is equipped with the physical hardware, as shown at the bottom of the figure. An example is an x-86 architecture desktop running its installed Windows OS, as shown in part of the figure. The VM can be provisioned for any hardware system. The VM is built with virtual resources managed by a guest OS to run a specific application. Between the VMs and the host platform, one needs to deploy a middleware layer called a virtual machine monitor (VMM).

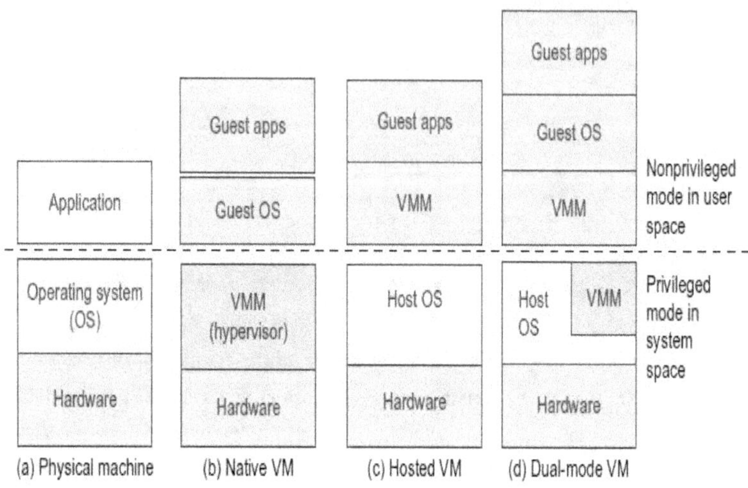

Three VM architectures in (b), (c), and (d), compared with the traditional physical machine shown in (a).

Shows a native VM installed with the use of a VMM called a hypervisor in privileged mode. For example, the hardware has x-86 architecture running the Windows system.

The guest OS could be a Linux system and the hypervisor is the XEN system developed at Cambridge University.

This hypervisor approach is also called bare-metal VM, because the hypervisor handles the bare hardware (CPU, memory, and I/O) directly.

Another Architecture is the host VM.

The VM approach offers hardware independence of the OS and applications. The user application running on its dedicated OS could be bundled together as a virtual appliance that can be ported to any hardware platform.

The VM could run on an OS different from that of the host computer.

VM Primitive Operations

The VMM provides the VM abstraction to the guest OS. With full virtualization, the VMM exports a VM abstraction identical to the physical machine so that a standard OS such as Windows 2000 or Linux can run just as it would on the physical hardware.

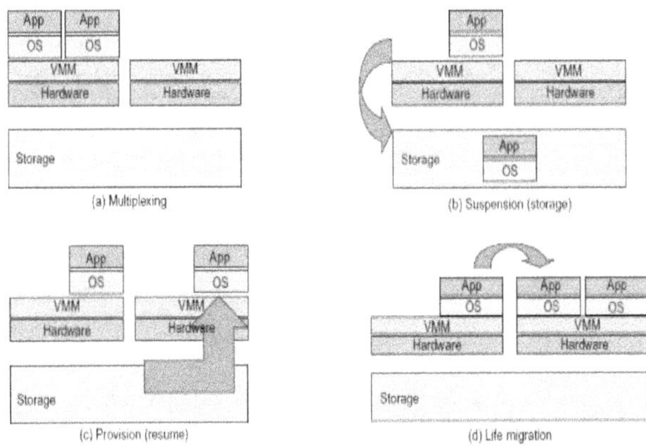

VM multiplexing, suspension, provision, and migration in a distributed computing environment.

These VM operations enable a VM to be provisioned to any available hardware platform. They also enable flexibility in porting distributed application executions. Furthermore, the VM approach will significantly enhance the utilization of server resources

Virtual Infrastructures

Physical resources for compute, storage, and networking at the bottom of are mapped to the needy applications embedded in various VMs at the top. Hardware and software are then separated. Virtual infrastructure is what connects resources to distributed applications. It is a dynamic mapping of system resources to specific applications. The result is decreased costs and increased efficiency and responsiveness.

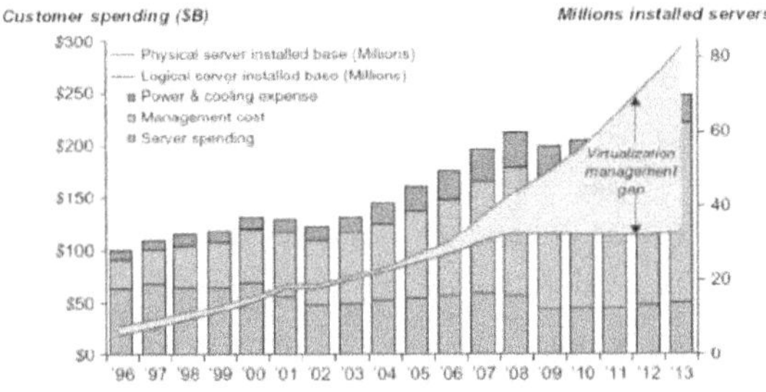

Growth and cost breakdown of data centers over the years.

5. ii) Explain in detail about Data Center Virtualization for Cloud Computing.

Basic architecture and design considerations of data centers. Cloud architecture is built with commodity hardware and network devices. Almost all cloud platforms choose the popular x86 processors. Low-cost terabyte disks and Gigabit Ethernet are used to build data centers. Data center design emphasizes the performance/price ratio over speed performance alone. In other words, storage and energy efficiency are more important than shear speed performance.

Data Center Growth and Cost Breakdown

A large data center may be built with thousands of servers. Smaller data centers are typically built with hundreds of servers. The cost to build and maintain data center servers has increased over the years. Typically only 30 percent of data center costs goes toward purchasing IT equipment (such as servers and disks), 33 percent is attributed to the chiller, 18 percent to the uninterruptible power supply (UPS), 9 percent to computer room air conditioning (CRAC), and the remaining 7 percent to power distribution, lighting, and transformer costs. Thus, about 60 percent of the cost to run a data center is allocated to management and maintenance The server purchase cost did not increase much with time. The cost of electricity and cooling did increase from 5 percent to 14 percent in 15 years.

Low-Cost Design Philosophy

High-end switches or routers may be too cost-prohibitive for building data centers. Thus, using high-bandwidth networks may not fit the economics of cloud computing. using commodity x86 servers is more desired over expensive mainframes. The software layer handles network traffic balancing, fault tolerance, and expandability. Currently, nearly all cloud computing data centers use Ethernet as their fundamental network technology

Convergence of Technologies

cloud computing is enabled by the convergence of technologies in four areas: (1) hardware virtualization and multi-core chips, (2) utility and grid computing, (3) SOA, Web 2.0, and WS mashups, and (4) atonomic computing and data center automation. Hardware virtualization and multicore chips enable the existence of dynamic configurations in the cloud. Utility and grid computing technologies lay the necessary foundation for computing clouds Recent advances in SOA, Web 2.0, and mashups of platforms are pushing the cloud another step forward.

Finally, achievements in autonomic computing and automated data center operations contribute to the rise of cloud computing.

Jim Gray once posted the following question: ─Science faces a data deluge. How to manage and analyze information?‖ This implies that science and our society face the same challenge of data deluge. Data comes from sensors, lab experiments, simulations, individual archives, and the web in all scales and formats. Preservation, movement, and access of massive data sets require generic tools supporting high-performance, scalable file systems, databases, algorithms, workflows, and visualization

On January 11, 2007, the Computer Science and Telecommunication Board (CSTB) recommended fostering tools for data capture, data creation, and data analysis. A cycle of interaction exists among four technical areas. First, cloud technology is driven by a surge of interest in data deluge. Also, cloud computing impacts e-science greatly, which explores multi core and parallel computing technologies.

By linking computer science and technologies with scientists, a spectrum of e-science or e-research applications in biology, chemistry, physics, the social sciences, and the humanities has generated new insights from interdisciplinary activities

Iterative MapReduce extends MapReduce to support a broader range of data mining algorithms commonly used in scientific applications. The cloud runs on an extremely large cluster of commodity computers. Internal to each cluster node, multithreading is practiced with a large number of cores in many-core GPU clusters

6. Explain in detail about clusters of cooperative computers

A computing cluster consists of interconnected stand-alone computers which work cooperatively as a single integrated computing resource. In the past, clustered computer systems have demonstrated impressive results in handling heavy workloads with large data sets.

Cluster Architecture

Architecture of a typical server cluster built around a low-latency, high band width interconnection network. This network can be as simple as a SAN (e.g., Myrinet) or a LAN (e.g., Ethernet). To build a larger cluster with more nodes, the interconnection network can be built with multiple levels of Gigabit Ethernet, Myrinet, or InfiniBand switches. Through hierarchical construction using a SAN, LAN, or WAN, one can build scalable clusters with an increasing number of nodes. The cluster is connected to the Internet via a virtual private network (VPN) gateway. The gateway IP address locates the cluster. The system image of a computer is decided by the way the OS manages the shared cluster resources. Most clusters have loosely coupled node computers. All resources of a server node are managed by their own OS. Thus, most clusters have multiple system images as a result of having many autonomous nodes under different OS control.

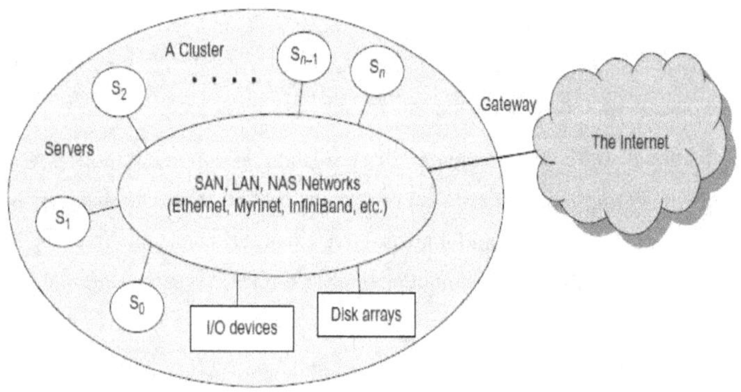

A cluster of servers interconnected by a high-bandwidth SAN or LAN with shared I/O devices and disk arrays; the cluster acts as a single computer attached to the Internet.

Single-System Image

An ideal cluster should merge multiple system images into a single-system image (SSI). Cluster designers desire a cluster operating system or some middleware to support SSI at various levels, including the sharing of CPUs, memory, and I/O across all cluster nodes.

An SSI is an illusion created by software or hardware that presents a collection of resources as one integrated, powerful resource. SSI makes the cluster appear like a single machine to the user. A cluster with multiple system images is nothing but a collection of independent computers.

Hardware, Software, and Middleware Support

Cluster design principles for both small and large clusters. Clusters exploring massive parallelism are commonly known as MPPs. Almost all HPC clusters in the Top 500 list are also MPPs. The building blocks are computer nodes (PCs, workstations, servers, or SMP), special communication software such as PVM or MPI, and a network interface card in each computer node. Most clusters run under the Linux OS.

Special cluster middleware supports are needed to create SSI or high availability (HA).

Both sequential and parallel applications can run on the cluster, and special parallel environments are needed to facilitate use of the cluster resources. For example, distributed memory has multiple images. Users may want all distributed memory to be shared by all servers by forming distributed shared memory (DSM).

Major Cluster Design Issues

A cluster-wide OS for complete resource sharing is not available yet. Middleware or OS extensions were developed at the user space to achieve SSI at selected functional levels. Without this middleware, cluster nodes cannot work together effectively to achieve cooperative computing.

7. Explain in detail about Grid computing Infrastructures

Users have experienced a natural growth path from Internet to web and grid computing services. Internet services such as the Telnet command enables a local computer to connect to a remote computer.

Web service such as HTTP enables remote access of remote web pages. Grid computing is envisioned to allow close interaction among applications running on distant computers simultaneously.

Computational Grids

Like an electric utility power grid, a computing grid offers an infrastructure that couples computers, software/middleware, special instruments, and people and sensors together. The grid is often constructed across LAN, WAN, or Internet backbone networks at a regional, national, or global scale Enterprises or organizations present grids as integrated computing resources. They can also be viewed as virtual platforms to support virtual organizations. The computers used in a grid are primarily workstations, servers, clusters, and supercomputers. Personal computers, laptops, and PDAs can be used as access devices to a grid system

Special instruments may be involved such as using the radio telescope in SETI@Home search of life in the galaxy and the austrophysics@Swineburne for pulsars. At the server end, the grid is a network.

Grid Families

Grid technology demands new distributed computing models, software/middleware support, network protocols, and hardware infrastructures. National grid projects are followed by industrial grid platform development by IBM, Microsoft, Sun, HP, Dell, Cisco, EMC, Platform Computing, and others. New grid service providers (GSPs) and new grid applications have emerged rapidly, similar to the growth of Internet and web services in the past two decades.

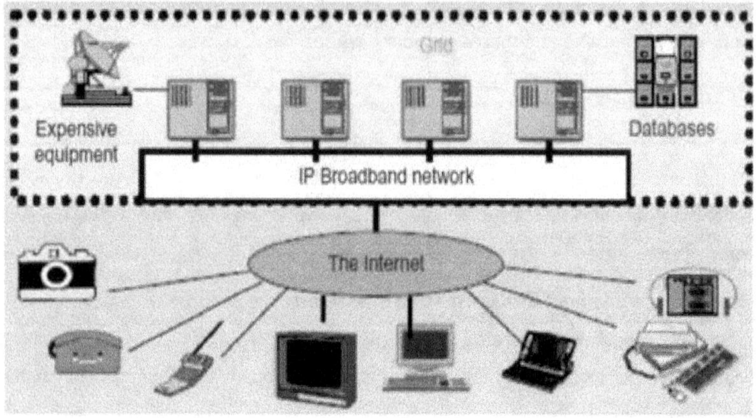

Computational grid or data grid providing computing utility, data, and information services through resource sharing and cooperation among participating organizations.

Table 1.4 Two Grid Computing Infrastructures and Representative Systems

Design Issues	Computational and Data Grids	P2P Grids
Grid Applications Reported	Distributed supercomputing, National Grid initiatives, etc.	Open grid with P2P flexibility, all resources from client machines
Representative Systems	TeraGrid built in US, ChinaGrid in China, and the e-Science grid built in UK	JXTA, FightAid@home, SETI@home
Development Lessons Learned	Restricted user groups, middleware bugs, protocols to acquire resources	Unreliable user-contributed resources, limited to a few apps

8. Explain in detail about service oriented architecture

In grids/web services, Java, and CORBA, an entity is, respectively, a service, a Java object, and a CORBA distributed object in a variety of languages. These architectures build on the traditional seven Open Systems Interconnection (OSI) layers that provide the base networking abstractions.

Layered Architecture for Web Services and Grids

The entity interfaces correspond to the Web Services Description Language (WSDL), Java method, and CORBA interface definition language (IDL) specifications in these example distributed systems. These interfaces are linked with customized, high-level communication systems: SOAP, RMI, and IIOP in the three examples. These communication systems support features including particular message patterns (such as Remote Procedure Call or RPC), fault recovery, and specialized routing the features in the Web Services Reliable Messaging (WSRM) framework mimic the OSI layer capability (as in TCP fault tolerance) modified to match the different abstractions (such as messages versus packets, virtualized addressing) at the entity levels. Security is a critical capability that either uses or reimplements the capabilities seen in concepts such as Internet Protocol Security (IPsec) and secure sockets in the OSI layers.

JNDI (Jini and Java Naming and Directory Interface) illustrating different approaches within the Java distributed object model. The CORBA Trading Service, UDDI (Universal Description, Discovery, and Integration), LDAP (Lightweight Directory Access Protocol), and ebXML (Electronic Business using eXtensible Markup Language) are other examples of discovery and information services described

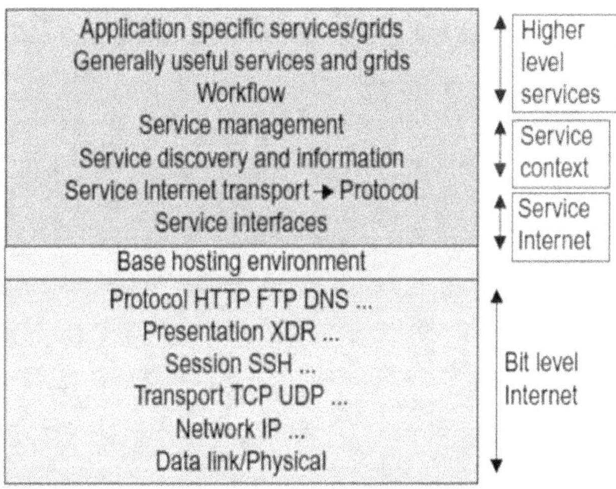

Layered achitecture for web services and the grids.

Web Services and Tools

Loose coupling and support of heterogeneous implementations make services more attractive than distributed objects. Corresponds to two choices of service architecture: web services or REST systems (these are further discussed in. Both web services and REST systems have very distinct approaches to building reliable interoperable systems. In web services, one aims to fully specify all aspects of the service and its environment.

In CORBA and Java, the distributed entities are linked with RPCs, and the simplest way to build composite applications is to view the entities as objects and use the traditional ways of linking them together. For Java, this could be as simple as writing a Java program with method calls replaced by Remote Method Invocation (RMI), while CORBA supports a similar model with a syntax reflecting the C++ style of its entity (object) interfaces.

The Evolution of SOA

Service-oriented architecture (SOA) has evolved over the years. SOA applies to building grids, clouds, grids of clouds, clouds of grids, clouds of clouds (also known as interclouds), and systems of systems in general.

A large number of sensors provide data-collection services, denoted in the figure as SS (sensor service).

A sensor can be a ZigBee device, a Bluetooth device, a WiFi access point, a personal computer, a GPA, or a wireless phone, among other things. Raw data is collected by sensor services.

The evolution of SOA: grids of clouds and grids, where —SS‖ refers to a sensor service and —fs‖ to a filter or transforming service Most distributed systems require a web interface or portal.

For raw data collected by a large number of sensors to be transformed into useful information or knowledge, the data stream may go through a sequence of compute, storage, filter, and discovery clouds. Finally, the inter-service messages converge at the portal, which is accessed by all users

Grids Versus Clouds

The boundary between grids and clouds are getting blurred in recent years. For web services, workflow technologies are used to coordinate or orchestrate services with certain specifications used to define critical business process models such as two-phase transactions

In general, a grid system applies static resources, while a cloud emphasizes elastic resources.

For some researchers, the differences between grids and clouds are limited only in dynamic resource allocation based on virtualization and autonomic computing. Thus one may end up building with a system of systems: such as a cloud of clouds, a grid of clouds, or a cloud of grids, or inter-clouds as a basic SOA architecture.

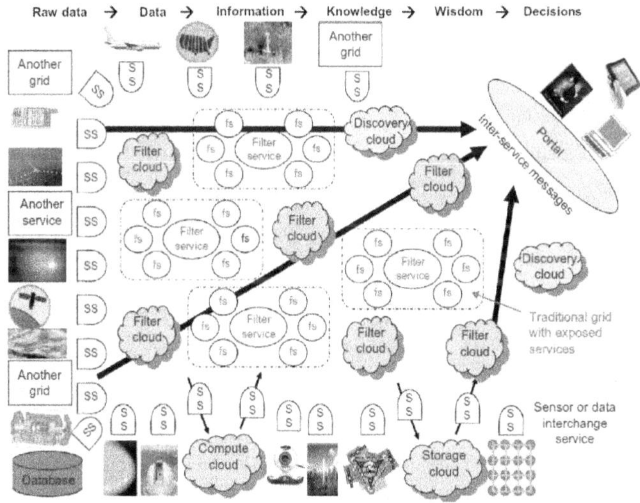

9. Explain in detail about Grid Architecture and standards

New architecture model and technology has been developed for the establishment and management of cross-organizational resource sharing. This new architecture, called *grid architecture*, identifies the basic components of a grid system. The grid architecture defines the purpose and functions of its components, while indicating how these components interact with one another.7 The main focus of the architecture is on interoperability among resource providers and users in order to establish the sharing relationships. This interoperability, in turn, necessitates common protocols at each layer of the architectural model, which leads to the definition of a grid protocol architecture as shown in Figure.

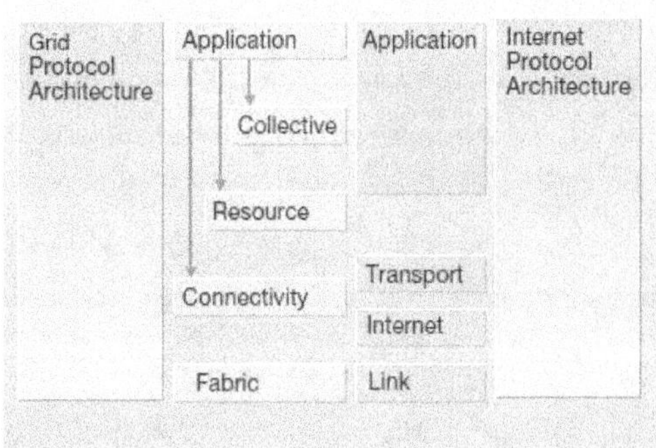

Reprinted with permission of Ian Foster

This protocol architecture defines common mechanisms, interfaces, schema, and protocols at each layer, by which users and resources can negotiate, establish, manage, and share resources. Figure 1 shows the component layers of the grid architecture and the capabilities of each layer. Each layer shares the behavior of the underlying component layers. The following describes the core features of each of these component layers, starting from the bottom of the stack and moving upward.

- *Fabric layer*—The fabric layer defines the interface to local resources, which may be shared. This includes computational resources, data storage, networks, catalogs, software modules, and other system resources.
- *Connectivity layer*—The connectivity layer defines the basic communication and authentication protocols required for grid-specific networking service transactions.
- *Resource layer*—This layer uses the communication and security protocols (defined by the connectivity layer) to control secure negotiation, initiation, monitoring, accounting, and payment for the sharing of functions of individual resources. The resource layer calls the fabric layer functions to access and control local resources. This layer only handles individual resources, ignoring global states and atomic actions across the resource collection pool, which are the responsibility of the collective layer.
- *Collective layer*—While the resource layer manages an individual resource, the collective layer is responsible for all global resource management and interaction with collections of resources. This protocol layer implements a wide variety of sharing behaviors using a small number of resource-layer and connectivity-layer protocols.
- *Application layer*—The application layer enables the use of resources in a grid environment through various collaboration and resource access protocols.

Thus far, our discussions have focused on the grid problem in the context of a virtual organization and the proposed grid computing architecture as a suggested solution to this problem. This architecture is designed for controlled resource sharing with improved interoperability among participants. In contrast, emerging architectures help the earlier-defined grid architecture quickly adapt to a wider (and strategically important) technology domain.

10. Explain in detail about Memory, Storage, and Wide-Area Networking

Memory Technology

Plots the growth of DRAM chip capacity from 16 KB in 1976 to 64 GB in 2011. This shows that memory chips have experienced a 4x increase in capacity every three years. Memory access time did not improve much in the past. In fact, the memory wall problem is getting worse as the processor gets faster. For hard drives, capacity increased from 260 MB in 1981 to 250 GB in 2004.

The Seagate Barracuda XT hard drive reached 3 TB in 2011. This represents an approximately 10x increase in capacity every eight years. The capacity increase of disk arrays will be even greater in the years to come. Faster processor speed and larger memory capacity result in a wider gap between processors and memory.

Disks and Storage Technology

Beyond 2011, disks or disk arrays have exceeded 3 TB in capacity. The lower curve in the disk storage growth in 7 orders of magnitude in 33 years. The rapid growth of flash memory and solid-state drives (SSDs) also impacts the future of HPC and HTC systems. The mortality rate of SSD is not bad at all. A typical SSD can handle 300,000 to 1 million write cycles per

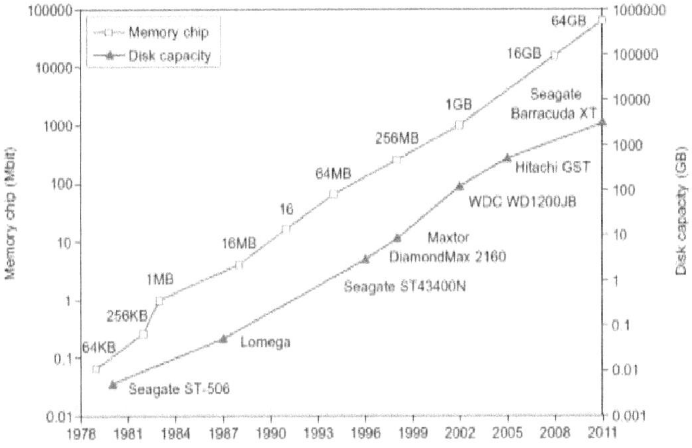

Improvement in memory and disk technologies over 33 years. The Seagate Barracuda XT disk has a capacity

System-Area Interconnects

The nodes in small clusters are mostly interconnected by an Ethernet switch or a local area network (LAN). a LAN typically is used to connect client hosts to big servers. A storage area network (SAN) connects servers to network storage such as disk arrays. Network attached storage (NAS) connects client hosts directly to the disk arrays.

All three types of networks often appear in a large cluster built with commercial network components. If no large distributed storage is shared, a small cluster could be built with a multiport Gigabit Ethernet switch plus copper cables to link the end machines.

Wide-Area Networking

An increase factor of two per year on network performance was reported, which is faster than Moore's law on CPU speed doubling every 18 months. The implication is that more computers will be used concurrently in the future. High-bandwidth networking increases the capability of building massively distributed systems.

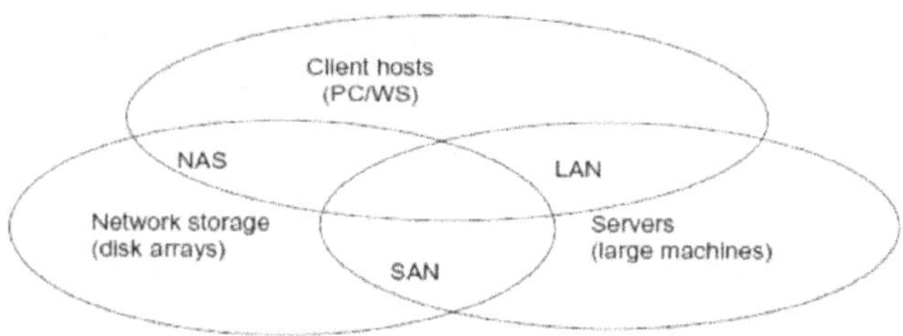

Three interconnection networks for connecting servers, client hosts, and storage devices; the LAN connects client hosts and servers, the SAN connects servers with disk arrays, and the NAS connects clients with large storage systems in the network environment.

UNIT II

Grid Services

Part A

1. List the OGSA grid service interfaces?

Port Type	Operation
Grid service	Find service data, Termination time and Destroy
Notification source	Subscribe to notification topic
Notification sink	Deliver notification
Registry	Register service and Unregister service
Factory	Create service
Handle map	Find by handle

2. Define Endpoint References in WSRF

The WSRF service addressing mechanism is defined in the WS-addressing standard and uses a term called an endpoint reference (EPR), which is an XML document that contains various information about the service and resource. Specifically, the endpoint reference includes both the service address (URI) and resource identification called a key.

3. What are the specifications of WSRF

WSRF is actually a collection of four specifications (standards):

- WS-ResourceProperties — specifies how resource properties are defined and accessed.
- WS-ResourceLifetime — specifies mechanisms to manage resource lifetimes.
- WS-ServiceGroup — specifies how to group services or WS-Resources together.
- WS-BaseFaults — specifies how to report faults.

4. Define Globus 4 information services

Globus 4 information services collectively is called the Monitoring and Discovering System (MDS4 in GT 4) and consists of a set of three WSRF information components:

- Index service
- Trigger service
- WebMDS

From which a framework can be constructed for collecting and using information. The three components are part of the full GT4 package.

5. Define WebMDS

WebMDS (Web Monitoring and Discovering System) is a servlet that provides a Web-based interface to display XML-based information such as resource property information, and as such can be a front-end to index services.

6. Write about the strategies of replication

The strategies of replication can be classified into method types: dynamic and static. For the static method, the locations and number of replicas are determined in advance and will not be modified.

Dynamic strategies can adjust locations and number of data replicas according to changes in conditions.

7. Define data grid? List the Grid Data Access Models

A data grid is a set of structured services that provides multiple services like the ability to access alter and transfer very large amounts of geographically separated data, especially for research and collaboration purposes.

1. Monadic model.
2. Hierarchical model
3. Federation model
4. Hybrid model

8. Define grid data access Federation model

This model is better suited for designing a data grid with multiple sources of data supplies. Sometimes this model is also known as a mesh model. The data sources are distributed to many different locations.

Although the data is shared, the data items are still owned and controlled by their original owners. According to predefined access policies, only authenticated users are authorized to request data from any data source.

9. Write about Parallel Data Transfer

Parallel data transfer opens multiple data streams for passing subdivided segments of a file simultaneously. Although the speed of each stream is the same as in sequential streaming, the total time to move data in all streams can be significantly reduced compared to FTP transfer.

10. Define Striped Data Transfer

Striped data transfer, a data object is partitioned into a number of sections, and each section is placed in an individual site in a data grid.

When a user requests this piece of data, a data stream is created for each site, and all the sections of data objects are transferred simultaneously.

11. Write about Monadic access model

This is a centralized data repository model. All the data is saved in a central data repository. When users want to access some data they have to submit requests directly to the central repository. No data is replicated for preserving data locality. This model is the simplest to implement for a small grid.

12. Explain grid data access Hierarchical model

This is suitable for building a large data grid which has only one large data access directory. The data may be transferred from the source to a second-level center. Then some data in the regional center is transferred to the third-level center. After being forwarded several times, specific data objects are accessed directly by users.

13. List the basic functionality requirements of grid service

* Discovery and brokering
* Metering and accounting
* Data sharing
* Deployment
* Virtual organizations
* Monitoring
* Policy

14. What are the security requirements of grid service

* Multiple security infrastructures
* Perimeter security solutions
* Authentication, Authorization, and Accounting
* Encryption
* Application and Network-Level Firewalls
* Certification

15. List the System Properties Requirements of grid service

* Fault tolerance
* Disaster recovery
* Self-healing capabilities
* Strong monitoring
* Legacy application management
* Administration.

- Agreement-based interaction

- Grouping/aggregation of services

16. What are the objectives of OGSA?

- Manage resources across distributed heterogeneous platforms

- Support QoS-oriented Service Level Agreements (SLAs).

- Provide a common base for autonomic management.

- Define open, published interfaces and protocols for the interoperability of diverse resources.

17. Define grid service instance

A grid service instance is a (potentially taransient) service that conforms to a set of conventions, expressed as WSDL interfaces, extensions, and behaviors, for such purposes as lifetime management, discovery of characteristics, and notification.

18. Define grid service handle (GSH)

A grid service handle (GSH) can be thought of as a permanent network pointer to a particular grid service instance. The GSH does not provide sufficient information to allow a client to access the service instance; the client needs to —resolve‖ a GSH into a grid service reference (GSR).

19. Define grid service reference (GSR).

The GSR contains all the necessary information to access the service instance. The GSR is not a —permanent‖ network pointer to the grid service instance because a GSR may become invalid for various reasons; for example, the grid service instance may be moved to a different server.

20. What is meant by grid service description

A grid service description describes how a client interacts with service instances. This description is independent of any particular instance. Within a WSDL document, the grid service description is embodied in the most derived of the instance, along with its associated port Types bindings, messages, and types definitions.

21. List the XML lifetime declaration properties

The three life time declaration properties are:

1. ogsi:goodFrom

2. ogsi:goodUntil

3. ogsi:availableUntil

22. Define Naming by Attributes in semantic name space

Attribute naming schemes associate various metadata with services and support retrieval via queries on attribute values. A registry implementing such a scheme allows service providers to publish the existence and properties of the services that they provide, so that service consumers can discover them.

23. Define naming by path in semantic name space

Path naming or directory schemes (as used, for example, in file systems) represent an alternative approach to attribute schemes for organizing services into a hierarchical name space that can be navigated.

Part B

1. Explain in detail about Open Grid Services Architecture

The OGSA is an open source grid service standard jointly developed by academia and the IT industry under coordination of a working group in the Global Grid Forum (GGF). The standard was specifically developed for the emerging grid and cloud service communities. The OGSA is extended from web service concepts and technologies.

The standard defines a common framework that allows businesses to build grid platforms across enterprises and business partners. The intent is to define the standards required for both open source and commercial software to support a global grid infrastructure

OGSA Framework

The OGSA was built on two basic software technologies: the Globus Toolkit widely adopted as a grid technology solution for scientific and technical computing, and web services (WS 2.0) as a popular standards-based framework for business and network applications. The OGSA is intended to support the creation, termination, management, and invocation of stateful, transient grid services via standard interfaces and conventions

OGSA Interfaces

The OGSA is centered on grid services. These services demand special well-defined application interfaces.

These interfaces provide resource discovery, dynamic service creation, lifetime management, notification, and manageability. These properties have significant implications regarding how a grid service is named, discovered, and managed.

Port Type	Operation	Brief Description
Grid service	Find service data	Query a grid service instance, including the handle, reference, primary key, home handle map, interface information, and service-specific information. Extensible support for various query languages.
	Termination time	Set (and get) termination time for grid service instance.
	Destroy	Terminate grid service instance.
Notification source	Subscribe to notification topic	Subscribe to notifications of service events. Allow delivery via third-party messaging services.
Notification sink	Deliver notification	Carry out asynchronous delivery of notification messages.
Registry	Register service	Conduct soft-state registration of Grid Service Handles (GSHs).
	Unregister service	Unregister a GSH.
Factory	Create service	Create a new grid service instance.
Handle map	Find by handle	Return the Grid Service Reference (GSR) associated with the GSH.

Grid Service Handle

A GSH is a globally unique name that distinguishes a specific grid service instance from all others. The status of a grid service instance could be that it exists now or that it will exist in the future.

These instances carry no protocol or instance-specific addresses or supported protocol bindings. Instead, these information items are encapsulated along with all other instance-specific information. In order to interact with a specific service instance, a single abstraction is defined as a GSR.

Grid Service Migration

This is a mechanism for creating new services and specifying assertions regarding the lifetime of a service. The OGSA model defines a standard interface, known as a factor, to implement this reference. This creates a requested grid service with a specified interface and returns the GSH and initial GSR for the new service instance.

If the time period expires without having received a reaffirmed interest from a client, the service instance can be terminated on its own and release the associated resources accordingly

OGSA Security Models

The grid works in a heterogeneous distributed environment, which is essentially open to the general public. We must be able to detect intrusions or stop viruses from spreading by implementing secure conversations, single logon, access control, and auditing for non repudiation.

At the security policy and user levels, we want to apply a service or endpoint policy, resource mapping rules, authorized access of critical resources, and privacy protection. At the Public Key Infrastructure (PKI) service level, the OGSA demands security binding with the security protocol stack and bridging of certificate authorities (CAs), use of multiple trusted intermediaries, and so on.

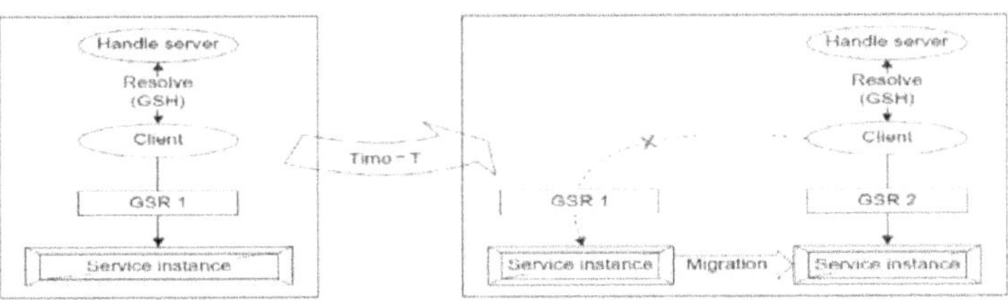

A GSH resolving to a different GSR for a migrated service instance before (shown on the left) and after (on the right) the migration at time T.

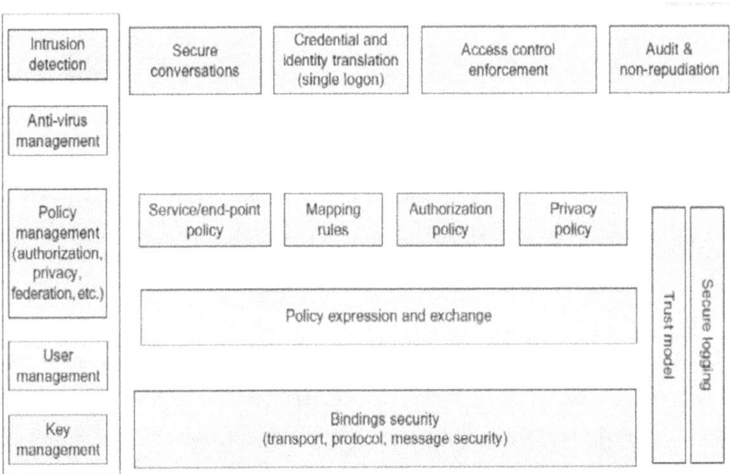

The OGSA security model implemented at various protection levels.

2. **Describe in detail about basic functionality requirements and System Properties Requirements**

Basic Functionality Requirements

Discovery and brokering Mechanisms are required for discovering and/or allocating services, data, and resources with desired properties. For example, clients need to discover network services before they are used, service brokers need to discover hardware and software availability, and service brokers must identify codes and platforms suitable for execution requested by the client

Metering and accounting. Applications and schemas for metering, auditing, and billing for IT infrastructure and management use cases. The metering function records the usage and duration, especially metering the usage of licenses. The auditing function audits usage and application profiles on machines, and the billing function bills the user based on metering.

Data sharing. Data sharing and data management are common as well as important grid applications. Chanisms are required for accessing and managing data archives, for caching data and managing its consistency, and for indexing and discovering data and metadata.

Deployment. Data is deployed to the hosting environment that will execute the job (or made available in or via a high-performance infrastructure). Also, applications (executable) are migrated to the computer that will execute them

Virtual organizations (VOs). The need to support collaborative VOs introduces a need for mechanisms to support VO creation and management, including group membership services [58]. For the commercial data center use case [55], the grid creates a VO in a data center that provides IT resources to the job upon the customer's job request.

Monitoring. A global, cross-organizational view of resources and assets for project and fiscal planning, troubleshooting, and other purposes. The users want to monitor their applications running on the grid. Also, the resource or service owners need to surface certain states so that the user of those resources or services may manage the usage using the state information

Policy. An error and event policy guides self-controlling management, including failover and provisioning. It is important to be able to represent policy at multiple stages in hierarchical systems, with the goal of automating the enforcement of policies that might otherwise be implemented as organizational processes or managed manually

System Properties Requirements

Fault tolerance. Support is required for failover, load redistribution, and other techniques used to achieve fault tolerance. Fault tolerance is particularly important for long running queries that can potentially return large amounts of data, for dynamic scientific applications, and for commercial data center applications.

Disaster recovery. Disaster recovery is a critical capability for complex distributed grid infrastructures. For distributed systems, failure must be considered one of the natural behaviors and disaster recovery mechanisms must be considered an essential component of the design.

Self-healing capabilities of resources, services and systems are required. Significant manual effort should not be required to monitor, diagnose, and repair faults.

Legacy application management. Legacy applications are those that cannot be changed, but they are too aluable to give up or to complex to rewrite. Grid infrastructure has to be built around them so that they can continue to be used

Administration. Be able to ―codify‖ and ―automate‖ the normal practices used to administer the environment. The goal is that systems should be able to self organize and self-describe to manage low-level configuration details based on higher-level configurations and management policies specified by administrators.

Agreement-based interaction. Some initiatives require agreement-based interactions capable of specifying and enacting agreements between clients and servers (not necessarily human) and then composing those agreements into higher-level end-user structures.

Grouping/aggregation of services. The ability to instantiate (compose) services using some set of existing services is a key requirement. There are two main types of composition techniques: selection and aggregation. Selection involves choosing to use a particular service among many services with the same operational interface.

3. **Explain the following functionality requirements**

a) Security Requirements

Grids also introduce a rich set of security requirements; some of these requirements are: ***Multiple security infrastructures.*** Distributed operation implies a need to interoperate with and manage multiple security infrastructures. For example, for a commercial data center application, isolation of customers in the same commercial data center is a crucial requirement; the grid should provide not only access control but also performance isolation.

Perimeter security solutions. Many use cases require applications to be deployed on the other side of firewalls from the intended user clients. Inter grid collaboration often requires crossing institutional firewalls.

Authentication, Authorization, and Accounting. Obtaining application programs and deploying them into a grid system may require authentication/authorization. In the commercial data center use case, the commercial data center authenticates the customer and authorizes the submitted request when the customer submits a job request.

Encryption. The IT infrastructure and management use case requires encrypting of the communications, at least of the payload

Application and Network-Level Firewalls. This is a long-standing problem; it is made particularly difficult by the many different policies one is dealing with and the particularly harsh restrictions at international sites.

Certification. A trusted party certifies that a particular service has certain semantic behavior. For example, a company could establish a policy of only using e-commerce services certified by Yahoo

b) Resource Management Requirements

Resource management is another multilevel requirement, encompassing SLA negotiation, provisioning, and scheduling for a variety of resource types and activities

Provisioning. Computer processors, applications, licenses, storage, networks, and instruments are all grid resources that require provisioning. OGSA needs a framework that allows resource provisioning to be done in a uniform, consistent manner.

Resource virtualization. Dynamic provisioning implies a need for resource virtualization mechanisms that allow resources to be transitioned flexibly to different tasks as required; for example, when bringing more Web servers on line as demand exceeds a threshold..

Optimization of resource usage while meeting cost targets (i.e., dealing with finite resources). Mechanisms to manage conflicting demands from various organizations, groups, projects, and users and implement a fair sharing of resources and access to the grid

Transport management. For applications that require some form of real-time scheduling, it can be important to be able to schedule or provision bandwidth dynamically for data transfers or in support of the other data sharing applications. In many (if not all) commercial applications, reliable transport management is essential to obtain the end-to-end QoS required by the application.

Management and monitoring. Support for the management and monitoring of resource usage and the detection of SLA or contract violations by all relevant parties. Also, conflict management is necessary.

Processor scavenging is an important tool that allows an enterprise or VO to use to aggregate computing power that would otherwise go to waste.

Scheduling of service tasks. Long recognized as an important capability for any information processing system, scheduling becomes extremely important and difficult for distributed grid systems.

Load balancing. In many applications, it is necessary to make sure make sure deadlines are met or resources are used uniformly. These are both forms of load balancing that must be made possible by the underlying infrastructure

Advanced reservation. This functionality may be required in order to execute the application on reserved resources.

Notification and messaging. Notification and messaging are critical in most dynamic scientific problems.

Logging. It may be desirable to log processes such as obtaining/deploying application programs because, for example, the information might be used for accounting. This functionality is represented as —metering and accounting.‖

Workflow management. Many applications can be wrapped in scripts or processes that require licenses and other resources from multiple sources. Applications coordinate using the file system based on events

Pricing. Mechanisms for determining how to render appropriate bills to users of a grid.

4. Describe in detail about Practical view of OGSA/OGSI

OGSA aims at addressing standardization (for interoperability) by defining the basic framework of a grid application structure.

Some of the mechanisms employed in the standards formulation of grid computing

The objectives of OGSA are:

Manage resources across distributed heterogeneous platforms.

Support QoS-oriented Service Level Agreements (SLAs). The topology of grids is often complex; the interactions between/among grid resources are almost invariably dynamic.

Provide a common base for autonomic management. A grid can contain a plethora of resources, along with an abundance of combinations of resource MPICH-G2: Grid-enabled message passing (Message Passing Interface).

1. CoG Kits, GridPort: Portal construction, based on N-tier architectures.
2. Condor-G: workflow management.
3. Legion: object models for grid computing.

4. Cactus: Grid-aware numerical solver framework.

Portals

1. N-tier architectures enabling thin clients, with middle tiers using grid functions _ Thin clients = web browsers.
2. Middle tier = e.g., Java Server Pages, with Java CoG Kit, GPDK, GridPort utilities _ Bottom tier = various grid resources.
3. Numerous applications and projects.
4. Unicore, Gateway, Discover, Mississippi Computational Web Portal, NPACI Grid Port, Lattice Portal, Nimrod-G, Cactus, NASA IPG Launchpad, Grid Resource.

Broker

High-Throughput Computing and Condor.

1. High-throughput computing.
2. Processor cycles/day (week, month, year?) under non ideal circumstances
3. How many times can I run simulation X in a month using all available machines?||
4. Condor converts collections of distributive owned workstations and dedicated clusters into a distributed high-throughput computing facility.
5. Emphasis on policy management and reliability.

Object-Based Approaches.

1. Grid-enabled CORBA
2. NASA Lewis, Rutgers, ANL, others
3. CORBA wrappers for grid protocols
4. Some initial successes
5. Legion
6. University of Virginia
7. Object models for grid components (e.g., ―vault|| = storage, ―host|| = computer) Cactus: Modular, portable framework for parallel, multidimensional simulations Construct codes by linking
8. Small core: management services
9. Selected modules: Numerical methods, grids and domain decomps, visualization and steering, etc.
10. Custom linking/configuration tools
11. Developed for astrophysics, but not astrophysics specific

Proposed OGSA grid service interfaces*

Port type	Operation	Description
GridService	FindServiceData	Query a variety of information about the grid service instance, including basic introspection information (handle, reference, primary key, home handle map: terms to be defined), richer per-interface information, and service-specific information (e.g., service instances known to a registry). Extensible support for various query languages.
	SetTermination Time	Set (and get) termination time for grid service instance
	Destroy	Terminate grid service instance.
Notification-Source	SubscribeTo-NotificationTopic	Subscribe to notifications of service-related events, based on message type and interest statement. Allows for delivery via third-party messaging services.
Notification-Sink	Deliver Notification	Carry out asynchronous delivery of notification messages.
Registry	RegisterService UnregisterService	Conduct soft-state registration of grid service handles. Deregister a grid service handle.
Factory	CreateService	Create new grid service instance.
Handle Map	FindByHandle	Return grid service reference currently associated

There are two fundamental requirements for describing Web services based on the OGSI

1. The ability to describe interface inheritance—a basic concept with most of the distributed object systems.

2. The ability to describe additional information elements with the interface definitions.

5. Explain in detail about Detailed view of OGSA/OGSI

Provides a more detailed view of OGSI based on the OGSI specification itself. For a more comprehensive description of these concepts, the reader should consult the specification OGSI defines a component model that extends WSDL and XML schema definition to incorporate the concepts of

State ful Web services.

1. Extension of Web services interfaces _ Asynchronous notification of state change _ References to instances of services _ Collections of service instances.

2. Service state data that augment the constraint capabilities of XML schema definition

    Setting the Context.

GGF calls OGSI the —base for OGSA.‖ Specifically, there is a relationship between OGSI and distributed object systems and also a relationship between OGSI and the existing (and evolving) Web services framework.

Relationship to Distributed Object Systems

Given grid service implementation is an addressable and potentially stateful instance that implements one or more interfaces described by WSDL portTypes. Grid service factories can be used to create instances implementing a given set of portType(s).

Client-Side Programming Patterns

Another important issue is how OGSI interfaces are likely to be invoked from client applications. OGSI exploits an important component of the Web services framework: the use of WSDL to describe multiple protocol bindings, encoding styles, messaging styles (RPC versus document oriented), and so on, for a given Web service.

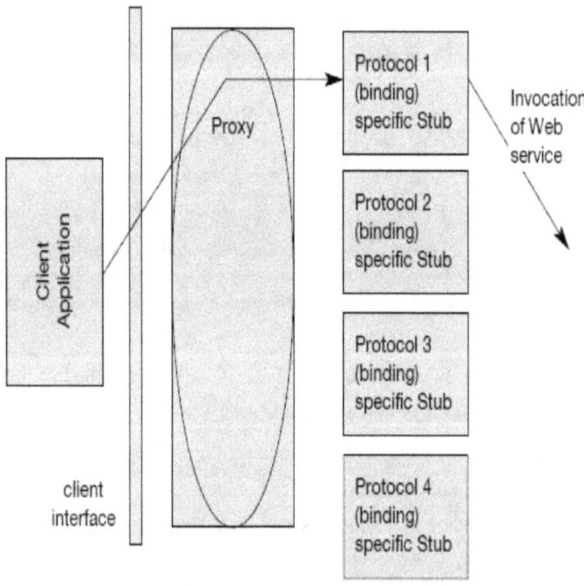

Possible client-side runtime architecture.

Client Use of Grid Service Handles and References

Client gains access to a grid service instance through grid service handles and grid service references. A grid service handle (GSH) can be thought of as a permanent network pointer to a particular grid service instance.

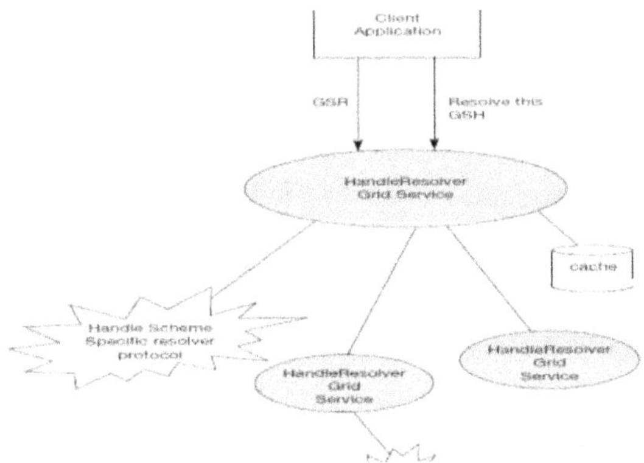

Resolving a GSH.

Relationship to Hosting Environment

OGSI does not dictate a particular service-provider-side implementation architecture. A variety of approaches are possible, ranging from implementing the grid service instance directly as an operating system process to a sophisticated server-side mponent model such as J2EE. In the former case, most or even all support for standard grid service behaviors (invocation, lifetime management, registration, etc.)

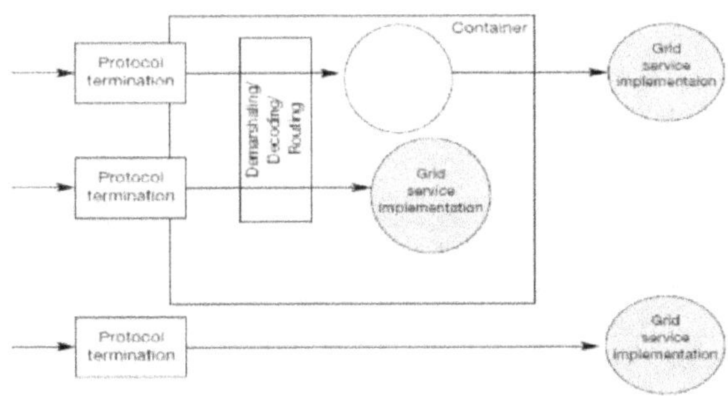

Two approaches to the implementation of argument demarshaling functions in a grid service hosting environment.

The Grid Service

The purpose of the OGSI document is to specify the (standardized) interfaces and behaviors that define a *grid service*

WSDL Extensions and Conventions

OGSI is based on Web services; in particular, it uses WSDL as the mechanism to describe the public interfaces of grid services.

Service Data

The approach to *stateful* Web services introduced in OGSI identified the need for a common mechanism to expose a service instance's state data to service requestors for query, update, and change notification.

Motivation and Comparison to JavaBean Properties

OGSI specification introduces the serviceData concept to provide a flexible, properties-style approach to accessing state data of a Web service.

The serviceData concept is similar to the notion of a public instance variable or field in object-oriented programming languages such as Java, Smalltalk, and C++.

Extending portType with ServiceData

ServiceData defines a Newport Type child element named serviceData, used to define serviceData elements, or SDEs, associated with that portType.

These serviceData element definitions are referred to as serviceData declarations, or SDDs.

Service Data Values

Each service instance is associated with a collection of serviceData elements: those serviceData elements defined within the various portTypes that form the service's interface, and also, potentially, additional service

SDE Aggregation within a portType Interface Hierarchy

WSDL 1.2 has introduced the notion of multiple portType extension, and one can model that construct within the GWSDL namespace.

A portType can extend zero or more other portTypes

Dynamic serviceData Elements

Although many serviceData elements are most naturally defined in a service's interface definition, situations can arise in which it is useful to add or move serviceData elements dynamically to or from an instance.

6. Short Notes on,

a) Core Grid Service Properties

Service Description and Service Instance

One can distinguish in OGSI between the *description* of a grid service and an *instance* of a grid service:

A *grid service description* describes how a client interacts with service instances.

This description is independent of any particular instance. Within a WSDL document, the grid service description is embodied in the most derived portType

A grid service description may be simultaneously used by any number of *grid service instances,* each of which

1. Embodies some state with which the service description describes how to interact _ Has one or more grid service handles.
2. Has one or more grid service references to it.

Modeling Time in OGSI

The need arises at various points throughout this specification to represent time that is meaningful to multiple parties in the distributed Grid.

The GMT global time standard is assumed for grid services, allowing operations to refer unambiguously to absolute times. However, assuming the GMT time standard to represent time does *not* imply any particular level of clock synchronization between clients and services in the grid. In fact, no specific accuracy of synchronization is specified or expected by OGSI, as this is a service-quality issue

XML Element Lifetime Declaration Properties

Service Data elements may represent instantaneous observations of the dynamic state of a service instance, it is critical that consumers of serviceData be able to understand the valid lifetimes of these observations.

The three lifetime declaration properties are:

1. ogsi:goodFrom. Declares the time from which the content of the element is said to be valid. This is typically the time at which the value was created.

2. ogsi:goodUntil. Declares the time until which the content of the element is said to be valid. This property must be greater than or equal to the goodFrom time.

3. ogsi:availableUntil. Declares the time until which this element itself is expected to be available, perhaps with updated values. Prior to this time, a client should be able to obtain an updated copy of this element.

b) Grid Service Handles and Grid Service References

Client gains access to a grid service instance through grid service handles and grid service references. A grid service handle (GSH) can be thought of as a permanent network pointer to a particular grid service instance.

The client resolves a GSH into a GSR by invoking a Handle Resolver grid service instance identified by some out-of-band mechanism. The Handle Resolver can use various means to do the resolution.

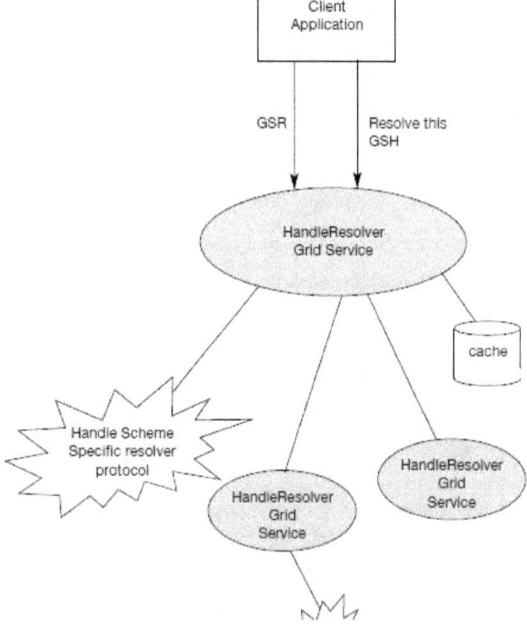

Resolving a GSH.

7. Explain in detail about Data-Intensive Grid Service Models

Applications in the grid are normally grouped into two categories: computation-intensive and data intensive. For data-intensive applications, we may have to deal with massive amounts of data. For example, the data produced annually by a Large Hadron Collider may exceed several petabytes (1015 bytes). The grid system must be specially designed to discover, transfer, and manipulate these massive data sets. Transferring massive data sets is a time-consuming task. Efficient data management demands low-cost storage and high-speed data movement

Data Replication and Unified Namespace

This data access method is also known as caching, which is often applied to enhance data efficiency in a grid environment. By replicating the same data blocks and scattering them in multiple regions of a grid, users can access the same data with locality of references. Replication strategies determine when and where to create a replica of the data. The factors to consider include data demand, network conditions, and transfer cost.

Grid Data Access Models

Multiple participants may want to share the same data collection. To retrieve any piece of data, we need a grid with a unique global namespace. Similarly, we desire to have unique file names.

To achieve these, we have to resolve inconsistencies among multiple data objects bearing the same name Monadic model: This is a centralized data repository model, All the data is saved in a central data repository.

When users want to access some data they have to submit requests directly to the central repository.

Hierarchical model: The hierarchical model, is suitable for building a large data grid which has only one large data access directory. The data may be transferred from the source to a second-level center.

Federation model: This data access model is better suited for designing a data grid with multiple sources of data supplies. Sometimes this model is also known as a mesh model.

Hybrid model: This data access model. The model combines the best features of the hierarchical and mesh models. Traditional data transfer technology, such as FTP, applies for networks with lower bandwidth.

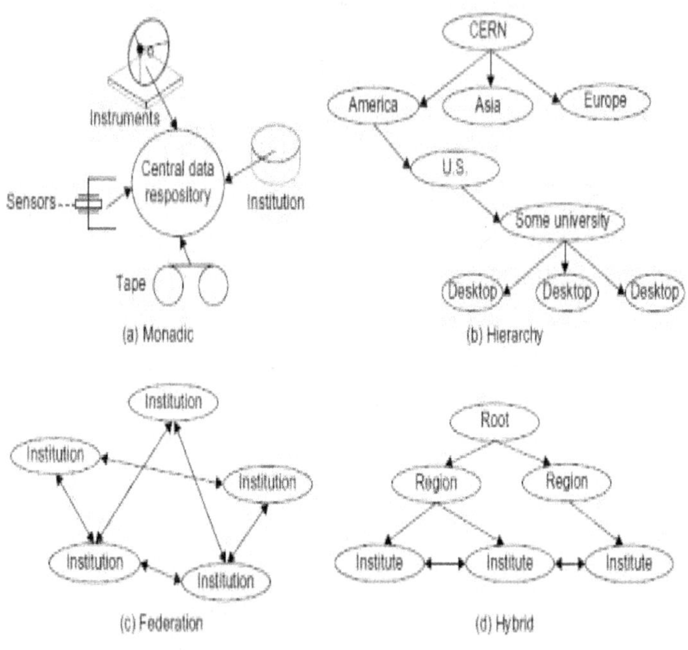

Four architectural models for building a data grid.

Parallel versus Striped Data Transfers

Compared with traditional FTP data transfer, parallel data transfer opens multiple data streams for passing subdivided segments of a file simultaneously. Although the speed of each stream is the same as in sequential streaming, the total time to move data in all streams can be significantly reduced compared to FTP transfer.

8. Short notes on OGSA Service

a) Metering Service

Different grid deployments may integrate different services and resources and feature different underlying economic motivations and models; however, regardless of these differences, it is a quasiuniversal requirement that resource utilization can be monitored, whether for purposes of cost allocation (i.e., charge back), capacity and trend analysis, dynamic provisioning, grid-service pricing, fraud and intrusion detection, and/or billing.

A grid service may consume multiple resources and a resource may be shared by multiple service instances. Ultimately, the sharing of underlying resources is managed by middleware and operating systems.

A metering interface provides access to a standard description of such aggregated data (metering serviceData). A key parameter is the time window over which measurements are aggregated. In commercial Unix systems, measurements are aggregated at administrator-defined intervals (chronological entry), usually daily, primarily for the purpose of accounting.

Several use cases require metering systems that support multitier, end-to-end flows involving multiple services. An OGSA metering service must be able to meter the resource consumption of configurable classes of these types of flows executing on widely distributed, loosely coupled server, storage, and network resources. Configurable classes should support, for example, a departmental charge-back scenario where incoming requests and their subsequent flows are partitioned into account classes determined by the department providing the service.

b) Service Groups and Discovery Services

GSHs and GSRs together realize a two-level naming scheme, with Handle Resolver services mapping from handles to references; however, GSHs are not intended to contain semantic information and indeed may be viewed for most purposes as opaque. Thus, other entities (both humans and applications) need other means for discovering services with particular properties, whether relating to interface, function, availability, location, policy

Attribute naming schemes associate various metadata with services and support retrieval via queries on attribute values. A registry implementing such a scheme allows service providers to publish the existence and properties of the services that they provide, so that service consumers can discover them

A Service Group is a collection of entries, where each entry is a grid service implementing the receive Group Entry interface. The Service Group interface also extends the Grid Service interface

It is also envisioned that many registries will inherit and implement the notification Source interface so as to facilitate client subscription to register state changes

Path naming or *directory* schemes (as used, for example, in file systems) represent an alternative approach to attribute schemes for organizing services into a hierarchical name space that can be navigated. The two approaches can be combined, as in LDAP.

c) Rating Service

A rating interface needs to address two types of behaviors. Once the metered information is available, it has to be translated into financial terms. That is, for each unit of usage, a price has to be associated with it. This step is accomplished by the rating interfaces, which provide operations that take the metered information and a rating package as input and output the usage in terms of chargeable amounts.

For example,

A commercial UNIX system indicates that 10 hours of prime-time resource and 10 hours on nonprime-time resource are consumed, and the rating package indicates that each hour of prime-time resource is priced at 2 dollars and each hour of nonprime- time resource is priced at 1 dollar, a rating service will apply the pricing indicated in the rating package.

Furthermore, when a business service is developed, a rating service is used to aggregate the costs of the components used to deliver the service, so that the service owner can determine the pricing, terms, and conditions under which the service will be offered to subscribe.

d) Other Data Services

A variety of higher-level data interfaces can and must be defined on top of the base data interfaces, to address functions such as: _ Data access and movement.

- Data replication and caching.
- Data and schema mediation.
- Metadata management and looking.

Data Replication. Data replication can be important as a means of meeting performance objectives by allowing local computer resources to have access to local data. Although closely related to caching (indeed, a —replica store‖ and a —cache‖may differ only in their policies), replicas may provide different interfaces.

Data Caching. In order to improve performance of access to remote data items, caching services will be employed. At the minimum, caching services for traditional flat file data will be employed. Caching of other data types, such as views on RDBMS data, streaming data, and application binaries, are also envisioned.

Consistency—Is the data in the cache the same as in the source? If not, what is the coherence window? Different applications have very different requirements. _ Cache invalidation protocols—How and when is cached data invalidated? _ Write through or write back? When are writes to the cache committed back to the original data source?

Security—How will access control to cached items be handled? Will access control enforcement be delegated to the cache, or will access control be somehow enforced by the original data source? _ Integrity of cached data—Is the cached data kept in memory or on disk? How is it protected from unauthorized access? Is it encrypted

Schema Transformation. Schema transformation interfaces support the transformation of data from one schema to another. For example, XML transformations as specified in XSLT.

9. Explain in detail about Open Grid Services Infrastructure and Distributed Logging

The OGSI defines fundamental mechanisms on which OGSA is constructed. These mechanisms address issues relating to the creation, naming, management, and exchange of information among entities called grid services. The following list recaps the key OGSI features and briefly discusses their relevance to OGSA.

Grid Service descriptions and instances. OGSI introduces the twin concepts of the grid service description and grid service instance as organizing principles of distributed systems.

Grid Service descriptions and instances. OGSI introduces the twin concepts of the grid service description and grid service instance as organizing principles of distributed systems.

Naming and name resolution. OGSI defines a two-level naming scheme for grid service instances based on abstract, long-lived *grid service* handles that can be mapped by Handle Mapper services to concrete but potentially lesslong- lived *grid service references.*

Fault model. OGSI defines a common approach for conveying fault information from operations.

Life cycle. OGSI defines mechanisms for managing the life cycle of a grid service instance, including both explicit destruction and soft-state lifetime management functions for grid service instances, and grid service factories that can be used to create instances implementing specified interfaces

Service groups. OGSI defines a means of organizing groups of service instances.

Distributed Logging

Distributed logging can be viewed as a typical messaging application in which *message producers* generate *log artifacts,* (atomic expressions of diagnostic information) that may or may not be used at a later time by other independent message *consumers.*

OGSA-based logging can leverage the notification mechanism available in OGSI as the transport for messages.

Logging services provide the extensions needed to deal with the following issues: *Decoupling.*

The logical separation of logging artifact creation from logging artifact consumption. The ultimate usage of the data (e.g., logging, tracing, management) is determined by the message consumer

Transformation and common representation. Logging packages commonly annotate the data that they generate with useful common information such as category, priority, time stamp, and location

Filtering and aggregation. The amount of logging data generated can be large, whereas the amount of data actually consumed can be small. Therefore, it can be desirable to have a mechanism for controlling the amount of data generated and for filtering out what is actually kept and where.

Configurable persistency. Depending on consumer needs, data may have different durability characteristics.

For example, in a real-time monitoring application, data may become irrelevant quickly, but be needed as soon as it is generated; data for an auditing program may be needed months or even years after it was generated.

Consumption patterns. Consumption patterns differ according to the needs of the consumer application. For example, a real-time monitoring application needs to be notified whenever a particular event occurs, whereas a postmortem problem determination program queries historical data, trying to find known patterns.

10. Short notes on

a) Job Agreement Service

The job agreement service is created by the agreement factory service with a set of job terms, including command line, resource requirements, execution environment, data staging, job control, scheduler directives, and accounting and notification term.

The job agreement service provides an interface for placing jobs on a resource manager (i.e., representing a machine or a cluster), and for interacting with the job once it has been dispatched to the resource manager.

The job agreement service provides basic matchmaking capabilities between the requirements of the job and the underlying resource manager available for running the job.

The interfaces provided by the job agreement service are:

- Manageability interface.
- Supported job terms: defines a set of service data used to publish the job terms supported by this job service, including the job definition (command line and application name), resource requirements, execution ironment, data staging, job control, scheduler directives, and accounting and notification terms.
- Workload status: total number of jobs, statuses such as number of jobs running or pending and suspended jobs.
- Job control: control the job after it has been instantiated. This would include the ability to suspend/resume, checkpoint, and kill the job.

b) *Reservation Agreement Service*

The reservation agreement service is created by the agreement factory service with a set of terms including time duration, resource requirement specification, and authorized user/project agreement terms. The reservation agreement service allows end users or a job agreement service to reserve resources under the control of a resource manager to guarantee their availability to run a job. The service allows reservations on any type of resource (e.g., hosts, software licenses, or network bandwidth). Reservations can be specific (e.g., provide access to host ─A‖ from noon to 5 PM), or more general (e.g., provide access to 16 Linux cpus on Sunday).

The reservation service makes use of information about the existing resource managers available and any policies that might be defined at the VO level, and will make use of a logging service to log reservations. It will use the resource manager adapter interfaces to make reservations and to delete existing reservations.

c) *Base Data Services*

OGSA data interfaces are intended to enable a service-oriented treatment of data so that data can be treated in the same way as other resources within the Web/grid services architecture

Four *base data interfaces* (WSDL port Types) can be used to implement a variety of different data service behaviors:

1. **Data Description** defines OGSI service data elements representing key parameters of the data virtualization encapsulated by the data service.

2. ***Data Access*** provides operations to access and/or modify the contents of the data virtualization encapsulated by the data service.

3. ***Data Factory*** provides an operation to create a new data service with a data virtualization derived from the data virtualization of the parent (factory) data service.

Data Management provides operations to monitor and manage the data service's data virtualization, including (depending on the implementation) the data sources (such as database management systems) that underlie the data service.

UNIT III

Virtualization

Part A

1. Define private cloud.

The *private cloud* is built within the domain of an intranet owned by a single organization. Therefore, they are client owned and managed. Their access is limited to the owning clients and their partners.

Their deployment was not meant to sell capacity over the Internet through publicly accessible interfaces. Private clouds give local users a flexible and agile private infrastructure to run service workloads within their administrative domains.

2. Define public cloud.

A *public cloud* is built over the Internet, which can be accessed by any user who has paid for the service.

Public clouds are owned by service providers. They are accessed by subscription. Many companies have built public clouds, namely Google App Engine, Amazon AWS, Microsoft Azure, IBM Blue Cloud, and Sales force Force.com.

These are commercial providers that offer a publicly accessible remote interface for creating and managing VM instances within their proprietary infrastructure.

3. Define hybrid cloud.

A *hybrid cloud* is built with both public and private clouds, Private clouds can also support a *hybrid cloud* model by supplementing local infrastructure with computing capacity from an external public cloud.

For example, the *research compute cloud* (RC2) is a private cloud built by IBM.

4. List the essential characteristics of cloud computing

1. On-demand capabilities .
2. Broad network access.
3. Resource pooling.
4. Rapid elasticity.
5. Measured service.

5. **List the design objectives of cloud computing.**

- Shifting Computing from Desktops to Datacenters

- Service Provisioning and Cloud Economics

- Scalability in Performance

- Data Privacy Protection.

- High Quality of Cloud Services.

6. **Define anything-as-a-service.**

Providing services to the client on the basis on meeting their demands at some pay per use cost such as data storage as a service, network as a service, communication as a service etc. it is generally denoted as anything as a service (XaaS).

7. **What is mean by SaaS?**

The software as a service refers to browser initiated application software over thousands of paid customer. The SaaS model applies to business process industry application, consumer relationship management (CRM), Enterprise resource Planning (ERP), Human Resources (HR) and collaborative application.

8. **What is mean by IaaS?**

The Infrastructure as a Service model puts together the infrastructure demanded by the user namely servers, storage, network and the data center fabric. The user can deploy and run on multiple VM's running guest OS on specific application.

9. **What is PaaS?**

The Platform as a Service model enables the user to deploy user built applications onto a virtualized cloud platform. It includes middleware, database, development tools and some runtime support such as web2.0 and java. It includes both hardware and software integrated with specific programming interface.

10. **What is mean by Virtualization?**

Virtualization is a computer architecture technology by which multiple virtual machines (VMs) are multiplexed in the same hardware machine.

The purpose of a VM is to enhance resource sharing by many users and improve computer performance in terms of resource utilization and application flexibility.

11. Define virtual machine monitor

A traditional computer runs with a host operating system specially tailored for its hardware architecture, After virtualization, different user applications managed by their own operating systems (guest OS) can run on the same hardware, independent of the host OS. This is often done by adding additional software, called a virtualization layer. This virtualization layer is known as hypervisor or virtual machine monitor (VMM).

12. List the requirements of VMM.

- VMM should provide an environment for programs which is essentially identical to the original machine.

- Programs run in this environment should show, at worst, only minor decreases in speed.

- VMM should be in complete control of the system resources. Any program run under a VMM should exhibit a function identical to that which it runs on the original machine directly.

13. Define Host OS and Guest OS.

The guest OS, which has control ability, is called Domain 0, and the others are called Domain U. Domain 0 is a privileged guest OS of Xen. It is first loaded when Xen boots without any file system drivers being available. Domain 0 is designed to access hardware directly and manage devices.

14. What are the responsibilities of VMM?

- The VMM is responsible for allocating hardware resources for programs.

- It is not possible for a program to access any resource not explicitly allocated to it.

- It is possible under certain circumstances for a VMM to regain control of resources already allocated.

15. Define CPU virtualization.

CPU architecture is virtualizable if it supports the ability to run the VM's privileged and unprivileged instructions in the CPU's user mode while the VMM runs in supervisor mode. When the privileged instructions including control- and behavior-sensitive instructions of a VM are executed, they are trapped in the VMM.

In this case, the VMM acts as a unified mediator for hardware access from different VMs to guarantee the correctness and stability of the whole system.

16. Define memory virtualization.

Virtual memory virtualization is similar to the virtual memory support provided by modern operating systems.

In a traditional execution environment, the operating system maintains mappings of virtual memory to machine memory using page tables, which is a one-stage mapping from virtual memory to machine memory.

All modern x86 CPUs include a memory management unit (MMU) and a translation look aside buffer (TLB) to optimize virtual memory performance.

17. What is mean by I/O virtualization?

I/O virtualization involves managing the routing of I/O requests between virtual devices and the shared physical hardware. There are three ways to implement I/O virtualization:

- Full device emulation, Full device emulation is the first approach for I/O virtualization
- Para-virtualization
- Direct I/O.

18. Distinguish the physical and virtual cluster. (Jan.2014)

A physical cluster is a collection of servers (physical machines) connected by a physical network such as a LAN. Virtual clusters have different properties and potential applications. There are three critical design issues of virtual clusters: live migration of virtual machines (VMs), memory and file migrations, and dynamic deployment of virtual clusters.

19. What is memory migration?

Moving the memory instance of a VM from one physical host to another can be approached in any number of ways.

Memory migration can be in a range of hundreds of megabytes to a few gigabytes in a typical system today, and it needs to be done in an efficient manner. The Internet Suspend-Resume (ISR) technique exploits temporal locality as memory states are likely to have considerable overlap in the suspended and the resumed instances of a VM.

20. What is mean by host based virtualization?

An alternative VM architecture is to install a virtualization layer on top of the host OS. This host OS is still responsible for managing the hardware. The guest OSes are installed and run on top of the virtualization layer.

Dedicated applications may run on the VMs. Certainly, some other applications can also run with the host OS directly.

21. Define KVM.

Kernel-Based VM:- This is a Linux para-virtualization system—a part of the Linux version 2.6.20 kernel. Memory management and scheduling activities are carried out by the existing Linux kernel.

The KVM does the rest, which makes it simpler than the hypervisor that controls the entire machine. KVM is a hardware-assisted para-virtualization tool, which improves performance and supports unmodified guest OSes such as Windows, Linux, Solaris, and other UNIX variants

Part B

1. Explain the cloud computing service and deployment models of cloud computing

    <u>**Cloud computing service**</u>

Infrastructure as a Service (IaaS)

The infrastructure layer builds on the virtualization layer by offering the virtual machines as a service to users.

Instead of purchasing servers or even hosted services, IaaS customers can create and remove virtual machines and network them together at will. Clients are billed for infrastructure services based on what resources are consumed. This eliminates the need to procure and operate physical servers, data storage systems, or networking resources.

Platform as a Service (PaaS)

The platform layer rests on the infrastructure layer's virtual machines. At this layer customers do not manage their virtual machines; they merely create applications within an existing API or programming language.

There is no need to manage an operating system, let alone the underlying hardware and virtualization layers. Clients merely create their own programs which are hosted by the platform services they are paying for.

Software as a Service (SaaS)

Services at the software level consist of complete applications that do not require development. Such applications can be email, customer relationship management, and other office productivity applications.

Enterprise services can be billed monthly or by usage, while software as service offered directly to consumers, such as email, is often provided for free.

Deployment Models of Cloud Computing

The Private Cloud

This model doesn't bring much in terms of cost efficiency: it is comparable to buying, building and managing your own infrastructure. Still, it brings in tremendous value from a security point of view.

During their initial adaptation to the cloud, many organizations face challenges and have concerns related to data security. These concerns are taken care of by this model, in which hosting is built and maintained for a specific client. The infrastructure required for hosting can be on-premises or at a third-party location. Security concerns are addressed through secure-access VPN or by the physical location within the client's firewall system.

Public Cloud

The public cloud deployment model represents true cloud hosting. In this deployment model, services and infrastructure are provided to various clients. Google is an example of a public cloud. This service can be provided by a vendor free of charge or on the basis of a pay-per-user license policy.

This model is best suited for business requirements wherein it is required to manage load spikes, host SaaS applications, utilize interim infrastructure for developing and testing applications, and manage applications which are consumed by many users that would otherwise require large investment in infrastructure from businesses.

Hybrid Cloud

This deployment model helps businesses to take advantage of secured applications and data hosting on a private cloud, while still enjoying cost benefits by keeping shared data and applications on the public cloud.

This model is also used for handling cloud bursting, which refers to a scenario where the existing private cloud infrastructure is not able to handle load spikes and requires a fallback option to support the load.

Hence, the cloud migrates workloads between public and private hosting without any inconvenience to the users. Many PaaS deployments expose their APIs, which can be further integrated with internal applications or applications hosted on a private cloud, while still maintaining the security aspects. Microsoft Azure and Force.com are two examples of this model.

Community Cloud

In the community deployment model, the cloud infrastructure is shared by several organizations with the same policy and compliance considerations. This helps to further reduce costs as compared to a private cloud, as it is shared by larger group.

Various state-level government departments requiring access to the same data relating to the local population or information related to infrastructure, such as hospitals, roads, electrical stations, etc., can utilize a community cloud to manage applications and data. Cloud computing is not a —silver–bullet‖ technology; hence, investment in any deployment model should be made based on business requirements, the criticality of the application and the level of support required.

2. A) Compare public cloud with private cloud

A private cloud hosting solution, also known as an internal or enterprise cloud, resides on company's intranet or hosted data center where all of your data is protected behind a firewall. This can be a great option for companies who already have expensive data centers because they can use their current infrastructure. However, the main drawback people see with a private cloud is that all management, maintenance and updating of data centers is the responsibility of the company. Over time, it's expected that your servers will need to be replaced, which can get very expensive. On the other hand, private clouds offer an increased level of security and they share very few, if any, resources with other organizations.

The main differentiator between public and private clouds is that you aren't responsible for any of the management of a public cloud hosting solution. Your data is stored in the provider's data center and the provider is responsible for the management and maintenance of the data center. This type of cloud environment is appealing to many companies because it reduces lead times in testing and deploying new products. However, the drawback is that many companies feel security could be lacking with a public cloud. Even though you don't control the security of a public cloud, all of your data remains separate from others and security breaches of public clouds are rare.

2. B) Pros and Cons of cloud computing

Pros

1. **Cloud Computing has lower software costs.** With Cloud Computing a lot of software is paid on a monthly basis which when compared to buying the software in the beginning, software through Cloud Computing is often a fraction of the cost.

2. Eventually your company may want to migrate to a new operating system, the associated **costs to migrate to a new operating system, is**often **less** than in a traditional server environment.

3. **Centralized data**- Another key benefit with Cloud Computing is having all the data (which could be **for multiple branch offices** or project sites) in a **single location** "the Cloud".

4. **Access from anywhere**- never leave another important document back at the office. With Cloud computing and an Internet connection, your data are always nearby, even if you are on the other side of the world.

5. **Internet connection** is a **required** for Cloud Computing. You must have an Internet connection to access your data.

Cons

1.   **Internet Connection Quality & Cloud Computing.**

Low Bandwidth -If you can only get low bandwidth Internet (like dial-up) then you **should not** consider using Cloud Computing. Bandwidth is commonly referred to as "how fast a connection is" or what the "speed" of your Internet is. The bandwidth to download data may not be the same as it is to send data.

Unreliable Internet connection -If you can get high speed Internet but it is unreliable (meaning your connection drops frequently and/or can be down for long periods at a time), depending on your business and how these outages will impact your operations, Cloud Computing may not be for you (or you may need to look into a more reliable and/or additional Internet connection).

Your company will **still need a Disaster Recovery Plan**, and if you have one now, it will need to be revised to address the changes for when you are using Cloud Computing.

3. Compare virtual and physical clusters. Explain how resource management done for virtual clusters.

A physical cluster is a collection of servers (physical machines) connected by a physical network such as a LAN. Virtual clusters have different properties and potential applications. There are three critical design issues of virtual clusters: live migration of virtual machines (VMs), memory and file migrations, and dynamic deployment of virtual clusters

Virtual clusters are built with VMs installed at distributed servers from one or more physical clusters. The VMs in a virtual cluster are interconnected logically by a virtual network across several physical networks. Below figure illustrates the concepts of virtual clusters and physical clusters. Each virtual cluster is formed with physical machines or a VM hosted by multiple physical clusters. The virtual cluster boundaries are shown as distinct boundaries.

The provisioning of VMs to a virtual cluster is done dynamically to have the following interesting properties:

- The virtual cluster nodes can be either physical or virtual machines. Multiple VMs running with different OSes can be deployed on the same physical node.
- A VM runs with a guest OS, which is often different from the host OS, that manages the resources in the physical machine, where the VM is implemented.
- The purpose of using VMs is to consolidate multiple functionalities on the same server. This will greatly enhance server utilization and application flexibility.

VMs can be colonized (replicated) in multiple servers for the purpose of promoting distributed parallelism, fault tolerance, and disaster recovery.

- The size (number of nodes) of a virtual cluster can grow or shrink dynamically, similar to the way an overlay network varies in size in a peer-to-peer (P2P) network.
- The failure of any physical nodes may disable some VMs installed on the failing nodes. But the failure of VMs will not pull down the host system.

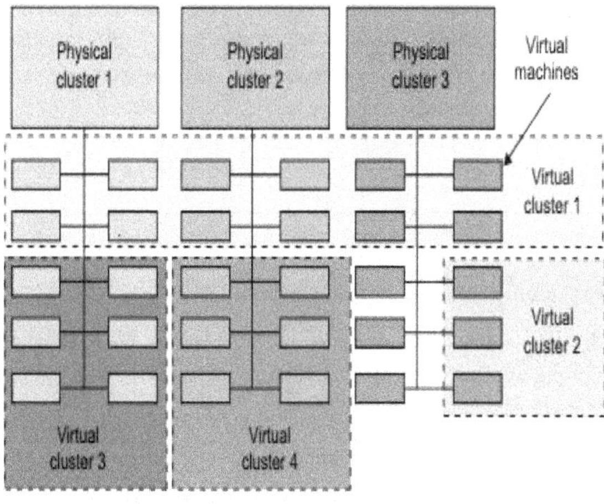

A cloud platform with four virtual clusters over three physical clusters shaded differently.

Below diagram shows the concept of a virtual cluster based on application partitioning or customization. The different colors in the figure represent the nodes in different virtual clusters. As a large number of VM images might be present, the most important thing is to determine how to store those images in the system efficiently. There are common installations for most users or applications, such as operating systems or user-level programming libraries. These software packages can be preinstalled as templates (called template VMs). With these templates, users can build their own software stacks. New OS instances can be copied from the template VM. User-specific components such as programming libraries and applications can be installed to those instances.

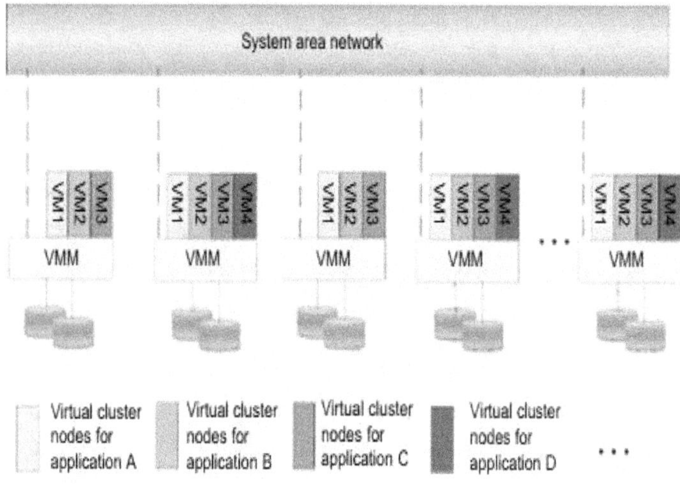

The concept of a virtual cluster based on application partitioning.

4. Explain the trust management in virtual clusters.

A VMM changes the computer architecture. It provides a layer of software between the operating systems and system hardware to create one or more VMs on a single physical platform. A VM entirely encapsulates the state of the guest operating system running inside it. Encapsulated machine state can be copied and shared over the network and removed like a normal file, which proposes a challenge to VM security. In general, a VMM can provide secure isolation and a VM accesses hardware resources through the control of the VMM, so the VMM is the base of the security of a virtual system. Normally, one VM is taken as a management VM to have some privileges such as creating, suspending, resuming, or deleting a VM.

Once a hacker successfully enters the VMM or management VM, the whole system is in danger. A subtler problem arises in protocols that rely on the ―freshness‖ of their random number source for generating session keys. Considering a VM, rolling back to a point after a random number has been chosen, but before it has been used, resumes execution; the random number, which must be ―fresh‖ for security purposes, is reused. With a stream cipher, two different plaintexts could be encrypted under the same key stream, which could, in turn, expose both plaintexts if the plaintexts have sufficient redundancy. Non-cryptographic protocols that rely on freshness are also at risk. For example, the reuse of TCP initial sequence numbers can raise TCP hijacking attacks.

VM-Based Intrusion Detection

Intrusions are unauthorized access to a certain computer from local or network users and intrusion detection is used to recognize the unauthorized access. An intrusion detection system (IDS) is built on operating systems, and is based on the characteristics of intrusion actions.

A typical IDS can be classified as a host-based IDS (HIDS) or a network-based IDS (NIDS), depending on the data source. A HIDS can be implemented on the monitored system. When the monitored system is attacked by hackers, the HIDS also faces the risk of being attacked. A NIDS is based on the flow of network traffic which can't detect fake actions. Virtualization-based intrusion detection can isolate guest VMs on the same hardware platform. Even some VMs can be invaded successfully; they never influence other VMs, which is similar to the way in which a NIDS operates.

Furthermore, a VMM monitors and audits access requests for hardware and system software. This can avoid fake actions and possess the merit of a HIDS. There are two different methods for implementing a VM-based IDS: Either the IDS is an independent process in each VM or a high-privileged VM on the VMM; or the IDS is integrated into the VMM and has the same privilege to access the hardware as well as the VMM.

The VM-based IDS contains a policy engine and a policy module. The policy framework can monitor events in different guest VMs by operating system interface library and PTrace indicates trace to secure policy of monitored host. It's difficult to predict and prevent all intrusions without delay.

Therefore, an analysis of the intrusion action is extremely important after an intrusion occurs. At the time of this writing, most computer systems use logs to analyze attack actions, but it is hard to ensure the credibility and integrity of a log. The IDS log service is based on the operating system kernel. Thus, when an operating system is invaded by attackers, the log service should be unaffected.

Besides IDS, honey pots and honey nets are also prevalent in intrusion detection. They attract and provide a fake system view to attackers in order to protect the real system. In addition, the attack action can be analyzed, and a secure IDS can be built. A honeypot is a purposely defective system that simulates an operating system to cheat and monitor the actions of an attacker.

A honeypot can be divided into physical and virtual forms. A guest operating system and the applications running on it constitute a VM. The host operating system and VMM must be guaranteed to prevent attacks from the VM in a virtual honeypot.

5. Explain the virtualization for data center automation.

The dynamic nature of cloud computing has pushed data center workload, server, and even hardware automation to whole new levels. Now, any data center provider looking to get into cloud computing must look at some form of automation to help them be as agile as possible in the cloud world.

New technologies are forcing data center providers to adopt new methods to increase efficiency, scalability and redundancy. Let's face facts; there are numerous big trends which have emphasized the increased use of data center facilities. These trends include:

- More users
- More devices
- More cloud
- More workloads
- A lot more data

As infrastructure improves, more companies have looked towards the data center provider to offload a big part of their IT infrastructure. With better cost structures and even better incentives in moving towards a data center environment, organizations of all sizes are looking at colocation as an option for their IT environment.

With that, data center administrators are teaming with networking, infrastructure and cloud architects to create an even more efficient environment. This means creating intelligent systems from the hardware to the software layer. This growth in data center dependency has resulted in direct growth around automation and orchestration technologies.

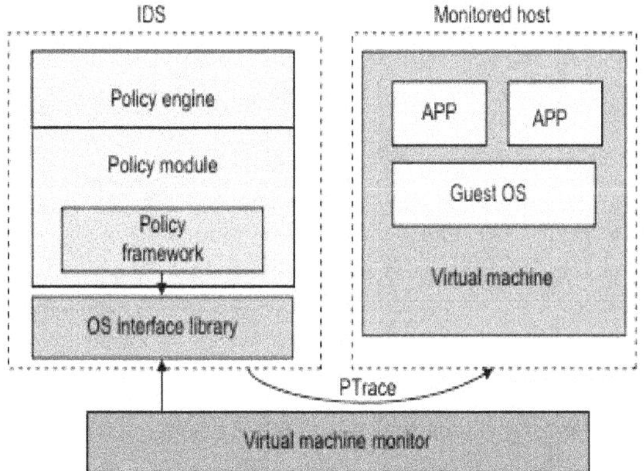

Now, organizations can granularly control resources, both internally and in the cloud. This type of automation can be seen at both the software layer as well as the hardware layer. Vendors like BMC, ServiceNow, and Microsoft SCCM/SCOM are working towards unifying massive systems under one management engine to provide a single pain of glass into the data center workload environment

Furthermore, technologies like the Cisco UCS platform allow administrators to virtualize the hardware layer and create completely automated hardware profiles for new blades and servers. This hardware automation can then be tied into software-based automation tools like SCCM. Already we're seeing direct integration between software management tools and the hardware layer.

Finally, from a cloud layer, platforms like CloudStack and OpenStack allow organizations to create orchestrated and automated fluid cloud environments capable of very dynamic scalability. Still, when a physical server or hardware component breaks – we still need a person to swap out that blade.

To break it down, it's important to understand what layers of automation and orchestration are available now – and what might be available in the future. The automation and orchestration layers

Server layer. Server and hardware automation have come a long way. As mentioned earlier, there are systems now available which take almost all of the configuration pieces out of deploying a server. Administrators only need to deploy one server profile and allow new servers to pick up those settings. More data centers are trying to get into the cloud business.

This means deploying high-density, fast-provisioned, servers and blades. With the on-demand nature of the cloud, being able to quickly deploy fully configured servers is a big plus for staying agile and very proactive.

Software layer. Entire applications can be automated and provisioned based on usage and resource utilization. Using the latest load-balancing tools, administrators are able to set thresholds for key applications running within the environment. If a load-balancer, a NetScaler for example, sees that a certain type of application is receiving too many connections, it can set off a process that will allow the administrator to provision another instance of the application or a new server which will host the app.

Virtual layer. The modern data center is now full of virtualization and virtual machines. In using solutions like Citrix's Provisioning Server or Unidesk's layering software technologies, administrators are able to take workload provisioning to a whole new level. Imagine being able to set a process that will kick-start the creation of a new virtual server when one starts to get over-utilized. Now, administrators can create truly automated virtual machine environments where each workload is monitored, managed and controlled.

Cloud layer. This is a new and still emerging field. Still, some very large organizations are already deploying technologies like CloudStack, OpenStack, and even OpenNebula. Furthermore, they're tying these platforms in with big data management solutions like MapReduce and Hadoop. What's happening now is true cloud-layer automation. Organizations can deploy distributed data centers and have the entire cloud layer managed by a cloud-control software platform. Engineers are able to monitor workloads, how data is being distributed, and the health of the cloud infrastructure. The great part about these technologies is that organizations can deploy a true private cloud, with as much control and redundancy as a public cloud instance.

Data center layer. Although entire data center automation technologies aren't quite here yet, we are seeing more robotics appear within the data center environment. Robotic arms already control massive tape libraries for Google and robotics automation is a thoroughly discussed concept among other large data center providers.

In a recent article, we discussed the concept of a —lights-out‖ data center in the future. Many experts agree that eventually, data center automation and robotics will likely make its way into the data center of tomorrow. For now, automation at the physical data center layer is only a developing concept.

The need to deploy more advanced cloud solution is only going to grow. More organizations of all verticals and sizes are seeing benefits of moving towards a cloud platform. At the end of the day, all of these resources, workloads and applications have to reside somewhere. That somewhere is always the data center.

In working with modern data center technologies administrators strive to be as efficient and agile as possible. This means deploying new types of automation solutions which span the entire technology stack. Over the upcoming couple of years, automation and orchestration technologies will continue to become popular as the data center becomes an even more core piece for any organization.

6. Explain implementation levels of virtualization in details.

Virtualization is computer architecture technology by which multiple virtual machines are multiplexed in the same hardware machine. The idea of VMs can be dated back to the 1960s. The purpose of a VM is to enhance resource sharing by many users and improve computer performance in terms of resource utilization and application flexibility. Hardware resources or software resources can be virtualized in various functional layers. Levels of virtualization implementation. A traditional computer runs with a host OS specially tailored for its hardware architecture. After virtualization different user applications managed by their own OS (Guest OS) can run on the same hardware, independent of the host OS. This is often done by adding additional software called virtualization layer. This virtualization layer is known as hypervisor or **Virtual Machine.**

Monitor

The main function of the software layer for virtualization is to virtualize the physical hardware of a host machine into virtual resources to be used by the VMs exclusively. Common virtualization layers include the instruction set architecture level, hardware level, OS Level, Library support level and application level.

Instruction Set Architecture

At the ISA level virtualization is performed by emulating a given ISA by the ISA of the host machine. For example, MIPS binary code can run on an 8086 based host machine with help of ISA emulation.

The basic emulation method is through code interpretation. An interpreter program interprets the source instructions to target instructions one by one. One source instruction may require tens or hundreds of native target instructions to perform its function.

Hardware Architecture

Hardware level virtualization is performed right on top of the bar hardware. On the one hand this approach generates a virtual hardware environment for a VM. On the other hand the process manages the underlying hardware through virtualization. The idea is to virtualize a computers resources, such as its processors, memory and I/O devices **OS Level.**

This refers to an abstraction layer between traditional OS and user application. OS level virtualization creates isolated containers on a single physical server and the OS instances to utilize the hardware and software in data centers.

Library Support Level

Most application use APIs exported by user level libraries rather than using lengthy system calls by the OS. Since most systems provide well documented APIs, such an interface becomes another candidate for virtualization. Virtualization with library interfaces is possible by controlling the communication link between applications and the rest of a system through API hooks.

User Application Level

Virtualization at the application level virtualizes an application as a VM. On a traditional OS, an application often runs as a process. Therefore, application level virtualization is known as process level virtualization. The most popular approach is to deploy high level language VMs.

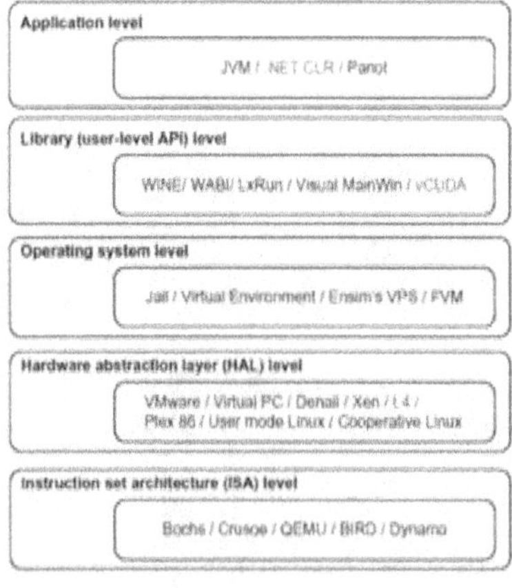

Virtualization ranging from hardware to applications in five abstraction levels.

7. Explain the virtualization of CPU, Memory and I/O devices Virtualization of CPU

A VM is a duplicate of an existing computer system in which a majority of the VM instructions are executed on the host processor in native mode. Thus, unprivileged instructions of VMs run directly on the host machine for higher efficiency. The critical instructions are divided into three categories.

- Privileged instructions
- Control sensitive instructions
- Behaviour sensitive instructions

Privileged instructions execute in a privileged mode and will be trapped if executes outside this mode.

Control sensitive instructions attempt to change the configuration of resources used.

Behavior sensitive instructions have different behaviors depending on the configuration of resources, including the load and store operations over the virtual memory.

A CPU architecture is virtualizable if it supports the ability to run the VM's privileged and unprivileged instructions in the CPU's user mode while the VMM run in supervisor mode. When the privileged instructions including control and behavior sensitive instructions of a VM are executed they are trapped in the VMM.

RISC CPU architectures can be naturally virtualized because all control and behavior sensitive instructions are privileged instruction.

Hardware Assisted CPU virtualization

- Processors with virtualization technology have extra instruction set called virtual machine extensions or VMX.
- There are two modes to run under virtualization: root operation and non-root operation. Usually only the virtualization controlling software, called Virtual Machine Monitor (VMM), runs under root operation, while operating systems running on top of the virtual machines run under non-root operation. Software running on top of virtual machines is also called 'guest software,.
- To enter virtualization mode, the software should execute the VMXON instruction and then call the VMM software. Then VMM software can enter each virtual machine using the VMLAUNCH instruction, and exit it by using the VMRESUME. If VMM wants to shut down and exit virtualization mode, it executes the VMXOFF instruction.

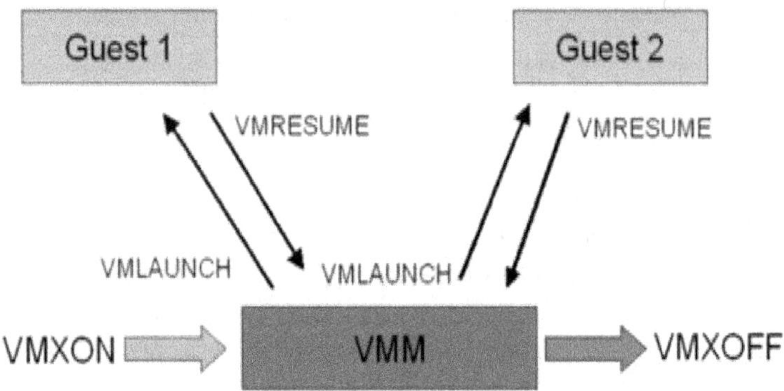

Memory Virtualization

Virtual memory virtualization is similar to the virtual memory support provided by modern operating systems. In a traditional execution environment the OS maintains mappings of virtual memory to machine memory using page tables, which is one stage mapping from virtual memory to machine memory.

All modern x86 CPUs include a Memory management Unit and a translation Look-aside Buffer to optimize virtual memory performance.

In virtual execution environment virtual memory virtualization involves sharing the physical system memory in RAM and dynamically allocating it to the physical memory of the VMs.

Guest OS sees flat ‚physical' address space.

Page tables within guest OS: Translate from virtual to physical addresses.

Second-level mapping: Physical addresses to machine addresses.

VMM can swap a VM's pages to disk.

Traditional way is to have the VMM maintain a shadow of the VM's page table.

The shadow page table controls which pages of machine memory are assigned to a given VM. When OS updates it's page table, VMM updates the shadow

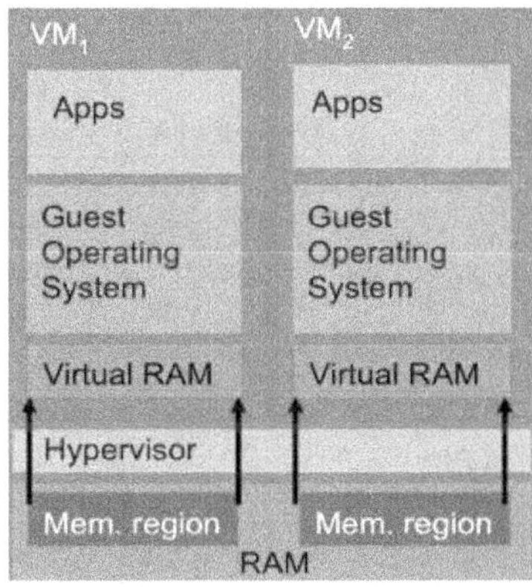

Memory Virtualization

I/O Virtualization

Input/output (I/O) virtualization is a methodology to simplify management, lower costs and improve performance of servers in enterprise environments. I/O virtualization environments are created by abstracting the upper layer protocols from the physical connections.

The technology enables one physical adapter card to appear as multiple virtual network interface cards (vNICs) and virtual host bus adapters (vHBAs). Virtual NICs and HBAs function as conventional NICs and HBAs, and are designed to be compatible with existing operating systems, hypervisors, and applications. To networking resources (LANs and SANs), they appear as normal cards.

In the physical view, virtual I/O replaces a server's multiple I/O cables with a single cable that provides a shared transport for all network and storage connections. That cable (or commonly two cables for redundancy) connects to an external device, which then provides connections to the data center networks.

Server I/O is a critical component to successful and effective server deployments, particularly with virtualized servers.

To accommodate multiple applications, virtualized servers demand more network bandwidth and connections to more networks and storage. According to a survey, 75% of virtualized servers require 7 or more I/O connections per device, and are likely to require more frequent I/O reconfigurations.

In virtualized data centers, I/O performance problems are caused by running numerous virtual machines (VMs) on one server. In early server virtualization implementations, the number of virtual machines per server was typically limited to six or less. But it was found that it could safely run seven or more applications per server, often using 80 percentage of total server capacity, an improvement over the average 5 to 15 percentage utilized with non-virtualized servers.

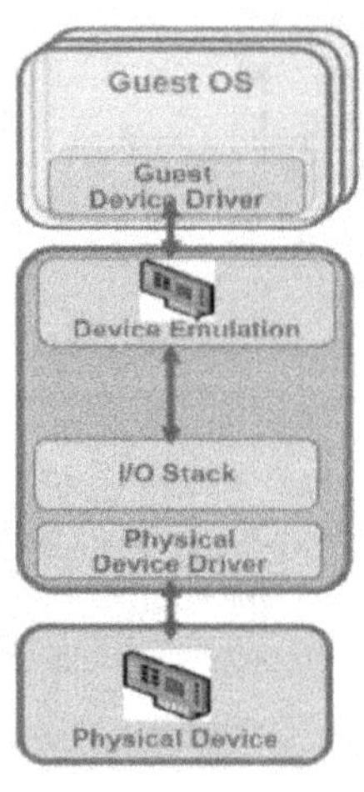

I/O Virtualization architecture consists of

➢ Guest driver

➢ Virtual device

➢ Communication mechanism between virtual device and virtualization stack

➢ Virtualization I/O stack

➢ Physical device driver

➢ Real device

Virtualization I/O stack

- Translates guest I/O addresses to host addresses
- Handles inter VM communication
- Multiplexes I/O requests from/to the physical device
- Provides enterprise-class I/O features to the Guest

8. A) Para-Virtualization with Compiler Support

Para-virtualization needs to modify the guest operating systems. A para-virtualized VM provides special APIs requiring substantial OS modifications in user applications. Performance degradation is a critical issue of a virtualized system. No one wants to use a VM if it is much slower than using a physical machine. The virtualization layer can be inserted at different positions in a machine software stack. However, para-virtualization attempts to reduce the virtualization overhead, and thus improve performance by modifying only the guest OS kernel. The concept of a para-virtualized VM architecture. The guest operating systems are para-virtualized.

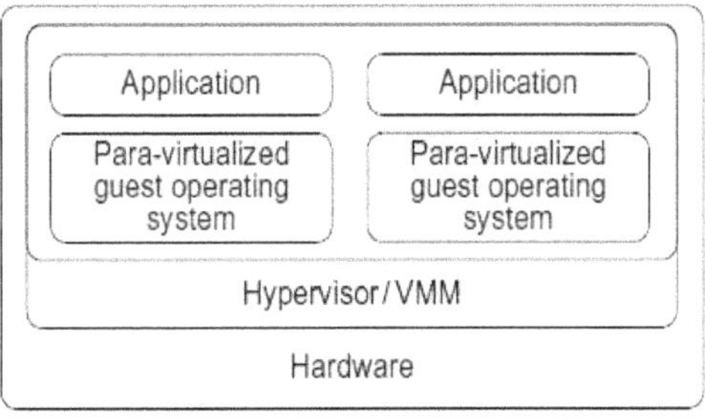

Para-virtualized VM architecture, which involves modifying the guest OS kernel to replace nonvirtualizable instructions with hypercalls for the hypervisor or the VMM to carry out the virtualization process

They are assisted by an intelligent compiler to replace the non virtualizable OS instructions by hyper calls as illustrated in below figure. The traditional x86 processor offers four instruction execution rings: Rings 0, 1, 2, and 3. The lower the ring number, the higher the privilege of instruction being executed. The OS is responsible for managing the hardware and the privileged instructions to execute at Ring 0, while user-level applications run at Ring 3.

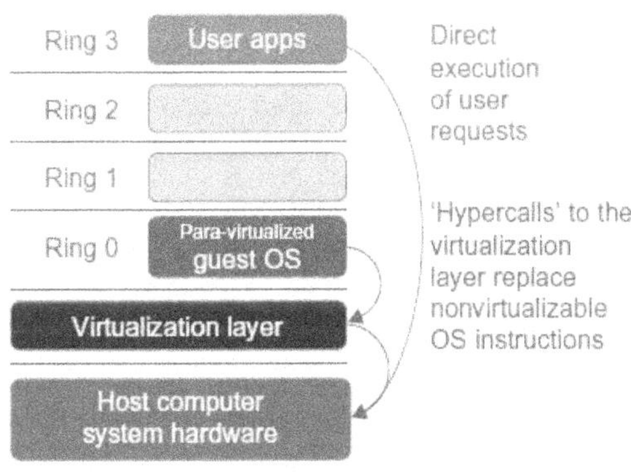

The use of a para-virtualized guest OS assisted by an intelligent compiler to replace nonvirtualizable OS instructions by hypercalls.

Para-Virtualization Architecture

When the x86 processor is virtualized, a virtualization layer is inserted between the hardware and the OS. According to the x86 ring definition, the virtualization layer should also be installed at Ring 0. Different instructions at Ring 0 may cause some problems. In above diagram, we show that para-virtualization replaces nonvirtualizable instructions with hypercalls that communicate directly with the hypervisor or VMM. However, when the guest OS kernel is modified for virtualization, it can no longer run on the hardware directly.

Although para-virtualization reduces the overhead, it has incurred other problems. First, its compatibility and portability may be in doubt, because it must support the unmodified OS as well. Second, the cost of maintaining para-virtualized OSes is high, because they may require deep OS kernel modifications. Finally, the performance advantage of para-virtualization varies greatly due to workload variations. Compared with full virtualization, para-virtualization is relatively easy and more practical. The main problem in full virtualization is its low performance in binary translation. To speed up binary translation is difficult. Therefore, many virtualization products employ the para-virtualization architecture. The popular Xen, KVM, and VMware ESX are good examples.

8. B) Binary Translation with Full Virtualization

Depending on implementation technologies, hardware virtualization can be classified into two categories:

Full virtualization and host-based virtualization. Full virtualization does not need to modify the host OS. It relies on binary translation to trap and to virtualize the execution of certain sensitive, nonvirtualizable instructions. The guest OSes and their applications consist of noncritical and critical instructions. In a host-based system, both a host OS and a guest OS are used. A virtualization software layer is built between the host OS and guest OS. These two classes of VM architecture are introduced next.

Full Virtualization

With full virtualization, noncritical instructions run on the hardware directly while critical instructions are discovered and replaced with traps into the VMM to be emulated by software. Both the hypervisor and VMM approaches are considered full virtualization. Why are only critical instructions trapped into the VMM? This is because binary translation can incur a large performance overhead. Noncritical instructions do not control hardware or threaten the security of the system, but critical instructions do. Therefore, running noncritical instructions on hardware not only can promote efficiency, but also can ensure system security.

Binary Translation of Guest OS Requests Using a VMM

This approach was implemented by VMware and many other software companies. VMware puts the VMM at Ring 0 and the guest OS at Ring 1. The VMM scans the instruction stream and identifies the privileged, control- and behavior-sensitive instructions. When these instructions are identified, they are trapped into the VMM, which emulates the behavior of these instructions. The method used in this emulation is called binary translation. Therefore, full virtualization combines binary translation and direct execution. The guest OS is completely decoupled from the underlying hardware. Consequently, the guest OS is unaware that it is being virtualized. The performance of full virtualization may not be ideal, because it involves binary translation which is rather time-consuming. In particular, the full virtualization of I/O-intensive applications is a really a big challenge. Binary translation employs a code cache to store translated hot instructions to improve performance, but it increases the cost of memory usage. At the time of this writing, the performance of full virtualization on the x86 architecture is typically 80 percent to 97 percent that of the host machine.

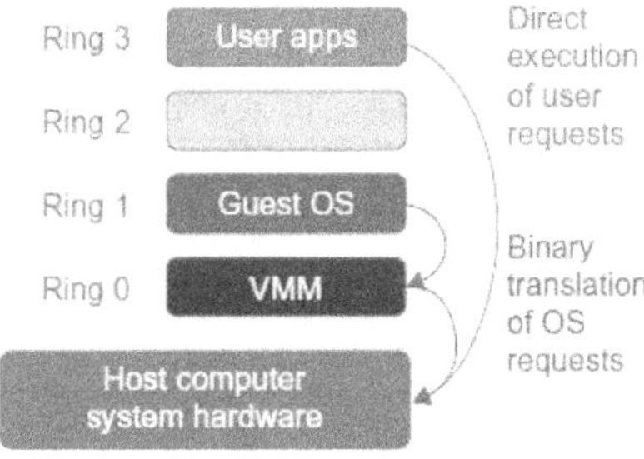

Indirect execution of complex instructions via binary translation of guest OS requests using the VMM plus direct execution of simple instructions on the same host.

Host-Based Virtualization

An alternative VM architecture is to install a virtualization layer on top of the host OS. This host OS is still responsible for managing the hardware. The guest OSes are installed and run on top of the virtualization layer. Dedicated applications may run on the VMs. Certainly, some other applications can also run with the host OS directly. This host based architecture has some distinct advantages, as enumerated next. First, the user can install this VM architecture without modifying the host OS. The virtualizing software can rely on the host OS to provide device drivers and other low-level services. This will simplify the VM design and ease its deployment. Second, the host-based approach appeals to many host machine configurations. Compared to the hypervisor/VMM architecture, the performance of the host-based architecture may also be low. When an application requests hardware access, it involves four layers of mapping which downgrades performance significantly. When the ISA of a guest OS is different from the ISA of the underlying hardware, binary translation must be adopted. Although the host-based architecture has flexibility, the performance is too low to be useful in practice.

9. Explain the characteristics and types of virtualization in cloud computing.

Virtualization is using computer resources to imitate other computer resources or whole computers. It separates resources and services from the underlying physical delivery environment.

Virtualization has three characteristics that make it ideal for cloud computing:

Partitioning: In virtualization, many applications and operating systems (OSes) are supported in a single physical system by partitioning (separating) the available resources.

Isolation: Each virtual machine is isolated from its host physical system and other virtualized machines. Because of this isolation, if one virtual-instance crashes, it doesn't affect the other virtual machines. In addition, data isn't shared between one virtual container and another.

Encapsulation: A virtual machine can be represented (and even stored) as a single file, so you can identify it easily based on the service it provides. In essence, the encapsulated process could be a business service. This encapsulated virtual machine can be presented to an application as a complete entity. Therefore, encapsulation can protect each application so that it doesn't interfere with another application.

Types

Virtualization can be utilized in many different ways and can take many forms aside from just server virtualization. The main types include application, desktop, user, storage and hardware. **Application virtualization** allows the user to access the application, not from their workstation, but from a remotely located server. The server stores all personal information and other characteristics of the application, but can still run on a local workstation. Technically, the application is not installed, but acts like it is.

Desktop virtualization allows the users' OS to be remotely stored on a server in the data center, allowing the user to then access their desktop virtually, from any location.

User virtualization is pretty similar to desktop, but allows users the ability to maintain a fully personalized virtual desktop when not on the company network. Users can basically log into their —desktop‖ from different types of devices like smart phones and tablets. With more companies migrating to a BYOD policy, desktop and user virtualization are becoming increasingly popular.

Storage virtualization is the process of grouping the physical storage from multiple network storage devices so that it acts as if it's on one storage device.

Hardware virtualization (also referred to as hardware-assisted virtualization) is a form of virtualization that uses one processor to act as if it were several different processors. The user can then run different operating systems on the same hardware, or more than one user can use the processor at the same time. This type of virtualization requires a virtual machine manager (VM) called a hypervisor.

10. Explain the NIST reference architecture of cloud computing in detail

The Conceptual Reference Model Figure 1 presents an overview of the NIST cloud computing reference architecture, which identifies the major actors, their activities and functions in cloud computing. The diagram depicts a generic high-level architecture and is intended to facilitate the understanding of the requirements, uses, characteristics and standards of cloud computing.

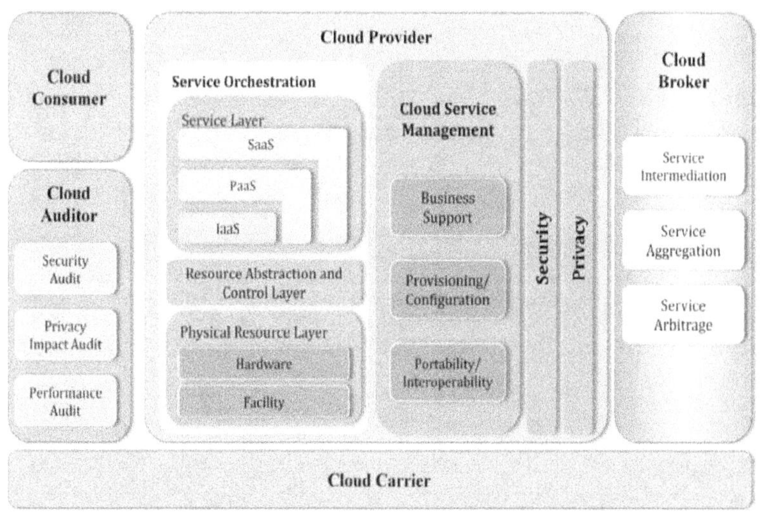

The Conceptual Reference Model

As shown in Figure 1, the NIST cloud computing reference architecture defines five major actors: cloud consumer, cloud provider, cloud carrier, cloud auditor and cloud broker. Each actor is an entity (a person or an organization) that participates in a transaction or process and/or performs tasks in cloud computing.

Actor	Definition
Cloud Consumer	A person or organization that maintains a business relationship with, and uses service from, Cloud Providers.
Cloud Provider	A person, organization, or entity responsible for making a service available to interested parties.
Cloud Auditor	A party that can conduct independent assessment of cloud services, information system operations, performance and security of the cloud implementation
Cloud Broker	An entity that manages the use, performance and delivery of cloud services, and negotiates relationships between *Cloud Providers* and *Cloud Consumers*
Cloud Carrier	An intermediary that provides connectivity and transport of cloud services from *Cloud Providers* to *Cloud Consumers*

UNIT IV

Programming Model

Part A

1. List out the grid middleware packages.

Package	Description
BOINC	Berkeley Open Infrastructure for Network Computing.
UNICORE	Middleware developed by the German grid computing community
Globus (GT4)	A middleware library jointly developed by Argonne National Lab.
CGSP in ChinaGrid	The CGSP (ChinaGrid Support Platform) is a middleware library developed by 20 top universities in China as part of the China Grid Project
Condor-G	Originally developed at the Univ. of Wisconsin for general distributed computing, and later extended to Condor-G for grid job management.
Sun Grid Engine (SGE)	Developed by Sun Microsystems for business grid applications. Applied to private grids and local clusters within enterprises or campuses.

2. Define MapReduce.

The mapreduce software framework provides an abstraction layer with the data flow and flow of control of users and hides implementation of all data flow steps such as data partitioning mapping, synchronization, communication and scheduling. The data flow is such framework is predefined the abstraction layer provides two well defined interface in the form of two functions map and reduce.

3. What is the role of Map function?

Each Map function receives the input data split as a set of (key, value) pairs to process and produce the intermediated (key, value) pairs.

4. What is the role of Reduce function?

The reduce worker iterates over the grouped (key, value) pairs, and for each unique key, it sends the key and corresponding values to the Reduce function. Then this function processes its input data and stores the output results in predetermined files in the user's program.

5. List out the Hadoop core fundamental layers.

The Hadoop core is divided into two fundamental layers: the MapReduce engine and HDFS. The MapReduce engine is the computation engine running on top of HDFS as its data storage manager. HDFS is a distributed file system inspired by GFS that organizes files and stores their data on a distributed computing system.

6. What are the features of HDFS?

HDFS is not a general-purpose file system, as it only executes specific types of applications, it does not need all the requirements of a general distributed file system. For example, security has never been supported for HDFS systems.

7. List the areas where HDFS cannot be used?

Low-latency data access.

Lots of small files.

Multiple writers, arbitrary file modifications.

8. Why is a block in HDFS so large?

HDFS blocks are large compared to disk blocks, and the reason is to minimize the cost of seeks. By making a block large enough, the time to transfer the data from the disk can be made to be significantly larger than the time to seek to the start of the block. Thus the time to transfer a large file made of multiple blocks operates at the disk transfer rate.

9. Define Namenode in HDFS

The name node manages the file system namespace. It maintains the file system tree and the metadata for all the files and directories in the tree.

This information is stored persistently on the local disk in the form of two files: the namespace image and the edit log. The name node also knows the data nodes on which all the blocks for a given file are located, however, it does not store block locations persistently, since this information is reconstructed from data nodes when the system starts.

10. Define Datanode in HDFS

Data nodes are the work horses of the file system. They store and retrieve blocks when they are told to (by clients or the name node), and they report back to the name node periodically with lists of blocks that they are storing.

11. What are the permission models for files and directories in HDFS

There are three types of permission: the read permission (r), the write permission (w) and the execute permission (x). The read permission is required to read files or list the contents of a directory.

The write permission is required to write a file, or for a directory, to create or delete files or directories in it. The execute permission is ignored for a file since you can't execute a file on HDFS (unlike POSIX), and for a directory it is required to access its children.

12. Define FUSE interface?

Filesystem in Userspace (FUSE) allows filesystems that are implemented in user space to be integrated as a Unix filesystem. Hadoop's Fuse-DFS contrib module allows any Hadoop filesystem (but typically HDFS) to be mounted as a standard filesystem. You can then use Unix utilities (such as ls and cat) to interact with the filesystem, as well as POSIX libraries to access the filesystem from any programming language. Fuse-DFS is implemented in C using *libhdfs* as the interface to HDFS.

13. Define globbing in HDFS?

It is a common requirement to process sets of files in a single operation.. To enumerate each file and directory to specify the input, it is convenient to use wildcard characters to match multiple files with a single expression, an operation that is known as *globbing*.

14. How to process globs in hadoop filesystem?

Hadoop provides two FileSystem methods for processing globs:

public FileStatus[] globStatus(Path pathPattern) throws IOException

public FileStatus[] globStatus(Path pathPattern, PathFilter filter) throws IOException

The globStatus() methods returns an array of FileStatus objects whose paths match the supplied pattern, sorted by path. An optional PathFilter can be specified to restrict the matches further

15. How to delete file or directory in hadoop filesystem?

Use the delete() method on FileSystem to permanently remove files or directories:

public boolean delete(Path f, boolean recursive) throws IOException

If *f* is a file or an empty directory, then the value of recursive is ignored. A nonempty directory is only deleted, along with its contents, if recursive is true (otherwise an IOException is thrown).

16. Define iterative MapReduce.

It is important to understand the performance of different runtime and in particular to compare MPI and map reduce.

The two major sources of parallel overhead are load imbalance and communication. The communication overhead in mapreduce can be high for two reasons.

- Mapreduce read and writes files whereas MPI transfer information directly between nodes over the network.
- MPI does not transfer all data from node to node.

17. Define HDFS.

HDFS is a distributed file system inspired by GFS that organizes files and stores their data on a distributed computing system. The hadoop implementation of mapreduce uses the hadoop distributed file system as in underlying layer rather than GFS.

18. List the characteristics of HDFS.

> HDFS fault tolerance
>
> Block replication
>
> Relica placement
>
> Heartbeat and block report messages
>
> HDFS high throughput access to large dataset.

19. What are the operations of HDFS?

The control flow of HDFS operation such as read and write can properly highlights role of the name node and data node in the managing operations. The control flow of the main operations of HDFS on file is further described to manifest the interaction between the users.

20. Define block replication.

The reliably store data in HDFS is the file blocks, it is replicated in this system. HDFS store a file as a set of blocks and each block is replicated and distributed across the whole cluster.

21. Define heart beat in Hadoop. What are the advantages of heart beat?

The heart beat are periodic messages sent to the name node by each data node in the cluster. Receipt of a heartbeat implies that data mode is functioning properly while each block report contains list of all blocks in a data mode. The name node receives such messages because it is the sole decision maker of all replicas in the system.

22. List out the functional modules in globus GT4 library

Service Functionality	Module Name	Functional Description
Global Resource Allocation Manager	GRAM	Grid Resource Access and Management (HTTP- based)
Communication	Nexus	Unicast and multicast communication
Grid Security Infrastructure	GSI	Authentication and related security services
Monitory and Discovery Service	MDS	Distributed access to structure and state information
Health and Status	HBM	Heartbeat monitoring of system components
Global Access of Secondary Storage	GASS	Grid access of data in remote secondary storage
Grid File Transfer	GridFTP	Inter-node fast file transfer

23. Define Globus Resource Allocation Manager

Globus Resource Allocation Manager (GRAM) provides resource allocation, process creation, monitoring, and management services. GRAM implementations map requests expressed in a resource specification language (RSL) into commands to local schedulers and computers.

24. Define Monitoring and Discovery Service

The Monitoring and Discovery Service (MDS) is an extensible grid information service that combines data discovery mechanisms with the LDAP (LDAP defines a data model, query language, and other related protocols). MDS provides a uniform framework for providing and accessing system configuration and status information such as computer server configuration, network status, or the locations of replicated datasets.

Part B

1. Explain in detail about Grid Middleware Packages

We first introduce some grid standards and popular APIs. Then we present the desired software support and middleware developed for grid computing.

Grid Standards and APIs

The Open Grid Forum (formally Global Grid Forum) and Object Management Group are two well-formed organizations behind those standards. we have also reported some grid standards including the GLUE for resource representation, SAGA (Simple API for Grid Applications), GSI (Grid Security Infrastructure), OGSI (Open Grid Service Infrastructure), and WSRE (Web Service Resource Framework).

Software Support and Middleware

Grid middleware is specifically designed a layer between hardware and the software. The middleware products enable the sharing of heterogeneous resources and managing virtual organizations created around the grid. Middleware glues the allocated resources with specific user applications. Popular grid middleware tools include the Globus Toolkits (USA), gLight, UNICORE (German), BOINC (Berkeley), CGSP (China), Condor-G, and Sun Grid Engine, etc.

Package	Description
BOINC	Berkeley Open Infrastructure for Network Computing.
UNICORE	Middleware developed by the German grid computing community
Globus (GT4)	A middleware library jointly developed by Argonne National Lab.
CGSP in China Grid	The CGSP (ChinaGrid Support Platform) is a middleware library developed by 20 top universities in China as part of the China Grid Project
Condor-G	Originally developed at the Univ. of Wisconsin for general distributed computing, and later extended to Condor-G for grid job management.
Sun Grid Engine (SGE)	Developed by Sun Microsystems for business grid applications. Applied to private grids and local clusters within enterprises or campuses.

2. The Globus Toolkit Architecture

GT4 is an open middleware library for the grid computing communities. These open source software libraries support many operational grids and their applications on an international basis. The toolkit addresses common problems and issues related to grid resource discovery, management, communication, security, fault detection, and portability. The software itself provides a variety of components and capabilities. The library includes a rich set of service implementations.

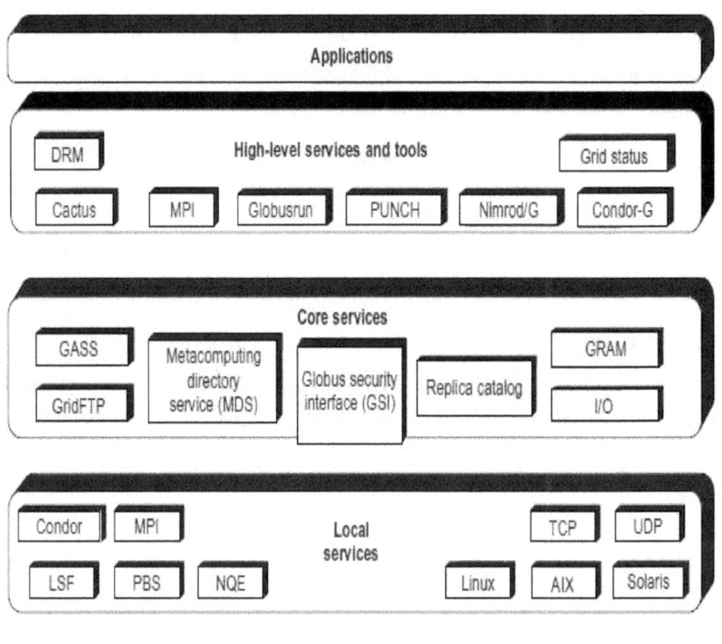

Globus Tookit GT4 supports distributed and cluster computing services.

(Courtesy of I. Foster [1.7])

The GT4 Library

GT4 offers the middle-level core services in grid applications. The high-level services and tools, such as MPI, Condor-G, and Nirod/G, are developed by third parties for general-purpose distributed computing applications.

The local services, such as LSF, TCP, Linux, and Condor, are at the bottom level and are fundamental tools supplied by other developers.

Service Functionality	Module Name	Functional Description
Global Resource Allocation Manager	GRAM	Grid Resource Access and Management (HTTP-based)
Communication	Nexus	Unicast and multicast communication
Grid Security Infrastructure	GSI	Authentication and related security services
Monitory and Discovery Service	MDS	Distributed access to structure and state information
Health and Status	HBM	Heartbeat monitoring of system components
Global Access of Secondary Storage	GASS	Grid access of data in remote secondary storage
Grid File Transfer	GridFTP	Inter-node fast file transfer

Globus Job Workflow

A typical job execution sequence proceeds as follows: The user delegates his credentials to a delegation service. The user submits a job request to GRAM with the delegation identifier as a parameter. GRAM parses the request, retrieves the user proxy certificate from the delegation service, and then acts on behalf of the user. GRAM sends a transfer request to the RFT (Reliable File Transfer), which applies GridFTP to bring in the necessary files. GRAM invokes a local scheduler via a GRAM adapter and the SEG (Scheduler Event Generator) initiates a set of user jobs. The local scheduler reports the job state to the SEG. Once the job is complete, GRAM uses RFT and GridFTP to stage out the resultant files. The grid monitors the progress of these operations and sends the user a notification when they succeed, fail, or are delayed.

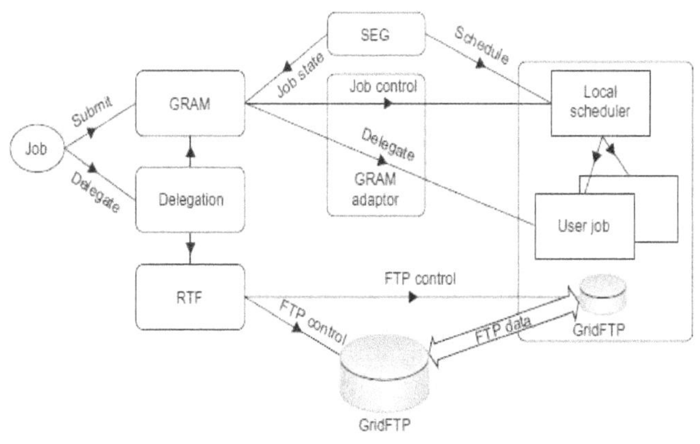

Globus job workflow among interactive functional modules.

Client-Globus Interactions

GT4 service programs are designed to support user applications. There are strong interactions between provider programs and user code. GT4 makes heavy use of industry-standard web service protocols and mechanisms in service description, discovery, access, authentication, authorization, and the like. GT4 makes extensive use of Java, C, and Python to write user code. Web service mechanisms define specific interfaces for grid computing. Web services provide flexible, extensible, and widely adopted XML-based interfaces.

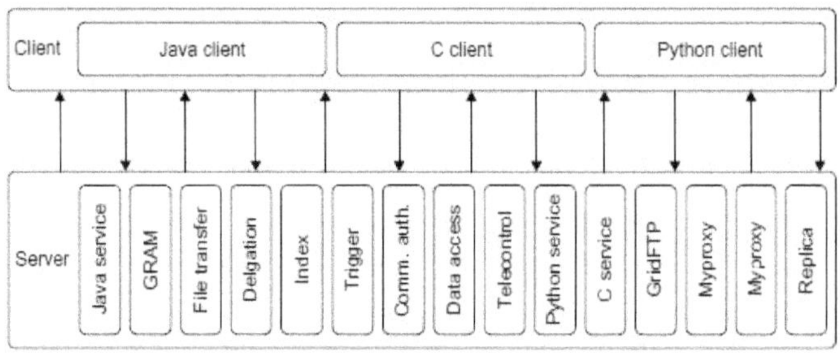

Client and GT4 server interactions; vertical boxes correspond to service programs and horizontal boxes represent the user codes.

3. Explain the MapReduce technique

MapReduce is a programming model and an associated implementation for processing and generating large data sets with a parallel, distributed algorithm on a cluster. A MapReduce program is composed of a **Map()** procedure that performs filtering and sorting (such as sorting students by first name into queues, one queue for each name) and a **Reduce()** procedure that performs a summary operation (such as counting the number of students in each queue, yielding name frequencies). The "MapReduce System" (also called "infrastructure" or "framework") orchestrates the processing by marshalling the distributed servers, running the various tasks in parallel, managing all communications and data transfers between the various parts of the system, and providing for redundancy and fault tolerance.

The model is inspired by the map and reduce functions commonly used in functional programming, although their purpose in the MapReduce framework is not the same as in their original forms. The key contributions of the MapReduce framework are not the actual map and reduce functions, but the scalability and fault-tolerance achieved for a variety of applications by optimizing the execution engine once. As such, a single-threaded implementation of MapReduce (such as MongoDB) will usually not be faster than a traditional (non-MapReduce) implementation, any gains are usually only seen with multi-threaded implementations. Only when the optimized distributed shuffle operation (which reduces network communication cost) and fault tolerance features of the MapReduce framework come into play, is the use of this model beneficial. Optimizing the communication cost is essential to a good MapReduce algorithm.

MapReduce libraries have been written in many programming languages, with different levels of optimization. A popular open-source implementation that has support for distributed shuffles is part of Apache Hadoop. The name MapReduce originally referred to the proprietary Google technology, but has since been genericized.

Hadoop is an open-source framework for writing and running distributed applications that process very large data sets. There has been a great deal of interest in the framework, and it is very popular in industry as well as in academia. Hadoop cases include: web indexing, scientific simulation, social network analysis, fraud analysis, recommendation engine, ad targeting, threat analysis, risk modeling and other. Hadoop is core part of a cloud computing infrastructure and is being used by companies like Yahoo, Facebook, IBM, LinkedIn, and Twitter. The main benefits of Hadoop framework can be summarized as follows:

Accessible: it runs on clusters of commodity servers Scalable: it scales linearly to handle larger data by adding nodes to the cluster

Fault-tolerant: it is designed with the assumption of frequent hardware failures

Simple: it allows user to quickly write efficiently parallel code

Global: it stores and analyzes data in its native format

Hadoop is designed for data-intensive processing tasks and for that reason it has adopted a move- code-to-data" philosophy. According to that philosophy, the programs to run, which are small in size, Are transferred to nodes that store the data. In that way, the framework achieves better performance and resource utilization. In addition, Hadoop solves the hard scaling problems caused by large amounts of complex data. As the amount of data in a cluster grows, new servers can be incrementally and inexpensively added to store and analyze it.

Hadoop has two major subsystems: the Hadoop Distributed File System (HDFS) and a distributed data processing framework called MapReduce. Apart from these two main components, Hadoop has grown into a complex ecosystem, including a range of software systems. Core related applications that are built on top of the HDFS are presented in figure and a short description per project is given in table.

MapReduce is a framework for processing parallelizable problems across huge datasets using a large number of computers (nodes), collectively referred to as a cluster (if all nodes are on the same local network and use similar hardware) or a grid (if the nodes are shared across geographically and administratively distributed systems, and use more heterogenous hardware). Processing can occur on data stored either in a filesystem (unstructured) or in a database (structured). MapReduce can take advantage of locality of data, processing it on or near the storage assets in order to reduce the distance over which it must be transmitted.

- **"Map" step:** Each worker node applies the "map()" function to the local data, and writes the output to a temporary storage. A master node orchestrates that for redundant copies of input data, only one is processed.

- **"Shuffle" step:** Worker nodes redistribute data based on the output keys (produced by the "map()" function), such that all data belonging to one key is located on the same worker node.

- **"Reduce" step:** Worker nodes now process each group of output data, per key, in parallel.

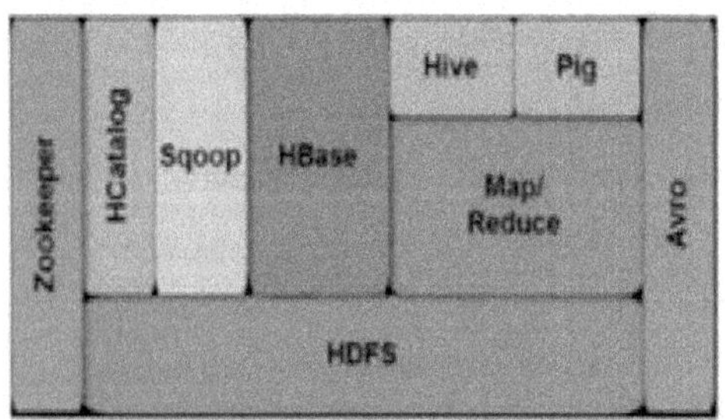

Figure . Hadoop Ecosystem

Project	Info
Hdfs	Hadoop distributed file system
Map reduce	Distributed computation framework
Zookeeper	High-performance collaboration service
Hbase	Column-oriented table service
Pig	Dataflow language and parallel execution
Hive	Data warehouse infrastructure
Hcatalog	Table and storage management service
Sqoop	Bulk data transfer
Avron	Data serialization system

Table . Project Descriptions

4. Explain the architecture of MapReduce in Hadoop?

The Hadoop MapReduce MRv1 framework is based on a centralized master/slave architecture. The architecture utilizes a single master server (JobTracker) and several slave servers (TaskTracker's). Please see Appendix A for a discussion on the MapReduce MRv2 framework. The JobTracker represents a centralized program that keeps track of the slave nodes, and provides an interface infrastructure for job submission. The TaskTracker executes on each of the slave nodes where the actual data is normally stored. In other words, the JobTracker reflects the interaction point among the users and the Hadoop framework. Users submit MapReduce jobs to the JobTracker, which inserts the jobs into the pending jobs queue and executes them (normally) on a FIFO basis (it has to be pointed out that other job schedulers are available - see Hadoop Schedulers below). The JobTracker manages the map and reduce task assignments with the TaskTracker's. The TaskTracker's execute the jobs based on the instructions from the JobTracker and handle the data movement between the maps and reduce phases, respectively. Any map/reduce construct basically reflects a special form of a Directed Acyclic Graph (DAG). A DAG can execute anywhere in parallel, as long as one entity is not an ancestor of another entity. In other words, parallelism is achieved when there are no hidden dependencies among shared states. In the MapReduce model, the internal organization is based on the map function that transforms a piece of data into entities of [key, value] pairs. Each of these elements is sorted (via their key) and ultimately reaches the same cluster node where a reduce function is used to merge the values (with the same key) into a single result (see code below). The Map/Reduce DAG is organized as depicted in Figure.

```
Map Function                         Reduce Function

map(input_record) {                  reduce(key, values) {
                                       while(values.has_next) {
  emit(k1,v1)                            aggregate=merge(values.next)
                                         }
  emit(k2,v2)                          collect(key,aggregate)
                                       }
}
```

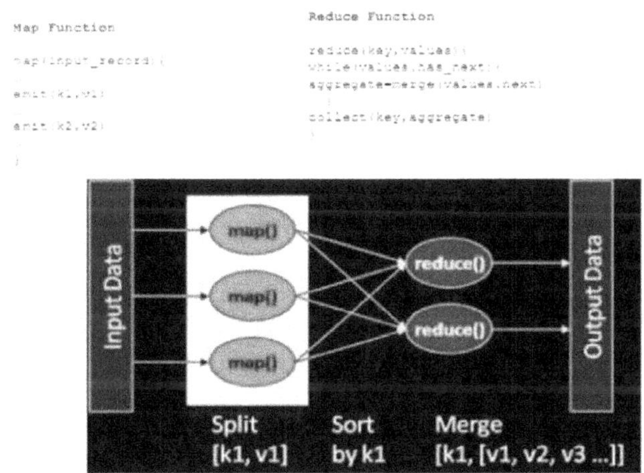

The Hadoop MapReduce framework is based on a pull model, where multiple TaskTracker's communicate with the JobTracker requesting tasks (either map or reduce tasks). After an initial setup phase, the JobTracker is informed about a job submission. The JobTracker provides a job ID to the client program, and starts allocating map tasks to idle TaskTracker's requesting work items (see below Figure).

Each TaskTracker contains a defined number of task slots based on the capacity potential of the system. Via the heartbeat protocol, the JobTracker knows the number of free slots in the TaskTracker (the TaskTracker's send heartbeat messages indicating the free slots true for the FIFO scheduler).

Hence, the JobTracker can determine the appropriate job setup for a TaskTracker based on the actual availability behavior. The assigned TaskTracker will fork a MapTask to execute the map processing cycle (the MapReduce framework spawns 1 MapTask for each InputSplit generated by the InputFormat).

In other words, the MapTask extracts the input data from the splits by using the RecordReader and InputFormat for the job, and it invokes the user provided map function, which emits a number of [key, value] pairs in the memory buffer.

After the MapTask finished executing all input records, the commit process cycle is initiated by flushing the memory buffer to the index and data file pair.

The next step consists of merging all the index and data file pairs into a single construct that is (once again) being divided up into local directories. As some map tasks are completed, the JobTracker starts initiating the reduce tasks phase.

The TaskTracker's involved in this step download the completed files from the map task nodes, and basically concatenate the files into a single entity. As more map tasks are being completed, the JobTracker notifies the involved TaskTracker's, requesting the download of the additional region files and to merge the files with the previous target file. Based on this design, the process of downloading the region files is interleaved with the on-going map task procedures.

Eventually, all the map tasks will be completed, at which point the JobTracker notifies the involved TaskTracker's to proceed with the reduce phase. Each TaskTracker will fork a ReduceTask (separate JVM's are used), read the downloaded file (that is already sorted by key), and invoke the reduce function that assembles the key and aggregated value structure into the final output file (there is one file per reducer node).

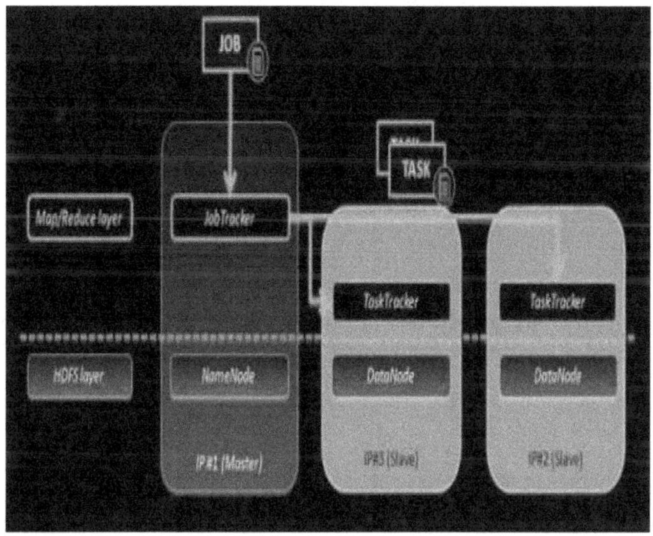

Each reduce task (or map task) is single threaded, and this thread invokes the reduce [key, values] function in either ascending or descending order. The output of each reducer task is written to a temp file in HDFS. When the reducer finishes processing all keys, the temp file is atomically renamed into its final destination file name.

As the MapReduce library is designed to process vast amounts of data by potentially utilizing hundreds or thousands of nodes, the library has to be able to gracefully handle any failure scenarios. The TaskTracker nodes periodically report their status to the JobTracker that oversees the overall job progress. In scenarios where the JobTracker has not been contacted by a TaskTracker for a certain amount of time, the JobTracker assumes a TaskTracker node failure and hence, reassigns the tasks to other available TaskTracker nodes. As the results of the map phase are stored locally, the data will no longer be available if a TaskTracker node goes offline.

In such a scenario, all the map tasks from the failed node (regardless of the actual completion percentage) will have to be reassigned to a different TaskTracker node that will re-execute all the newly assigned splits. The results of the reduce phase are stored in HDFS and hence, the data is globally available even if a TaskTracker node goes offline. Hence, in a scenario where during the reduce phase a TaskTracker node goes offline, only the set of incomplete reduce tasks have to be reassigned to a different TaskTracker node for re-execution.

5. Explain the dataflow and control flow of MapReduce

MapReduce is the heart of Hadoop. It is a programming model designed for processing large volumes of data in parallel by dividing the work into a set of independent tasks.

The framework possesses the feature of data locality. Data locality means movement of algorithm to the data instead of data to algorithm. When the processing is done on the data algorithm is moved across the DataNodes rather than data to the algorithm. The architecture is so constructed because Moving Computation is Cheaper than Moving Data.

It is fault tolerant which is achieved by its daemons using the concept of replication. The daemons associated with the MapReduce phase are job-tracker and task-trackers.

Map-Reduce jobs are submitted on job-tracker. The JobTracker pushes work out to available TaskTracker nodes in the cluster, striving to keep the work as close to the data as possible. A heartbeat is sent from the TaskTracker to the JobTracker every few minutes to check its status whether the node is dead or alive. Whenever there is negative status, the job tracker assigns the task to another node on the replicated data of the failed node stored in this node. Let's see how the data flows:

MapReduce has a simple model of data processing: inputs and outputs for the map and reduce functions are key-value pairs. The map and reduce functions in Hadoop MapReduce have the following general form:

map: (K1, V1) → list(K2, V2)

reduce: (K2, list(V2)) → list(K3, V3)

Now before processing it needs to know on which data to process, this is achieved with the InputFormat class. InputFormat is the class which selects file from HDFS that should be input to the map function. An InputFormat is also responsible for creating theinput splits and dividing them into records. The data is divided into number of splits (typically 64/128mb) in HDFS. An input split is a chunk of the input that is processed by a single map.

InputFormat class calls the getSplits() function and computes splits for each file and then sends them to the jobtracker, which uses their storage locations to schedule map tasks to process them on the tasktrackers. On a tasktracker, the map task passes the split to the createRecordReader() method on InputFormat to obtain a RecordReader for that split. The RecordReader loads data from its source and converts into key-value pairs suitable for reading by mapper. The default InputFormat is TextInputFormat which treats each value of input a new value and the associated key is byte offset.

A RecordReader is little more than an iterator over records, and the map task uses one to generate record key-value pairs, which it passes to the map function. We can see this by looking at the Mapper's run() method:

```
public void run(Context context) throws IOException, InterruptedException {
setup(context);
while (context.nextKeyValue()) {
map(context.getCurrentKey(), context.getCurrentValue(), context);
}
cleanup(context);
}
```

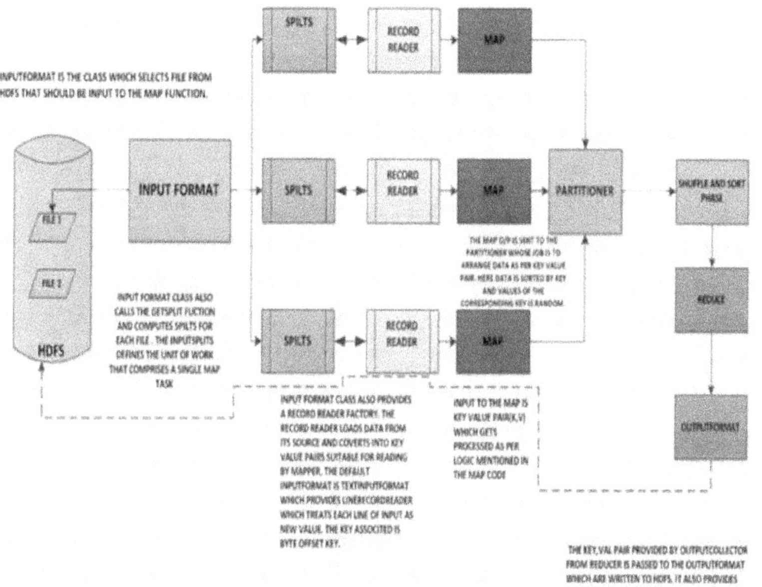

After running setup(), the nextKeyValue() is called repeatedly on the Context, (which delegates to the identically-named method on the the RecordReader) to populate the key and value objects for the mapper. The key and value are retrieved from the Record Reader by way of the Context, and passed to the map() method for it to do its work. Input to the map function which is the key-value pair (K, V) gets processed as per the logic mentioned in the map code.

When the reader gets to the end of the stream, the nextKeyValue() method returns false, and the map task runs its cleanup() method.

The output of the mapper is sent to the partitioner. Partitioner controls the partitioning of the keys of the intermediate map-outputs. The key (or a subset of the key) is used to derive the partition, typically by a hash function. The total number of partitions is the same as the number of reduce tasks for the job. Hence this controls which of the m reduce tasks the intermediate key (and hence the record) is sent for reduction. The use of partitioners is optional.

6. Describe in detail about dataflow of file read in HDFS

To get an idea of how data flows between the client interacting with HDFS, the namenode and the datanode, consider the below diagram, which shows the main sequence of events when reading a file.

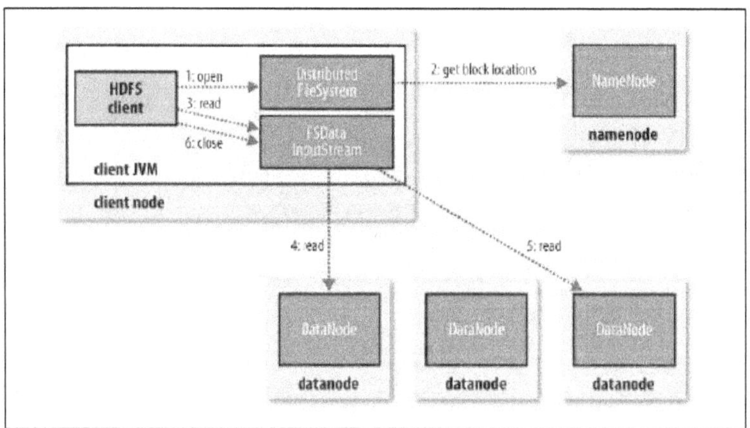

A client reading data from HDFS

The client opens the file it wishes to read by calling open() on the FileSystem object, which for HDFS is an instance of DistributedFileSystem (step 1). DistributedFileSystem calls the namenode, using RPC, to determine the locations of the blocks for the first few blocks in the file (step 2). For each block, the namenode returns the addresses of the datanodes that have a copy of that block. Furthermore, the datanodes are sorted according to their proximity to the client. If the client is itself a datanode (in the case of a MapReduce task, for instance), then it will read from the local datanode.

The DistributedFileSystem returns a FSDataInputStream to the client for it to read data from. FSDataInputStream in turn wraps a DFSInputStream, which manages the datanode and namenode I/O. The client then calls read() on the stream (step 3). DFSInputStream, which has stored the datanode addresses for the first few blocks in the file, then connects to the first (closest) datanode for the first block in the file. Data is streamed from the datanode back to the client, which calls read() repeatedly on the stream (step 4). When the end of the block is reached, DFSInputStream will close the connection to the datanode, then find the best datanode for the next block (step 5). This happens transparently to the client, which from its point of view is just reading a continuous stream. Blocks are read in order with the DFSInputStream opening new connections to datanodes as the client reads through the stream. It will also call the namenode to retrieve the datanode locations for the next batch of blocks as needed. When the client has finished reading, it calls close() on the FSDataInputStream (step 6).

One important aspect of this design is that the client contacts datanodes directly to retrieve data, and is guided by the namenode to the best datanode for each block. This design allows HDFS to scale to large number of concurrent clients, since the data traffic is spread across all the datanodes in the cluster. The namenode meanwhile merely has to service block location requests (which it stores in memory, making them very efficient), and does not, for example, serve data, which would quickly become a bottleneck as the number of clients grew.

7. Describe in detail about dataflow of file write in HDFS

The case we're going to consider is the case of creating a new file, writing data to it, then closing the file

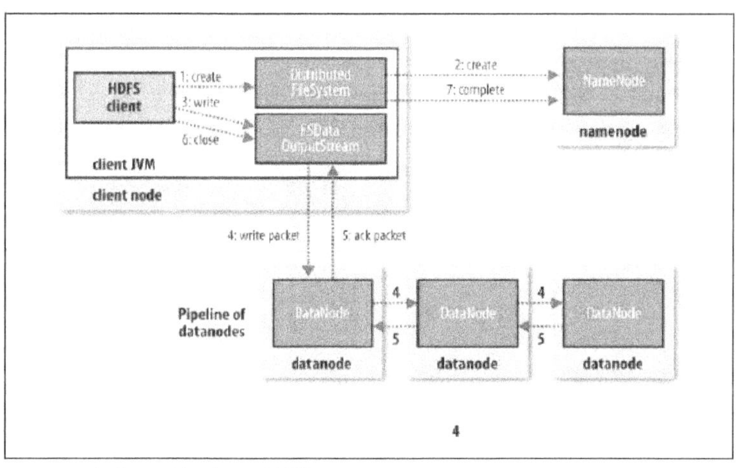

A client writing data to HDFS

The client creates the file by calling create() on DistributedFileSystem (step 1). DistributedFileSystem makes an RPC call to the namenode to create a new file in the file system's namespace, with no blocks associated with it (step 2). The namenode performs various checks to make sure the file doesn't already exist, and that the client has the right permissions to create the file. If these checks pass, the namenode makes a record of the new file; otherwise, file creation fails and the client is thrown an IOException. The DistributedFileSystem returns a SDataOutputStream for the client to start writing data to. Just as in the read case, FSDataOutputStream wraps a DFSOutputStream, which handles communication with the datanodes and namenode.

As the client writes data (step 3), DFSOutputStream splits it into packets, which it writes to an internal queue, called the *data queue*. The data queue is consumed by the DataStreamer, whose responsibility it is to ask the namenode to allocate new blocks by picking a list of suitable datanodes to store the replicas. The list of datanodes forms a pipeline—we'll assume the replication level is 3, so there are three nodes in the pipeline. The DataStreamer streams the packets to the first datanode in the pipeline, which stores the packet and forwards it to the second datanode in the pipeline.

Similarly, the second datanode stores the packet and forwards it to the third (and last) datanode in the pipeline (step 4). DFSOutputStream also maintains an internal queue of packets that are waiting to be acknowledged by datanodes, called the *ack queue*. A packet is removed from the ack queue only when it has been acknowledged by all the datanodes in the pipeline (step 5).

If a datanode fails while data is being written to it, then the following actions are taken, which are transparent to the client writing the data. First the pipeline is closed, and any packets in the ack queue are added to the front of the data queue so that datanodes that are downstream from the failed node will not miss any packets.

The current block on the good datanodes is given a new identity, which is communicated to the namenode, so that the partial block on the failed datanode will be deleted if the failed datanode recovers later on.

The failed datanode is removed from the pipeline and the remainder of the block's data is written to the two good datanodes in the pipeline. The namenode notices that the block is under-replicated, and it arranges for a further replica to be created on another node. Subsequent blocks are then treated as normal.

When the client has finished writing data it calls close() on the stream (step 6). This action flushes all the remaining packets to the datanode pipeline and waits for acknowledgments before contacting the namenode to signal that the file is complete (step7). The namenode already knows which blocks the file is made up of (via Data Streamer asking for block allocations), so it only has to wait for blocks to be minimally replicated before returning successfully.

8. Explain Reading Data from a Hadoop URL and Deleting Data

The Hadoop's FileSystem class: the API for interacting with one of Hadoop's filesystems. While we focus mainly on the HDFS implementation, DistributedFileSystem, in general you should strive to write your code against the FileSystem abstract class, to retain portability across filesystems. This is very useful when testing your program.

One of the simplest ways to read a file from a Hadoop filesystem is by using a java.net.URL object to open a stream to read the data from. The general idiom is:

```
try {
in = new URL("hdfs://host/path").openStream();
process in } finally { IOUtils.closeStream(in);
}
```

There's a little bit more work required to make Java recognize Hadoop's hdfs URL scheme. This is achieved by calling the setURLStreamHandlerFactory method on URL with an instance of FsUrlStreamHandlerFactory. This method can only be called once per JVM, so it is typically executed in a static block.

This limitation means that if some other part of your program perhaps a third-party component outside your control sets RLStreamHandlerFactory, you won't be able to use this approach for reading data from Hadoop.

The next section discusses an alternative. A program for displaying files from Hadoop filesystems on standard output, like the Unix cat command.

We make use of the handy IOUtils class that comes with Hadoop for closing the stream in the finally clause, and also for copying bytes between the input stream and the output stream (System.out in this case).

The last two arguments to the copyBytes method are the buffer size used for copying, and whether to close the streams when the copy is complete. We close the input stream ourselves, and System.out doesn't need to be closed.

```
public class URLCat {

  static {
    URL.setURLStreamHandlerFactory(new FsUrlStreamHandlerFactory());
  }

  public static void main(String[] args) throws Exception {
    InputStream in = null;
    try {
      in = new URL(args[0]).openStream();
      IOUtils.copyBytes(in, System.out, 4096, false);
    } finally {
      IOUtils.closeStream(in);
    }
  }
}
```

Deleting Data

Use the delete() method on FileSystem to permanently remove files or directories: public boolean delete(Path f, boolean recursive) throws IOException. If f is a file or an empty directory, then the value of recursive is ignored. A nonempty directory is only deleted, along with its contents, if recursive is true (otherwise an IOException is thrown).

9.   a) File pattern in HDFS

It is a common requirement to process sets of files in a single operation. For example, a MapReduce job for log processing might analyze a month worth of files, contained in a number of directories. Rather than having to enumerate each file and directory to specify the input, it is convenient to use wildcard characters to match multiple files with a single expression, an operation that is known as *globbing*. Hadoop provides two FileSystem methods for processing globs:

public FileStatus[] globStatus(Path pathPattern) throws IOException

public FileStatus[] globStatus(Path pathPattern, PathFilter filter) throws IOException

The globStatus() methods returns an array of FileStatus objects whose paths match the supplied pattern, sorted by path. An optional PathFilter can be specified to restrict the matches further.

Glob characters and their meanings

Glob	Name	Matches
*	*asterisk*	Matches zero or more characters
?	*question mark*	Matches a single character
[ab]	*character class*	Matches a single character in the set {a, b}
[^ab]	*negated character class*	Matches a single character that is not in the set {a, b}
[a-b]	*character range*	Matches a single character in the (closed) range [a, b], where a is lexicographically less than or equal to b
[^a-b]	*negated character range*	Matches a single character that is not in the (closed) range [a, b], where a is lexicographically less than or equal to b
{a,b}	*alternation*	Matches either expression a or b
\c	*escaped character*	Matches character c when it is a metacharacter

Hadoop supports the same set of glob characters as Unix *bash.*

Imagine that logfiles are stored in a directory structure organized hierarchically by date.

So, for example, logfiles for the last day of 2007 would go in a directory named */2007/12/31.*

Suppose that the full file listing is:

>*/2007/12/30*
>*/2007/12/31*
>*/2008/01/01*
>*/2008/01/02*

9. b) Path filter

Glob patterns are not always powerful enough to describe a set of files you want to access. For example, it is not generally possible to exclude a particular file using a glob pattern. The listStatus() and globStatus() methods of FileSystem take an optional PathFilter, which allows programmatic control over matching:

```
package org.apache.hadoop.fs;
public interface PathFilter
{
boolean accept(Path path);
}
```

PathFilter is the equivalent of java.io.FileFilter for Path objects rather than File objects.

A PathFilter for excluding paths that match a regular expression

```java
public class RegexExcludePathFilter implements PathFilter {

  private final String regex;

  public RegexExcludePathFilter(String regex) {
    this.regex = regex;
  }

  public boolean accept(Path path) {
    return !path.toString().matches(regex);
  }
}
```

The filter passes only files that *don't* match the regular expression. We use the filter in conjunction with a glob that picks out an initial set of files to include: the filter is used to refine the results. For example:

fs.globStatus(new Path("/2007/*/*"), new RegexExcludeFilter("^.*/2007/12/31$"))

Will expand to *2007/12/30*. Filters can only act on a file's name, as represented by a Path. They can't use a file's properties, such as creation time, as the basis of the filter. Nevertheless, they can perform matching that neither glob patterns nor regular expressions can achieve.

10. Explain in detail about command line interface in HDFS

There are many other interfaces to HDFS, but the command line is one of the simplest, and to many developers the most familiar.

We are going to run HDFS on one machine, so first follow the instructions for setting up Hadoop in pseudo-distributed mode.Later you'll see how to run on a cluster of machines to give us scalability and fault tolerance.

There are two properties that we set in the pseudo-distributed configuration that deserve further explanation. The first is fs.default.name, set to *hdfs://localhost/*, which is used to set a default filesystem for Hadoop.

Filesystems are specified by a URI, and here we have used a hdfs URI to configure Hadoop to use HDFS by default.

The HDFS daemons will use this property to determine the host and port for the HDFS namenode. We'll be running it on localhost, on the default HDFS port, 8020. And HDFS clients will use this property to work out where the namenode is running so they can connect to it.

We set the second property, dfs.replication, to one so that HDFS doesn't replicate filesystem blocks by the usual default of three. When running with a single datanode, HDFS can't replicate blocks to three datanodes, so it would perpetually warn about blocks being under-replicated. This setting solves that problem.

Basic Filesystem Operations

The filesystem is ready to be used, and we can do all of the usual filesystem operations such as reading files, creating directories, moving files, deleting data, and listing directories. You can type hadoop fs -help to get detailed help on every command. Start by copying a file from the local filesystem to HDFS:

% hadoop fs -copyFromLocal input/docs/quangle.txt hdfs://localhost/user/tom/quangle.txt

This command invokes Hadoop's filesystem shell command fs, which supports a number of subcommands—in this case, we are running -copyFromLocal. The local file *quangle.txt* is copied to the file */user/tom/quangle.txt* on the HDFS instance running on localhost. In fact, we could have omitted the scheme and host of the URI and picked up the default, hdfs://localhost, as specified in *core-site.xml*.

hadoop fs -copyFromLocal input/docs/quangle.txt /user/tom/quangle.txt

We could also have used a relative path, and copied the file to our home directory in HDFS, which in this case is */user/tom*:

hadoop fs -copyFromLocal input/docs/quangle.txt quangle.txt

Let's copy the file back to the local filesystem and check whether it's the same:

% hadoop fs -copyToLocal quangle.txt quangle.copy.txt

% md5 input/docs/quangle.txt quangle.copy.txt

MD5 (input/docs/quangle.txt) = a16f231da6b05e2ba7a339320e7dacd9 MD5 (quangle.copy.txt) = a16f231da6b05e2ba7a339320e7dacd9

The MD5 digests are the same, showing that the file survived its trip to HDFS and is back intact.

Finally, let's look at an HDFS file listing. We create a directory first just to see how it is displayed in the listing:

% hadoop fs -mkdir books

% hadoop fs -ls.

Found 2 items

    drwxr-xr-x - tom supergroup 0 2009-04-02 22:41 /user/tom/books
    -rw-r--r-- 1 tom supergroup 118 2009-04-02 22:29 /user/tom/quangle.txt

The information returned is very similar to the Unix command ls -l, with a few minor differences. The first column shows the file mode. The second column is the replication factor of the file (something a traditional Unix filesystems does not have). Remember we set the default replication factor in the site-wide configuration to be 1, which is why we see the same value here. The entry in this column is empty for directories since the concept of replication does not apply to them—directories are treated as metadata and stored by the namenode, not the datanodes. The third and fourth columns show the file owner and group. The fifth column is the size of the file in bytes, or zero for directories. The six and seventh columns are the last modified date and time. Finally, the eighth column is the absolute name of the file or directory.

UNIT V

Security

Part A

1. What are the challenges of grid sites

- The first challenge is integration with existing systems and technologies.
- The second challenge is interoperability with different hosting environments.
- The third challenge is to construct trust relationships among interacting hosting environments.

2. Define Reputation-Based Trust Model

In a reputation-based model, jobs are sent to a resource site only when the site is trustworthy to meet users' demands. The site trustworthiness is usually calculated from the following information: the defense capability, direct reputation, and recommendation trust.

3. Define direct reputation

Direct reputation is based on experiences of prior jobs previously submitted to the site. The reputation is measured by many factors such as prior job execution success rate, cumulative site utilization, job turnaround time, job slowdown ratio, and so on. A positive experience associated with a site will improve its reputation. On the contrary, a negative experience with a site will decrease its reputation.

4. What are the major authentication methods in the grid?

The major authentication methods in the grid include passwords, PKI, and Kerberos. The password is the simplest method to identify users, but the most vulnerable one to use. The PKI is the most popular method supported by GSI.

5. List the types of authority in grid

The authority can be classified into three categories: attribute authorities, policy authorities, and identity authorities. Attribute authorities issue attribute assertions; policy authorities issue authorization policies; identity authorities issue certificates. The authorization server makes the final authorization decision.

6. Define grid security infrastructure

The Grid Security Infrastructure (GSI), formerly called the Globus Security Infrastructure, is a specification for secret, tamper-proof, delegatable communication between software in a grid computing environment. Secure, authenticatable communication is enabled using asymmetric encryption.

7. What are the functions present in GSI

GSI may be thought of as being composed of four distinct functions: message protection, authentication, delegation, and authorization.

8. List the protection mechanisms in GSI

GSI allows three additional protection mechanisms. The first is integrity protection, by which a receiver can verify that messages were not altered in transit from the sender. The second is encryption, by which messages can be protected to provide confidentiality. The third is replay prevention, by which a receiver can verify that it has not.

9. What is the primary information of GSI

GSI authentication, a certificate includes four primary pieces of information:

1. A subject name, which identifies the person or object that the certificate represents.
2. The public key belonging to the subject.
3. The identity of a CA that has signed the certificate to certify that the public key and the identity both belong to the subject.
4. The digital signature of the named CA.

10. Define blue pill

The blue pill is malware that executes as a hypervisor to gain control of computer resources.

The hypervisor installs without requiring a restart and the computer functions normally, without degradation of speed or services, which makes detection difficult.

11. What are the host security threats in public IaaS

- Stealing keys used to access and manage hosts (e.g., SSH private keys).
- Attacking unpatched, vulnerable services listening on standard ports (e.g., FTP, SSH).
- Hijacking accounts that are not properly secured (i.e., no passwords for standard accounts).
- Attacking systems that are not properly secured by host firewalls.
- Deploying Trojans embedded in the software component in the VM or within the VM image (the OS) itself.

12. List the Public Cloud Security Limitations

- There are limitations to the public cloud when it comes to support for custom security features. Security requirements such as an application firewall, SSL accelerator, cryptography, or rights management using a device that supports PKCS 12 are not supported in a public SaaS, PaaS, or IaaS cloud.

- Any mitigation controls that require deployment of an appliance or locally attached peripheral devices in the public IaaS/PaaS cloud are not feasible.

13. Define Data lineage

Data lineage is defined as a data life cycle that includes the data's origins and where it moves over time.

It describes what happens to data as it goes through diverse processes. It **helps** provide visibility into the analytics pipeline and simplifies tracing errors back to their sources.

14. Define Data remanence

Data remanence is the residual representation of data that has been in some way nominally erased or removed.

15. What are the IAM processes operational activities.

- Provisioning
- Credential and attribute management
- Entitlement management
- Compliance management
- Identity federation management

16. What are the functions of Cloud identity administrative

Cloud identity administrative functions should focus on life cycle management of user identities in the cloud—provisioning, deprovisioning, identity federation, SSO, password or credentials management, profile management, and administrative management. Organizations that are not capable of supporting federation should explore cloud-based identity management services.

17. List the factors to manage the IaaS virtual infrastructure in the cloud

- Availability of a CSP network, host, storage, and support application infrastructure.
- Availability of your virtual servers and the attached storage (persistent and ephemeral) for compute services
- Availability of virtual storage that your users and virtual server depend on for storage Service
- Availability of your network connectivity to the Internet or virtual network connectivity to IaaS services.
- Availability of network services

18. What is meant by the terms data-in-transit

It is the process of the transfer of the data between all of the versions of the original file, especially when data may be in transit on the Internet. It is data that is exiting the network via email, web, or other Internet protocols.

19. List the IAM process business category

- User management
- Authentication management
- Authorization management
- Access management
- Data management and provisioning
- Monitoring and auditing

20. What are the key components of IAM automation process?

- User Management, New Users.
- User Management, User Modifications.
- Authentication Management.
- Authorization Management.

Part B

1. Trust Models for Grid Security

A user job demands the resource site to provide security assurance by issuing a security demand (SD). On the other hand, the site needs to reveal its trustworthiness, called its trust index (TI). These two parameters must satisfy a security-assurance condition: TI $\geq$ SD during the job mapping process. When determining its security demand, users usually care about some typical attributes. These attributes and their values are dynamically changing and depend heavily on the trust model, security policy, accumulated reputation, self-defense capability, attack history, and site vulnerability.

Three challenges are outlined below to establish the trust among grid sites.

The first challenge is integration with existing systems and technologies. The resources sites in a grid are usually heterogeneous and autonomous. It is unrealistic to expect that a single type of security can be compatible with and adopted by every hosting environment. At the same time, existing security infrastructure on the sites cannot be replaced overnight. Thus, to be successful, grid security architecture needs to step up to the challenge of integrating with existing security architecture and models across platforms and hosting environments.

The second challenge is interoperability with different —hosting environments.‖ Services are often invoked across multiple domains, and need to be able to interact with one another. The interoperation is demanded at the protocol, policy, and identity levels. For all these levels, interoperation must be protected securely. The third challenge is to construct trust relationships among interacting hosting environments. Grid service requests can be handled by combining resources on multiple security domains. Trust relationships are required by these domains during the end-to-end traversals. A service needs to be open to friendly and interested entities so that they can submit requests and access securely.

The grid aims to construct a large-scale network computing system by integrating distributed, heterogeneous, and autonomous resources. The security challenges faced by the grid are much greater than other computing systems. Before any effective sharing and cooperation occurs, a trust relationship has to be established among participants. A Generalized Trust Model.

At the bottom, we identify three major factors which influence the trustworthiness of a resource site. An inference module is required to aggregate these factors. Followings are some existing inference or aggregation methods. An intra-site fuzzy inference procedure is called to assess defense capability and direct reputation. Defense capability is decided by the firewall, intrusion detection system (IDS), intrusion response capability, and anti-virus capacity of the individual resource site. Direct reputation is decided based on the job success rate, site utilization, job turnaround time, and job slowdown ratio measured. Recommended trust is also known as secondary trust and is obtained indirectly over the grid network. Reputation-Based Trust Model.

In a reputation-based model, jobs are sent to a resource site only when the site is trustworthy to meet users' demands. The site trustworthiness is usually calculated from the following information: the defense capability, direct reputation, and recommendation trust. The defense capability refers to the site's ability to protect itself from danger. It is assessed according to such factors as intrusion detection, firewall, response capabilities, anti-virus capacity, and so on. Direct reputation is based on experiences of prior jobs previously submitted to the site.

The reputation is measured by many factors such as prior job execution success rate, cumulative site utilization, job turnaround time, job slowdown ratio, and so on. A positive experience associated with a site will improve its reputation. On the contrary, a negative experience with a site will decrease its reputation.

A Fuzzy-Trust Model

The job security demand (SD) is supplied by the user programs. The trust index (TI) of a resource site is aggregated through the fuzzy-logic inference process over all related parameters. Specifically, one can use a two-level fuzzy logic to estimate the aggregation of numerous trust parameters and security attributes into scalar quantities that are easy to use in the job scheduling and resource mapping process. The TI is normalized as a single real number with 0 representing the condition with the highest risk at a site and 1 representing the condition which is totally risk-free or fully trusted.

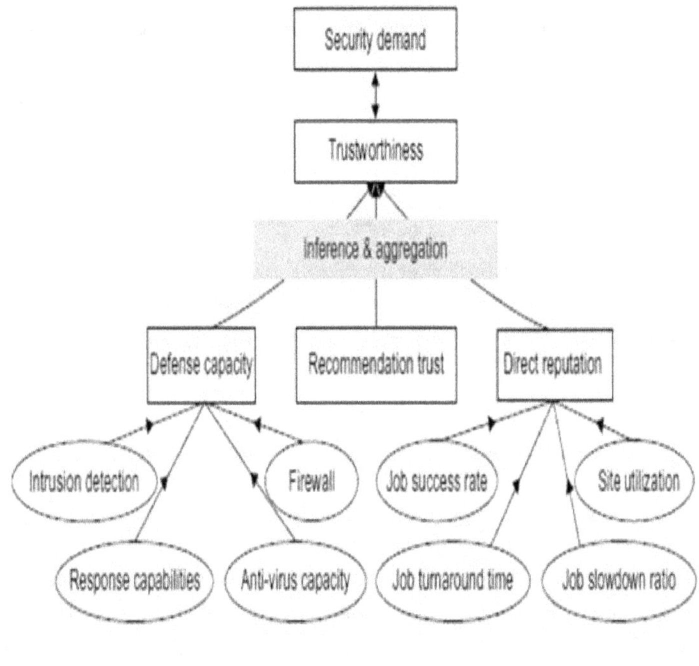

A general trust model for grid computing.

The fuzzy inference is accomplished through four steps: fuzzification, inference, aggregation, and defuzzification.

The second salient feature of the trust model is that if a site's trust index cannot match the job security demand (i.e., SD > TI), the trust model could deduce detailed security features to guide the site security upgrade as a result of tuning the fuzzy system.

2. Authentication and Authorization Methods

The major authentication methods in the grid include passwords, PKI, and Kerberos. The password is the simplest method to identify users, but the most vulnerable one to use. The PKI is the most popular method supported by GSI. To implement PKI, we use a trusted third party, called the certificate authority (CA). Each user applies a unique pair of public and private keys. The public keys are issued by the CA by issuing a certificate, after recognizing a legitimate user. The private key is exclusive for each user to use, and is unknown to any other users. A digital certificate in IEEE X.509 format consists of the user name, user public key, CA name, and a secrete signature of the user. The following example illustrates the use of a PKI service in a grid environment.

Authorization for Access Control

The authorization is a process to exercise access control of shared resources. Decisions can be made either at the access point of service or at a centralized place. Typically, the resource is a host that provides processors and storage for services deployed on it. Based on a set predefined policies or rules, the resource may enforce access for local services. The central authority is a special entity which is capable of issuing and revoking polices of access rights granted to remote accesses. The authority can be classified into three categories: attribute authorities, policy authorities, and identity authorities. Attribute authorities issue attribute assertions; policy authorities issue authorization policies; identity authorities issue certificates. The authorization server makes the final authorization decision.

Three Authorization Models

Three authorization models are shown in diagram. The subject is the user and the resource refers to the machine side.

The subject-push model is shown at the top diagram. The user conducts handshake with the authority first and then with the resource site in a sequence. The resource-pulling model puts the resource in the middle.

The user checks the resource first. Then the resource contacts its authority to verify the request, and the authority authorizes at step 3. Finally the resource accepts or rejects the request from the subject at step 4.

The authorization agent model puts the authority in the middle. The subject check with the authority at step 1 and the authority makes decisions on the access of the requested resources. The authorization process is complete at steps 3 and 4 in the reverse direction.

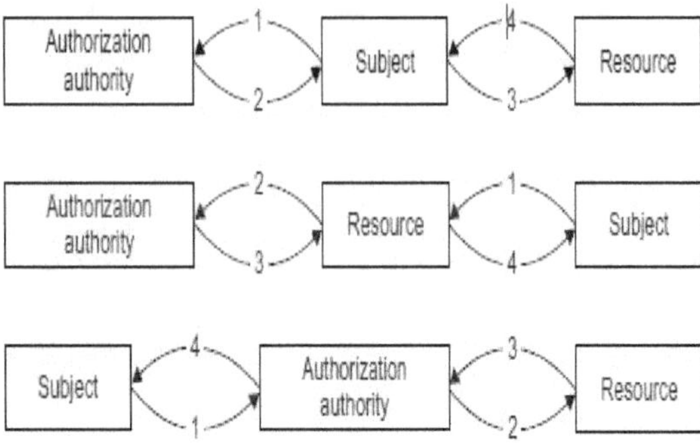

Three authorization models: the subject-push model, resource-pulling model, and the authorization agent model.

3. Explain in detail about Grid Security Infrastructure

GSI is a portion of the Globus Toolkit and provides fundamental security services needed to support grids, including supporting for message protection, authentication and delegation, and authorization. GSI enables secure authentication and communication over an open network, and permits mutual authentication across and among distributed sites with single sign-on capability.

No centrally managed security system is required, and the grid maintains the integrity of its members' local policies. GSI supports both message-level security, which supports the WS-Security standard and the WS-Secure Conversation specification to provide message protection for SOAP messages, and transport-level security, which means authentication via TLS with support for X.509 proxy certificates.

GSI Functional Layers

GT4 provides distinct WS and pre-WS authentication and authorization capabilities. Both build on the same base, namely the X.509 standard and entity certificates and proxy certificates, which are used to identify persistent entities such as users and servers and to support the temporary delegation of privileges to other entities, respectively.

As shown in diagram, GSI may be thought of as being composed of four distinct functions: message protection, authentication, delegation, and authorization.

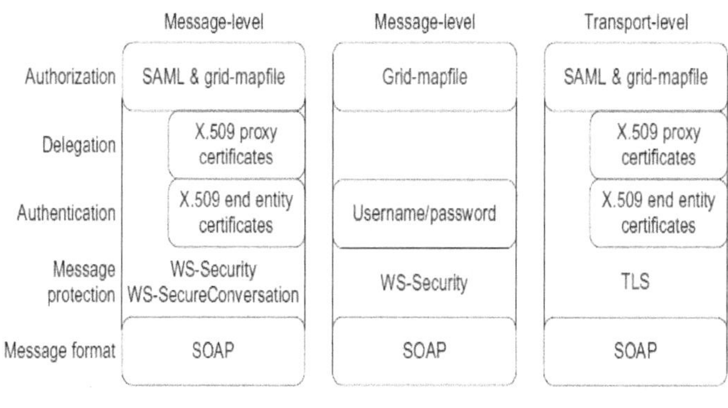

GSI functional layers at the message and transport levels.

Transport-Level Security

Transport-level security entails SOAP messages conveyed over a network connection protected by TLS. TLS provides for both integrity protection and privacy (via encryption). Transport-level security is normally used in conjunction with X.509 credentials for authentication, but can also be used without such credentials to provide message protection without authentication, often referred to as ―anonymous transport-level security.‖ In this mode of operation, authentication may be done by username and password in a SOAP message

GSI also provides message-level security for message protection for SOAP messages by implementing the WS-Security standard and the WS-Secure Conversation specification. The WS-Security standard from OASIS defines a framework for applying security to individual SOAP messages; WS-Secure Conversation is a proposed standard from IBM and Microsoft that allows for an initial exchange of messages to establish a security context which can then be used to protect subsequent messages in a manner that requires less computational overhead (i.e., it allows the trade-off of initial overhead for setting up the session for lower overhead for messages).

GSI conforms to this standard. GSI uses these mechanisms to provide security on a per-message basis, that is, to an individual message without any preexisting context between the sender and receiver (outside of sharing some set of trust roots). GSI, as described further in the subsequent section on authentication, allows for both X.509 public key credentials and the combination of username and password for authentication; however, differences still exist.

With username/password, only the WS-Security standard can be used to allow for authentication; that is, a receiver can verify the identity of the communication initiator.

GSI allows three additional protection mechanisms. The first is integrity protection, by which a receiver can verify that messages were not altered in transit from the sender. The second is encryption, by which messages can be protected to provide confidentiality. The third is replay prevention, by which a receiver can verify that it has not received the same message previously. These protections are provided between WS-Security and WS-Secure Conversation. The former applies the keys associated with the sender and receiver's X.509 credentials. The X.509 credentials are used to establish a session key that is used to provide the message protection.

Authentication and Delegation

GSI has traditionally supported authentication and delegation through the use of X.509 certificates and public keys. As a new feature in GT4, GSI also supports authentication through plain usernames and passwords as a deployment option. We discuss both methods in this section. GSI uses X.509 certificates to identify persistent users and services.

As a central concept in GSI authentication, a certificate includes four primary pieces of information: (1) a subject name, which identifies the person or object that the certificate represents; (2) the public key belonging to the subject; (3) the identity of a CA that has signed the certificate to certify that the public key and the identity both belong to the subject; and (4) the digital signature of the named CA. X.509 provides each entity with a unique identifier (i.e., a distinguished name) and a method to assert that identifier to another party through the use of an asymmetric key pair bound to the identifier by the certificate.

Trust Delegation

To reduce or even avoid the number of times the user must enter his passphrase when several grids are used or have agents (local or remote) requesting services on behalf of a user, GSI provides a delegation capability and a delegation service that provides an interface to allow clients to delegate (and renew) X.509 proxy certificates to a service. The interface to this service is based on the WS-Trust specification. A proxy consists of a new certificate and a private key. The key pair that is used for the proxy, that is, the public key embedded in the certificate and the private key, may either be regenerated for each proxy or be obtained by other means. The new certificate contains the owner's identity, modified slightly to indicate that it is a proxy. The new certificate is signed by the owner, rather than a CA

4. Explain cloud infrastructure security at application level

We will limit our discussion to web application security: web applications in the cloud accessed by users with standard Internet browsers, such as Firefox, Internet Explorer, or Safari, from any computer connected to the Internet.

Application-Level Security Threats

The existing threats exploit well-known application vulnerabilities including cross-site scripting (XSS), SQL injection, malicious file execution, and other vulnerabilities resulting from programming errors and design flaws. Armed with knowledge and tools, hackers are constantly scanning web applications (accessible from the Internet) for application vulnerabilities.

It has been a common practice to use a combination of perimeter security controls and network- and host-based access controls to protect web applications deployed in a tightly controlled environment, including corporate intranets and private clouds, from external hackers.

Web applications built and deployed in a public cloud platform will be subjected to a high threat level, attacked, and potentially exploited by hackers to support fraudulent and illegal activities. In that threat model, web applications deployed in a public cloud (the SPI model) must be designed for an Internet threat model, and security must be embedded into the Software Development Life Cycle (SDLC)

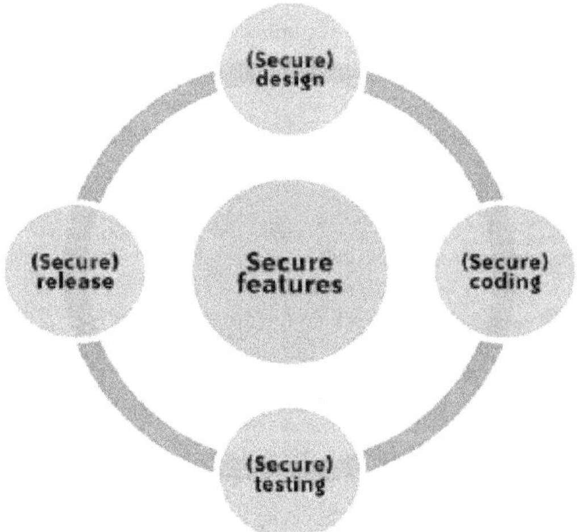

DoS and EDoS

Additionally, you should be cognizant of application-level DoS and EDDoS attacks that can potentially disrupt cloud services for an extended time. These attacks typically originate from compromised computer systems attached to the Internet.

Application-level DoS attacks could manifest themselves as high-volume web page reloads, XML* web services requests (over HTTP or HTTPS), or protocol-specific requests supported by a cloud service.

Since these malicious requests blend with the legitimate traffic, it is extremely difficult to selectively filter the malicious traffic without impacting the service as a whole

DoS attacks on pay-as-you-go cloud applications will result in a dramatic increase in your cloud utility bill: you'll see increased use of network bandwidth, CPU, and storage consumption. This type of attack is also being characterized as *economic denial of sustainability* (EDoS)

End User Security

A customer of a cloud service, are responsible for end user security tasks—security procedures to protect your Internet-connected PC—and for practicing —safe surfing.‖ Protection measures include use of security software, such as anti-malware, antivirus, personal firewalls, security patches, and IPS-type software on your Internet-connected computer.

The new mantra of —the browser is your operating system‖ appropriately conveys the message that browsers have become the ubiquitous —operating systems‖ for consuming cloud services.

All Internet browsers routinely suffer from software vulnerabilities that make them vulnerable to end user security attacks.

Hence, our recommendation is that cloud customers take appropriate steps to protect browsers from attacks.

To achieve end-to-end security in a cloud, it is essential for customers to maintain good browser hygiene. The means keeping the browser (e.g., Internet Explorer, Firefox, Safari) patched and updated to mitigate threats related to browser vulnerabilities.

Currently, although browser security add-ons are not commercially available, users are encouraged to frequently check their browser vendor's website for security updates, use the auto-update feature, and install patches on a timely basis to maintain end user security.

SaaS Application Security

The SaaS model dictates that the provider manages the entire suite of applications delivered to users. Therefore, SaaS providers are largely responsible for securing the applications and components they offer to customers. Customers are usually responsible for operational security functions, including user and access management as supported by the provider. Extra attention needs to be paid to the authentication and access control features offered by SaaS CSPs. Usually that is the only security control available to manage risk to information. Most services, including those from Salesforce.com and Google, offer a web-based administration user interface tool to manage authentication and access control of the application. Cloud customers should try to understand cloud-specific access control mechanisms— including support for strong authentication and privilege management based on user roles and functions—and take the steps necessary to protect information hosted in the cloud. Additional controls should be implemented to manage privileged access to the SaaS administration tool, and enforce segregation of duties to protect the application from insider threats. In line with security standard practices, customers should implement a strong password policy—one that forces users to choose strong passwords when authenticating to an application.

PaaS Application Security

PaaS vendors broadly fall into the following two major categories:

• Software vendors (e.g., Bungee, Etelos, GigaSpaces, Eucalyptus)
• CSPs (e.g., Google App Engine, Salesforce.com's Force.com, Microsoft Azure, Intuit QuickBase)

A PaaS cloud (public or private) offers an integrated environment to design, develop, test, deploy, and support custom applications developed in the language the platform supports.

PaaS application security encompasses two software layers:

• Security of the PaaS platform itself (i.e., runtime engine)
• Security of customer applications deployed on a PaaS platform

PaaS CSPs (e.g., Google, Microsoft, and Force.com) are responsible for securing the platform software stack that includes the runtime engine that runs the customer applications. Since PaaS applications may use third-party applications, components, or web services, the third-party application provider may be responsible for securing their services. Hence, customers should understand the dependency of their application on all services and assess risks pertaining to third-party service providers.

IaaS Application Security

IaaS cloud providers (e.g., Amazon EC2, GoGrid, and Joyent) treat the applications on customer virtual instances as a black box, and therefore are completely agnostic to the operations and management of the customer's applications.

The entire stack—customer applications, runtime application platform (Java, .NET, PHP, Ruby on Rails, etc.), and so on— runs on the customer's virtual servers and is deployed and managed by customers. To that end, customers have full responsibility for securing their applications deployed in the IaaS cloud.

Web applications deployed in a public cloud must be designed for an Internet threat model, embedded with standard security countermeasures against common web vulnerabilities. In adherence with common security development practices, they should also be periodically tested for vulnerabilities, and most importantly, security should be embedded into the SDLC. Customers are solely responsible for keeping their applications and runtime platform patched to protect the system from malware and hackers scanning for vulnerabilities to gain unauthorized access to their data in the cloud. It is highly recommended that you design and implement applications with a —least-privileged‖ runtime model.

Developers writing applications for IaaS clouds must implement their own features to handle authentication and authorization. In line with enterprise identity management practices, cloud applications should be designed to leverage delegated authentication service features supported by an enterprise Identity Provider (e.g., OpenSSO, Oracle IAM, IBM, CA) or third-party identity service provider (e.g., Ping Identity, Symplified, TriCipher). Any custom implementations of Authentication, Authorization, and Accounting (AAA) features can become a weak link if they are not properly implemented, and you should avoid them when possible.

5. Describe in detail about provider data and its security

Customers should also be concerned about what data the provider collects and how the CSP protects that data. Additionally, your provider collects and must protect a huge amount of security-related data.

Storage

For data stored in the cloud (i.e., storage-as-a-service), we are referring to IaaS and not data associated with an application running in the cloud on PaaS or SaaS. The same three information security concerns are associated with this data stored in the cloud (e.g., Amazon's S3) as with data stored elsewhere: confidentiality, integrity, and availability.

Confidentiality

When it comes to the confidentiality of data stored in a public cloud, you have two potential concerns. First, what access control exists to protect the data? Access control consists of both authentication and authorization.

CSPs generally use weak authentication mechanisms (e.g., username + password), and the authorization (—access‖) controls available to users tend to be quite coarse and not very granular. For large organizations, this coarse authorization presents significant security concerns unto itself. Often, the only authorization levels cloud vendors provide are administrator authorization (i.e., the owner of the account itself) and user authorization (i.e., all other authorized users)—with no levels in between (e.g., business unit administrators, who are authorized to approve access for their own business unit personnel).

If a CSP does encrypt a customer's data, the next consideration concerns what encryption algorithm it uses. Not all encryption algorithms are created equal. Cryptographically, many algorithms provide insufficient security. Only algorithms that have been publicly vetted by a formal standards body (e.g., NIST) or at least informally by the cryptographic community should be used. Any algorithm that is proprietary should absolutely be avoided.

Symmetric encryption involves the use of a single secret key for both the encryption and decryption of data. Only symmetric encryption has the speed and computational efficiency to handle encryption of large volumes of data. It would be highly unusual to use an asymmetric algorithm for this encryption use case.

Although the example in diagram is related to email, the same concept (i.e., a single shared, secret key) is used in data storage encryption.

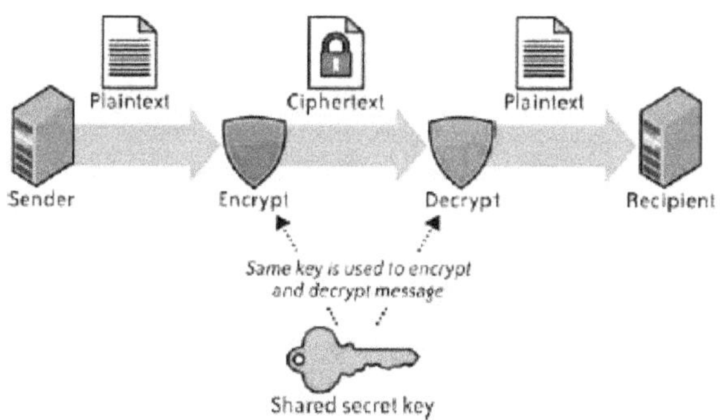

Symmetric encryption

Although the example in diagram is related to email, the same concept (i.e., a public key and a private key) is *not* used in data storage encryption.

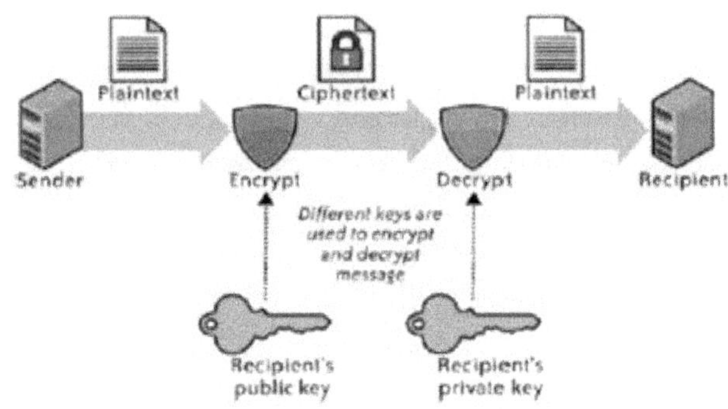

Asymmetric encryption

Integrity

Confidentiality does not imply integrity; data can be encrypted for confidentiality purposes, and yet you might not have a way to verify the integrity of that data. Encryption alone is sufficient for confidentiality, but integrity also requires the use of message authentication codes (MACs). The simplest way to use MACs on encrypted data is to use a block symmetric algorithm (as opposed to a streaming symmetric algorithm) in cipher block chaining (CBC) mode, and to include a one-way hash function.

Another aspect of data integrity is important, especially with bulk storage using IaaS. Once a customer has several gigabytes (or more) of its data up in the cloud for storage, how does the customer check on the integrity of the data stored there? There are IaaS transfer costs associated with moving data into and back down from the cloud,* as well as network utilization (bandwidth) considerations for the customer's own network. What a customer really wants to do is to validate the integrity of its data while that data remains in the cloud— without having to download and re-upload that data.

Availability

Assuming that a customer's data has maintained its confidentiality and integrity, you must also be concerned about the availability of your data. There are currently three major threats in this regard—none of which are new to computing, but all of which take on increased importance in cloud computing because of increased risk.

The first threat to availability is network-based attacks.

The second threat to availability is the CSP's own availability.

Cloud storage customers must be certain to ascertain just what services their provider is actually offering. Cloud storage does not mean the stored data is actually backed up. Some cloud storage providers do back up customer data, in addition to providing storage. However, many cloud storage providers do not back up customer data, or do so only as an additional service for an additional cost.

All three of these considerations (confidentiality, integrity, and availability) should be encapsulated in a CSP's service-level agreement (SLA) to its customers. However, at this time, CSP SLAs are extremely weak—in fact, for all practical purposes, they are essentially worthless.

Even where a CSP appears to have at least a partially sufficient SLA, how that SLA actually gets measured is problematic. For all of these reasons, data security considerations and how data is actually stored in the cloud should merit considerable attention by customers.

6. Explain identity and access management functional architecture

We'll present the basic concepts and definitions of IAM functions for any service:

Authentication

Authentication is the process of verifying the identity of a user or system. Authentication usually connotes a more robust form of identification. In some use cases, such as service-to-service interaction, authentication involves verifying the network service requesting access to information served by another service.

Authorization

Authorization is the process of determining the privileges the user or system is entitled to once the identity is established. —in other words, authorization is the process of enforcing policies.

Auditing

In the context of IAM, auditing entails the process of review and examination of authentication, authorization records, and activities to determine the adequacy of IAM system controls, to verify compliance with established security policies and procedures (e.g., separation of duties), to detect breaches in security services (e.g., privilege escalation), and to recommend any changes that are indicated for countermeasures.

IAM Architecture

Standard enterprise IAM architecture encompasses several layers of technology, services, and processes. At the core of the deployment architecture is a directory service (such as LDAP or Active Directory) that acts as a repository for the identity, credential, and user attributes of the organization's user pool.

The directory interacts with IAM technology components such as authentication, user management, provisioning, and federation services that support the standard IAM practice and processes within the organization. It is not uncommon for organizations to use several directories that were deployed for environment-specific reasons (e.g., Windows systems using Active Directory, Unix systems using LDAP) or that were integrated into the environment by way of business mergers and acquisitions.

The IAM processes to support the business can be broadly categorized as follows:

User Management

Activities for the effective governance and management of identity life cycles

Authentication Management

Activities for the effective governance and management of the process for determining that an entity is who or what it claims.

Authorization Management

Activities for the effective governance and management of the process for determining entitlement rights that decide what resources an entity is permitted to access in accordance with the organization's policies.

Access Management

Enforcement of policies for access control in response to a request from an entity (user, services) wanting to access an IT resource within the organization

Data Management and Provisioning

Propagation of identity and data for authorization to IT resources via automated or manual processes

Monitoring and Auditing

Monitoring, auditing, and reporting compliance by users regarding access to resources within the organization based on the defined policies.

IAM Processes Support the Following Operational Activities

Provisioning

This is the process of on-boarding users to systems and applications. These processes provide users with necessary access to data and technology resources. The term typically is used in reference to enterprise-level resource management.

Credential and Attribute Management

These processes are designed to manage the life cycle of credentials and user attributes—create, issue, manage, revoke—to minimize the business risk associated with identity impersonation and inappropriate account use. Credentials are usually bound to an individual and are verified during the authentication process. The processes include provisioning of attributes, static (e.g., standard text password) and dynamic (e.g., one-time password) credentials that comply with a password standard (e.g., passwords resistant to dictionary attacks), handling password expiration, encryption management of credentials during transit and at rest, and access policies of user attributes.

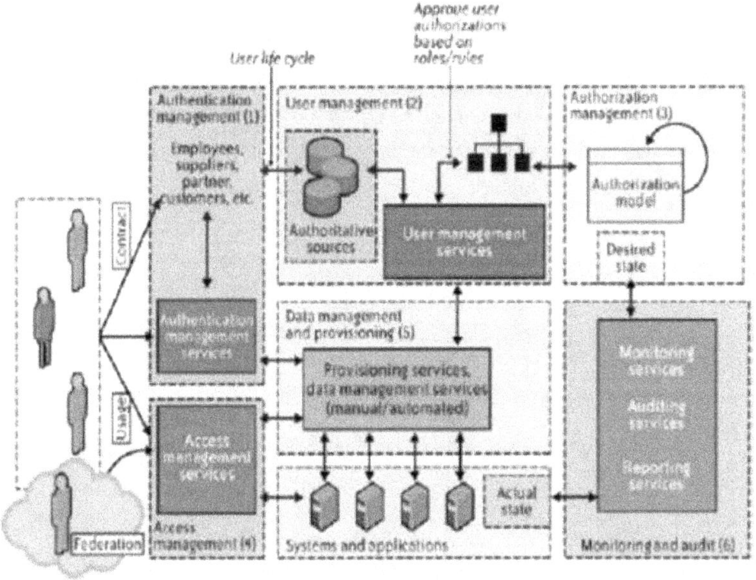

Enterprise IAM functional architecture

Entitlement Management

Entitlements are also referred to as *authorization policies*. The processes in this domain address the provisioning and de-provisioning of privileges needed for the user to access resources including systems, applications, and databases.

Compliance Management

This process implies that access rights and privileges are monitored and tracked to ensure the security of an enterprise's resources. The process also helps auditors verify compliance to various internal access control policies, and standards that include practices such as segregation of duties, access monitoring, periodic auditing, and reporting.

Identity Federation Management

Federation is the process of managing the trust relationships established beyond the internal network boundaries or administrative domain boundaries among distinct organizations. A federation is an association of organizations that come together to exchange information about their users and resources to enable collaborations and transactions

Centralization of Authentication (authN) and Authorization (authZ)

A central authentication and authorization infrastructure alleviates the need for application developers to build custom authentication and authorization features into their applications. Furthermore, it promotes a loose coupling architecture where applications become agnostic to the authentication methods and policies. This approach is also called an —externalization of authN and authZ‖ from applications.

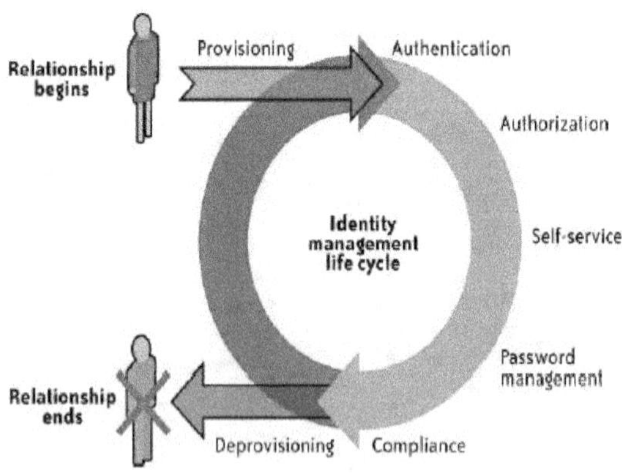

Identity life cycle

7. Explain user management functions in the cloud

User management functions in the cloud can be categorized as follows:

1. Cloud identity administration
2. Federation or SSO
3. Authorization management
4. Compliance management

Cloud Identity Administration

Cloud identity administrative functions should focus on life cycle management of user identities in the cloud—provisioning, de-provisioning, identity federation, SSO, password or credentials management, profile management, and administrative management. Organizations that are not capable of supporting federation should explore cloud-based identity management services.

By federating identities using either an internal Internet-facing IdP or a cloud identity management service provider, organizations can avoid duplicating identities and attributes and storing them with the CSP. Given the inconsistent and sparse support for identity standards among CSPs, customers may have to devise custom methods to address user management functions in the cloud. Provisioning users when federation is not supported can be complex and laborious.

Federated Identity (SSO)

Organizations planning to implement identity federation that enables SSO for users can take one of the following two paths (architectures):

1. Implement an enterprise IdP within an organization perimeter.
2. Integrate with a trusted cloud-based identity management service provider.

Enterprise Identity Provider

In this architecture, cloud services will delegate authentication to an organization's IdP. In this delegated authentication architecture, the organization federates identities within a trusted circle of CSP domains. A circle of trust can be created with all the domains that are authorized to delegate authentication to the IdP. In this deployment architecture, where the organization will provide and support an IdP, greater control can be exercised over user identities, attributes, credentials, and policies for authenticating and authorizing users to a cloud service.

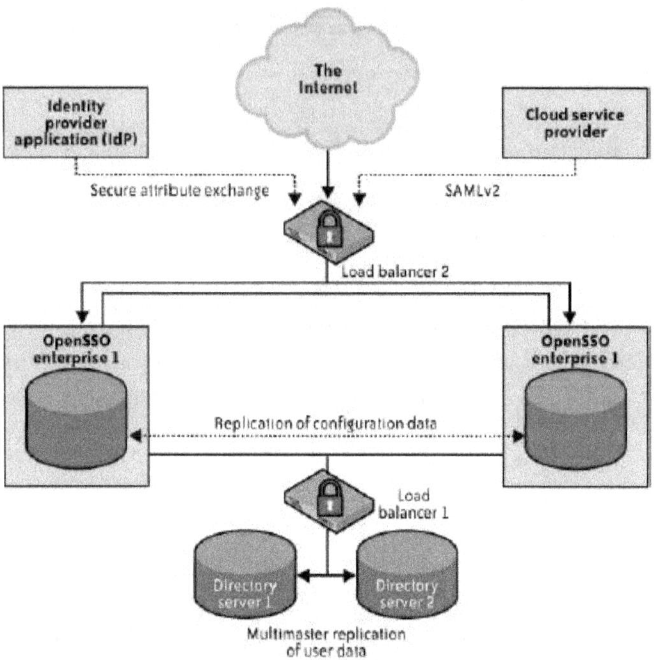

Identity provider deployment architecture

Identity Management-as-a-Service

In this architecture, cloud services can delegate authentication to an identity management-as-a- service (IDaaS) provider. In this model, organizations outsource the federated identity management technology and user management processes to a third-party service provider. In essence, this is a SaaS model for identity management, where the SaaS IdP stores identities in a —trusted identity store‖ and acts as a proxy for the organization's users accessing cloud services.

The identity store in the cloud is kept in sync with the corporate directory through a provider proprietary scheme (e.g., agents running on the customer's premises synchronizing a subset of an organization's identity store to the identity store in the cloud using SSL VPNs). Once the IdP is established in the cloud, the organization should work with the CSP to delegate authentication to the cloud identity service provider. The cloud IdP will authenticate the cloud users prior to them accessing any cloud services.

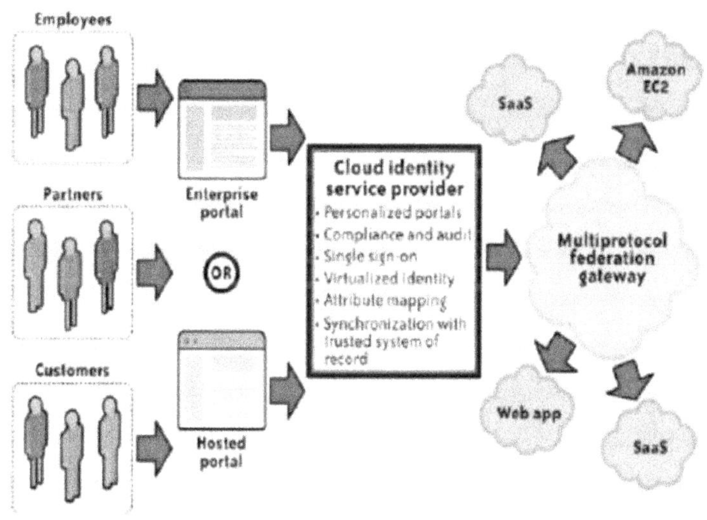

Identity management-as-a-service (IDaaS)

Cloud Authorization Management

Most cloud services support at least dual roles (privileges): administrator and end user. It is a normal practice among CSPs to provision the administrator role with administrative privileges. These privileges allow administrators to provision and de-provision identities, basic attribute profiles, and, in some cases, to set access control policies such as password strength and trusted networks from which connections are accepted.

As we mentioned earlier, XACML is the preferred standard for expressing and enforcing authorization and user authentication policies. As of this writing, we are not aware of any cloud services supporting XACML to express authorization policies for users.

IAM Support for Compliance Management

As much as cloud IAM architecture and practices impact the efficiency of internal IT processes, they also play a major role in managing compliance within the enterprise. Properly implemented IAM practices and processes can help improve the effectiveness of the controls identified by compliance frameworks.

IAM practices and processes offer a centralized view of business operations and an automated process that can stop insider threats before they occur. However, given the sparse support for IAM standards such as SAML (federation), SPML (provisioning), and XACML (authorization) by the CSP, you should assess the CSP capabilities on a case-by-case basis and institute processes for managing compliance related to identity (including attribute) and access management.

8.   a) PaaS Availability Management

In a typical PaaS service, customers (developers) build and deploy PaaS applications on top of the CSP-supplied PaaS platform. The PaaS platform is typically built on a CSP owned and managed network, servers, operating systems, storage infrastructure, and application components (web services). Given that the customer PaaS applications are assembled with CSP-supplied application components and, in some cases, third-party web services components (mash-up applications), availability management of the PaaS application can be complicated

PaaS applications may rely on other third-party web services components that are not part of the PaaS service offerings; hence, understanding the dependency of your application on third-party services, including services supplied by the PaaS vendor, is essential. PaaS providers may also offer a set of web services, including a message queue service, identity and authentication service, and database service, and your application may depend on the availability of those service components. App Engine resource is measured against one of two kinds of quotas: a billable quota or a fixed quota.

Billable quotas are resource maximums set by you, the application's administrator, to prevent the cost of the application from exceeding your budget. Every application gets an amount of each billable quota for free. You can increase billable quotas for your application by enabling billing, setting a daily budget, and then allocating the budget to the quotas. You will be charged only for the resources your app actually uses, and only for the amount of resources used above the free quota thresholds.

Fixed quotas are resource maximums set by the App Engine to ensure the integrity of the system. These resources describe the boundaries of the architecture, and all applications are expected to run within the same limits. They ensure that another app that is consuming too many resources will not affect the performance of your app.

Customer Responsibility

The PaaS application customer should carefully analyze the dependencies of the application on the third-party web services (components) and outline a holistic management strategy to manage and monitor all the dependencies.

PaaS Platform Service Levels

Customers should carefully review the terms and conditions of the CSP's SLAs and understand the availability constraints.

Third-Party Web Services Provider Service Levels

When your PaaS application depends on a third-party service, it is critical to understand the SLA of that service.

PaaS Health Monitoring

The following options are available to customers to monitor the health of their service:

- Service health dashboard published by the CSP.
- CSP customer mailing list that notifies customers of occurring and recently occurred outages.
- RSS feed for RSS readers with availability and outage information.
- Internal or third-party-based service monitoring tools that periodically check your PaaS application, as well as third-party web services that monitor your application.

8. b) IaaS Availability Management

Availability considerations for the IaaS delivery model should include both a computing and storage (persistent and ephemeral) infrastructure in the cloud. IaaS providers may also offer other services such as account management, a message queue service, an identity and authentication service, a database service, a billing service, and monitoring services. Managing your IaaS virtual infrastructure in the cloud depends on five factors:

- Availability of a CSP network, host, storage, and support application infrastructure. This factor depends on the following:
    1. CSP data center architecture, including a geographically diverse and fault-tolerance architecture.
    2. Reliability, diversity, and redundancy of Internet connectivity used by the customer and the CSP.
    3. Reliability and redundancy architecture of the hardware and software components used for delivering compute and storage services.
    4. Availability management process and procedures, including business continuity processes established by the CSP.
- Availability of your virtual servers and the attached storage (persistent and ephemeral) for compute services.

*Availability of virtual storage that your users and virtual server depend on for storage service. This includes both synchronous and asynchronous storage access use cases. Synchronous storage access use cases demand low data access latency and continuous availability, whereas asynchronous use cases are more tolerant to latency and availability.

*Availability of your network connectivity to the Internet or virtual network connectivity to IaaS services. In some cases, this can involve virtual private network (VPN) connectivity between your internal private data center and the public IaaS cloud.

*Availability of network services, including a DNS, routing services, and authentication services required to connect to the IaaS service.

IaaS Health Monitoring

- Service health dashboard published by the CSP.
- CSP customer mailing list that notifies customers of occurring and recently occurred outages.
- Web console or API that publishes the current health status of your virtual servers and network.

9. a) What Are the Key Privacy Concerns in the Cloud?

These concerns typically mix security and privacy. Here are some additional considerations to be aware of,

Access

Data subjects have a right to know what personal information is held and, in some cases, can make a request to stop processing it. This is especially important with regard to marketing activities; in some jurisdictions, marketing activities are subject to additional regulations and are almost always addressed in the end user privacy policy for applicable organizations. In the cloud, the main concern is the organization's ability to provide the individual with access to all personal information, and to comply with stated requests.

Compliance

What are the privacy compliance requirements in the cloud? What are the applicable laws, regulations, standards, and contractual commitments that govern this information, and who is responsible for maintaining the compliance?

How are existing privacy compliance requirements impacted by the move to the cloud? Clouds can cross multiple jurisdictions.

Storage

Where is the data in the cloud stored? Was it transferred to another data center in another country? Is it commingled with information from other organizations that use the same CSP? Privacy laws in various countries place limitations on the ability of organizations to transfer some types of personal information to other countries. When the data is stored in the cloud, such a transfer may occur without the knowledge of the organization, resulting in a potential violation of the local law.

Retention

How long is personal information (that is transferred to the cloud) retained? Which retention policy governs the data? Does the organization own the data, or the CSP? Who enforces the retention policy in the cloud, and how are exceptions to this policy (such as litigation holds) managed?

Destruction

How does the cloud provider destroy PII at the end of the retention period? How do organizations ensure that their PII is destroyed by the CSP at the right point and is not available to other cloud users? How do they know that the CSP didn't retain additional copies? Cloud storage providers usually replicate the data across multiple systems and sites—increased availability is one of the benefits they provide. This benefit turns into a challenge when the organization tries to destroy the data—can you truly destroy information once it is in the cloud? Did the CSP really destroy the data, or just make it inaccessible to the organization? Is the CSP keeping the information longer than necessary so that it can mine the data for its own use?

Audit and monitoring

How can organizations monitor their CSP and provide assurance to relevant stakeholders that privacy requirements are met when their PII is in the cloud?

Privacy breaches

How do you know that a breach has occurred, how do you ensure that the CSP notifies you when a breach occurs, and who is responsible for managing the breach notification process (and costs associated with the process)? If contracts include liability for breaches resulting from negligence of the CSP, how is the contract enforced and how is it determined who is at fault?

9. b) SaaS Availability Management

SaaS service providers are responsible for business continuity, application, and infrastructure security management processes. This means the tasks your IT organization once handled will now be handled by the CSP. Some mature organizations that are aligned with industry standards, such as ITIL, will be faced with new challenges of governance of SaaS services as they try to map internal service-level categories to a CSP.

Customer Responsibility

Customers should understand the SLA and communication methods (e.g., email, RSS feed, website URL with outage information) to stay informed on service outages. When possible, customers should use automated tools such as Nagios or Siteuptime.com to verify the availability of the SaaS service. As of this writing, customers of a SaaS service have a limited number of options to support availability management. Hence, customers should seek to understand the availability management factors, including the SLA of the service, and clarify with the CSP any gaps in SLA exclusions and service credits when disruptions occur.

SaaS Health Monitoring

The following options are available to customers to stay informed on the health of their service:

- Service health dashboard published by the CSP. Usually SaaS providers, such as Salesforce.com, publish the current state of the service, current outages that may impact customers, and upcoming scheduled maintenance services on their website
- The Cloud Computing Incidents Database (CCID).
- Customer mailing list that notifies customers of occurring and recently occurred outages.
- Internal or third-party-based service monitoring tools that periodically check SaaS provider health and alert customers when service becomes unavailable
- RSS feed hosted at the SaaS service provider.

10. Explain cloud infrastructure security at network level

Although your organization's IT architecture may change with the implementation of a private cloud, your current network topology will probably not change significantly. If you have a private extranet in place (e.g., for premium customers or strategic partners), for practical purposes you probably have the network topology for a private cloud in place already.

The security considerations you have today apply to a private cloud infrastructure, too. And the security tools you have in place (or should have in place) are also necessary for a private cloud and operate in the same way.

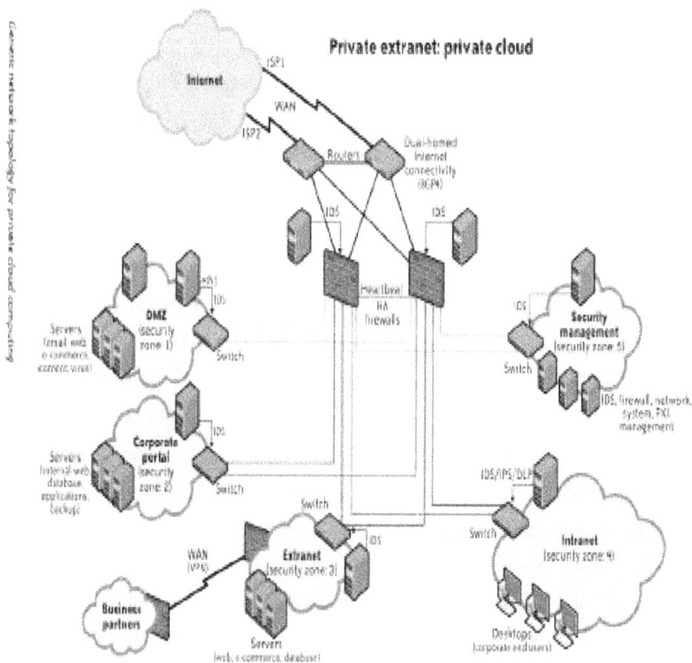

If you choose to use public cloud services, changing security requirements will require changes to your network topology. You must address how your existing network topology interacts with your cloud provider's network topology. There are four significant risk factors in this use case:

- Ensuring the confidentiality and integrity of your organization's data-in-transit to and from your public cloud provider.
- Ensuring proper access control (authentication, authorization, and auditing) to whatever resources you are using at your public cloud provider.
- Ensuring the availability of the Internet-facing resources in a public cloud that are being used by your organization, or have been assigned to your organization by your public cloud providers.
- Replacing the established model of network zones and tiers with domains.

Ensuring Data Confidentiality and Integrity

Some resources and data previously confined to a private network are now exposed to the Internet, and to a shared public network belonging to a third-party cloud provider. Although use of HTTPS (instead of HTTP) would have mitigated the integrity risk, users not using HTTPS (but using HTTP) did face an increased risk that their data could have been altered in transit without their knowledge.

Ensuring Proper Access Control

Since some subset of these resources (or maybe even all of them) is now exposed to the Internet, an organization using a public cloud faces a significant increase in risk to its data. The ability to audit the operations of your cloud provider's network (let alone to conduct any real time monitoring, such as on your own network), even after the fact, is probably non-existent. You will have decreased access to relevant network-level logs and data, and a limited ability to thoroughly conduct investigations and gather forensic data.

However, the issue of —non-aged‖ IP addresses and unauthorized network access to resources does not apply only to routable IP addresses (i.e., resources intended to be reachable directly from the Internet). The issue also applies to cloud providers' internal networks for customer use and the assignment of non-routable IP addresses.

Ensuring the Availability of Internet-Facing Resources

There are deliberate attacks as well. Although prefix hijacking due to deliberate attacks is far less common than mis configurations, it still occurs and can block access to data. According to the same study presented to NANOG, attacks occur fewer than 100 times per month. Although prefix hijackings are not new, that attack figure will certainly rise, and probably significantly, along with a rise in cloud computing.

DNS attacks are another example of problems associated with this third risk factor. In fact, there are several forms of DNS attacks to worry about with regard to cloud computing. Although DNS attacks are not new and are not directly related to the use of cloud computing, the issue with DNS and cloud computing is an increase in an organization's risk at the network level because of increased external DNS querying.

CS6703 Grid and Cloud Computing–Question Bank–IV Year CSE-7TH Semester

Question Bank

Unit I

Part A

1. Define distributed system
2. What is distributed computing?
3. List the features of distributed computing
4. Give the issues in distributed computing
5. Define clusters
6. Distinguish between centralized and distributed computing
7. Differentiate HPC and HTC.
8. What is multi core Architecture?
9. Define multithreading.
10. What is GPU computing
11. Give the features of GPU
12. What are the issues faced in exascale processing?
13. Define virtual machine.
14. What is hypervisor?
15. Define Map reduce.
16. Give the basic operations of VM
17. What is cloud computing?
18. Differ private and public cloud.
19. Compare IAAS,PAAS & SAAS
20. What is grid service?
21. What is OGSA?

Part B

1. Explain the evolution of grid computing?
2. Describe the multi core and multithreading architecture?
3. Briefly write about GPU computing?
4. Write in detail about VMs & its operations, structures.
5. Describe in detail about the Grid infrastructure.
6. Describe the Cluster architecture in detail.
7. Write briefly about SOA and its evolution.
8. Explain in detail about grid architecture, its standards, and its elements.

Unit II

Part A

1. Define grid architecture.
2. list the requirements of resource sharing?
3. What are the job execution requirements.
4. What are data requirements?
5. What are security requirements?
6. What is policy based management?
7. What is application content management?
8. List the features of OGSI.
9. What is GSR?
10. What is GSH?
11. What is grid migration?
12. Define grid security architecture?.
13. List out the OGSA services.
14. Compare Federation model and hybrid model.
15. What is data replication?
16. Define unified namespace?
17. List the Grid data access models.
18. Differentiate Monadic and hierarchical model?
19. Give the categories of Grid applications.
20. Write about the two basic software technologies of OGSA framework.

Part B

1. Explain in detail about OGSA.
2. Explain in detail about the requirements of OGSA.
3. Breifly explain about the data intensive grid service models.
4. Explain briefly about the various OGSA services.
5. Describe in detail about grid migration services and its security services.
6. Write briefly about the detailed and practical view of OGSA.

Unit III

Part A

1. What is cloud computing?
2. Define Cloud provider.
3. List the characteristics of feature cloud.
4. What are cloud deployment models?
5. List the advantages of public cloud.
6. What is hybrid cloud?
7. What are the types of cloud providers?
8. Define virtulaization.
9. Give the types of virtualization.
10. Compare full and para virtualization.
11. What is hypercall?
12. Define data center automation.
13. List the different levels of virtualization implementation.
14. Define VMM.
15. What is I/O vitualization.
16. Distinguish Physical Vs Virtual Clusters.
17. What is memory migration?
18. Write about live migration of VM using Xen.
19. What is virtual storage management.
20. Define VM based Intrusion Detection.

Part B

1. Describe in detail about the cloud categories and its deployment models?
2. Explain briefly about the various implementation levels of virtualization?
3. Explain about Virtualization structure and show how virtualization is achieved in CPU, memory and I/O devices.
4. Explain in detail about Virtual clusters.
5. Explain how resource management is done in cloud and virtualization is implemented in data centers?.

Unit IV

Part A

1. What is middleware?
2. Define GT4.
3. List the advantages of Sun grid engine.
4. Give the use of GRAM.
5. What is MDS?
6. Define Hadoop.
7. Give the modules in hadoop framework.
8. What is input splitting?
9. Give the operational modes of Hadoop?
10. List the Features of Hadoop?
11. Name some Open source grid Middleware packages.
12. Give any four Grid Standards and APIs.
13. List any five Production grids.
14. What is globus job workflow?
15. What is partial file transfer?
16. What are the factors to be provided by a high security subsystem?
17. Draw the view of GT4 components.
18. Define mapreduce.
19. How will you configure SSH?
20. Compare synchronization and communication.

Part B

1. With a neat sketch, explain briefly the GT4 Architecture?
2. Write briefly about the programming model of GT4?
3. Describe in detail about the Hadoop framework with a neat diagram?
4. Explain the concepts of Mapreduce, Configure and running a job in Hadoop?
5. Explain hadoop file system and briefly discuss the file area and write process in Hadoop?

Unit V

Part A

1. List the challenges in building trust management?

2. What are the security requirements of grid?

3. What are the types of message level security?

4. What is IAM?

5. List the components in IAM architecture provider.

6. What is privacy in cloud?

7. List the important tasks in the management of identities in cloud?

8. What is SD?

9. What is TI?

10. List Some potential security issues.

11. What is security assurance condition?

12. Give the steps accomplished in fuzzy inference.

13. Which information's are taken into account for calculating site trust worthiness?

14. What are the major authenticated methods?

15. Give the category classifications of authority?

16. What is the role of GSI functional layers?

17. What are the additional protection mechanisms of GSI?

18. Give the various levels of security.

19. Name the Cloud security controls.

20. Give some of the data security issues.

21. List the types of PHRs.

Part B

1. Discuss in detail about the various trust models in grids?.

2. Write about Authorization and Delegation in Grids?

3. Explain briefly about Grid Security Infrastructure?

4. Explain briefly about the aspects of data security, provider data and security.

5. Describe in detail about the IAM architecture and its practices in cloud.

6. Write about the various key privacy issues in the cloud?

Content beyond Syllabus

Garuda–Global Access to Resource Using Distributed Architecture

Objectives

In pursuit of scientific and technological excellence, GARUDA PoC has also brought together the critical mass of well-established researchers. PoC and Foundation phase has accomplished its target:

- Successfully created heterogeneous test bed of various operating systems, platforms, software's
- Brought together major Research, Development and User groups to GARUDA.
- Addressing long term research issues and applications in Grid computing.

The strategic objectives of operational phase being:

- Promoting active collaboration among Research, Industry, Academia, and Government through nationwide NKN
- Providing stable link, high bandwidth and low latency to the developer's community.
- Bringing in new partners both with/ without resources to maximize the utilization of GARUDA and to avail technological benefits using GARUDA.
- Focus on identifying, developing and promoting globally challenging applications/research issues.
- Enabling compute and data intensive applications of developer's on the Grid.
- Delivering guaranteed Quality of Service (QoS) and finalizing Service Level Agreements (SLA).
- Strengthening mechanisms to maximize benefits of GARUDA
- Providing stable and robust Grid environment

GARUDA Architecture

GARUDA architecture based on Service-Oriented Approach (SOA), comprises of - a set of core system components that provide system-wide services and a set of common interface definitions that resources or services may implement in order to provide users with familiar and consistent interfaces to build their applications.

Core system components of GARUDA include.

1. Network - Dependent on National Knowledge Network (NKN), connectivity through high - speed communication fabric.

2. Resources - Heterogeneous and distributed computing resources, pooling of compute and storage resources and special devices provided by C-DAC and its partners.

3. GARUDA (Federated) Information Service - keeps track of distributed GARUDA resources,

4. Security with Authentication and Authorization service - VOMS for Virtual organization and My Proxy for certificate management,

5. Job Management - Access Portal, CLI, Workflow tools and PSE form the job management interface. It deals with data movement, scheduling, reservation and accounting of jobs.

6. Access mechanisms

    a) Access Portal which primarily acts as a GUI interface for the core systems.

    b) Command line Interfaces (CLI).

    c) Workflow tools.

    d) Problem Solving Environments (PSE)

Deliverables

Grid computing technologies for operational GARUDA, covers:

- Architecture, Framework and Standards.
- Middleware and Associated tools: Development, deployment and operational support.
- Migration to inter operation with international Grids.
- Resource aggregation and coordination with resources initiative.
- Operational pilot of applications and coordination with new application initiatives.

Reg. No. : [ ][ ][ ][ ][ ][ ][ ][ ][ ][ ][ ][ ][ ]

Question Paper Code : 21294

B.E./B.Tech. DEGREE EXAMINATION, MAY/JUNE 2013.

Eighth Semester

Computer Science and Engineering

CS 2063/CS 810 — GRID COMPUTING

(Common to Seventh Semester Information Technology)

(Regulation 2008)

Time : Three hours   Maximum : 100 marks

Answer ALL questions.

PART A — (10 × 2 = 20 marks)

1. How is grid computing different from cluster and P2P computing?

2. What is the relationship between OGSA, OGSI and Web Services?

3. Specify whether OGSI/WSRF :
    (a) Communication with service instances about service data
    (b) Communication with service about resources and properties
    (c) Extensibility through inheritance
    (d) Explicitly differentiates between a stateless web service and stateful resources.

4. What is the goal of grid monitoring?

5. Which monitoring system will you prefer for the following :
    (a) Federate clusters and aggregate their states
    (b) Utilizes a relational system
    (c) Provides information service for GT3

6. Suggest component of GSI for the following :
    (a) Allows remote processes and resources to act on user's behalf
    (b) Maintains a list of authorized users on server side

7.   What are the job types supported by LSF?

8.   What is a portlet?

9.   List 2 usecases each for a datagrid and a computational grid.

10. List any two grid middleware and their functionalities

PART B — (5 × 16 = 80 marks)

11. (a) (i)   Explain the architecture of second generation grids with a neat diagram. (10)

         (ii) List out the advantages and disadvantages of the same. (6)

Or

    (b)   What architecture of grid is open technology and service-based? Explain in detail its core platform component.

12. (a) (i)   What is the purpose of a directory service in GMA? (6)

         (ii) What is GridICE? Describe its architecture. (10)

Or

    (b) (i)   What is Network Weather service? Describe its architecture with the functionality of each component. (8)

         (ii) Evaluate the same for scalability, fault tolerance, monitoring, presentation, searching and security highlighting its pros and cons in comparison with other grid monitors. (8)

13. (a) (i)   What type of scheduling is used for each of the following? Describe them (8)

              (1)   GT3

              (2)   Cluster environment.

         (ii) Describe Job lifecycle in Condor. (8)

Or

    (b) (i)   Consider two jobs – J1 and J2. Job J1 requires a resource to be atleast 80% effective and J2 requires a resource to be atleast 50% effective.

              Consider 3 resources R1, R2 and R3 whose Resource information matrix details is provided in the table below. Let CPU weight be 6 and RAM weight be 4. The minimum CPU speed is 1 GHz and the minimum RAM size is 256 MB

	CPU speed (GHz)	CPU load (%)	RAM size (MB)	RAM usage (%)
R1	1.8	50	256	50
R2	2.6	70	512	60
R3	1.2	40	512	30

Identify the resource best suited for J1 and J2. (8)

   (ii) What are the QoS that NimrodG supports? What are the components to offer these? (8)

14. (a) (i) Give the architecture of first generation of portals. What are the limitations of the same? (8)

   (ii) Describe the classes of data oriented services (8)

Or

(b) (i) Describe how the grid resources can be accessed via grid portlets, with a figure. (8)

   (ii) What extra services is needed in grid environment to manage data. Discuss data management and information services in GT3. (8)

15. (a) Describe in detail the architecture of GT3. Write the core services supported by the same.

Or

(b) What is gLite? Describe its architecture with the functionality of various components.

———————

Roll No. ☐☐☐☐☐☐☐☐☐☐☐

B.E / B.Tech (Full Time) DEGREE END SEMESTER EXAMINATIONS, APRIL / MAY 2014

INFORMATION TECHNOLOGY

Semester VI

IT9354 - Grid Computing

(Regulation 2008)

Time: 3 Hours　　　　　Answer ALL Questions　　　　　Max. Marks 100

PART-A (10 x 2 = 20 Marks)

1. Compare and contrast grid computing with cluster computing

2. How do the web services benefit the grid environment?

3. State the advantages of OGSI over WSRF.

4. What are the responsibilities of Ganglia Monitoring Daemon?

5. Write about the functionalities of Sensors and Sensor Manager of JAMM System.

6. How are the private keys secured in GSI?

7. State the three authorization modes of GSI in the server side.

8. Write the advantages of distributed scheduling over centralized scheduling in a grid environment.

9. List and specify the three execution modes of job run-time environments in Sun Grid Engine.

10. What is a Grid Portal?

Part – B (5 x 16 = 80 marks)

11. Discuss in detail the core services and base services of GT3.　　　　(16)

12. a) Explain the Grid Monitoring Architecture (GMA), its components and monitoring data.

(16)

(OR)

b) Compare and contrast between the grid monitoring tools, Monitoring and Discovery Services (MDS) and Network Weather Service (NWS) with respect to various features.

(16)

13. a) Discuss in detail the four main stages of grid scheduling. (16)

(OR)

   b) Explain the architecture of LSF grid scheduling system, its daemons, job life cycle, job management and resource management. (16)

14. a) (i) Discuss the various resource matching services provided by Portable Batch System (PBS). (8)

   (ii) Discuss the various job scheduling policies adopted in LSF. (8)

(OR)

   b) (i) Explain how mutual authentication and credential delegation are achieved in GSI. (8)

   (ii) Explain how heuristics like genetic algorithm and simulated annealing can be used in Grid Scheduling Optimization. (8)

15. a) Discuss in detail the three tier architecture of first generation grid portals, services and implementations. (16)

(OR)

   b) (i) Write a note on various categories of structured data. (8)

   (ii) Discuss the challenges associated with data management services in grid environment. (8)

Question Paper Code : 63561

M.E./M.Tech. DEGREE EXAMINATION, MAY/JUNE 2014.

Second Semester

Computer Science and Engineering

IF 7202 — CLOUD COMPUTING

(Common to M.E. Software Engineering, M.E. Mobile and Pervasive Computing,
M.E. Biometrics and Cyber Security, M.E. Multimedia Technology and
M.Tech. Information Technology)

(Regulation 2013)

Time : Three hours   Maximum : 100 marks

Answer ALL questions.

PART A — (10 × 2 = 20 marks)

1. Define Cloud Computing.

2. How does Cloud Computing provides on-demand functionality?

3. What is Information Architecture?

4. What is the use of Architectural Page Mockups?

5. Why Cloud Computing architecture has to be loose-coupled, stateless, fail-in-place computing?

6. What are the benefits offered by global exchange of cloud resources?

7. What is meant by horizontal scaling?

8. What are the modules does Apache Hadoop library includes?

9. What is trusted cloud computing?

10. What are the server security issues?

PART B — (5 × 16 = 80 marks)

11. (a) (i) Explain the NIST reference architecture of Cloud computing in detail. (10)

    (ii) Discuss about the Pros and Cons of Cloud Computing. (6)

Or

    (b) (i) Explain the Cloud deployment models and the different layers of cloud computing. (10)

    (ii) Why is cloud called as ecosystem? Justify. (6)

12. (a) (i) Explain the characteristics and types of Virtualization in Cloud Computing. (10)

    (ii) Enlist and explain some of the come pitfalls that comes with virtualization. (6)

Or

    (b) (i) Describe the various steps for live VM migration and its performance effects. (10)

    (ii) Differentiate between process virtual machines, host VMMs, native VMMs. (6)

13. (a) (i) Explain about layered cloud architecture. (10)

    (ii) Discuss about the various challenges during architectural design. (6)

Or

    (b) (i) Explain briefly about the Inter cloud resources management. (10)

    (ii) Discuss about the implementation of Elasticity while designing the cloud. (6)

14. (a) (i) What are the parallel and distributed programming paradigms? Explain the map reduce technique. (10)

    (ii) Discuss about the services offered by Amazon AWS. (6)

Or

    (b) (i) What are the programming supports of Google App Engine? Explain Google File System. (10)

    (ii) Explain the various emerging cloud software environment and explain briefly about anyone. (6)

5. (a) (i)   Explain about security controls classified in a tiered model.   (8)

        (ii)   Discuss about the virtual machine security.   (8)

                                        Or

    (b) (i)   Explain about identity management arid access control which are
               required for secure cloud computing.   (8)

        (ii)   Explain risks from multi-tenancy, with respect to various cloud
               environments.   (8)

____

Reg. No. :

Question Paper Code : 50401

B.E./B.Tech. DEGREE EXAMINATION, NOVEMBER/DECEMBER 2017

Seventh Semester

Computer Science and Engineering

CS 6703-GRID AND CLOUD COMPUTING

(Common to : Information Technology)

(Regulations 2013)

Time : Three Hours   www.recentquestion paper.com   Maximum : 100 Marks

Answer ALL questions

PART – A   (10×2=20 Marks)

1. "Grid inherits features of P2P and cluster computing systems". Is the statement true ? Validate your answer.

2. Differentiate between grid and cloud computing.

3. Compare GSH with GSR.

4. What is the purpose of grid service description ?

5. List the requirements of VMM.

6. Distinguish between physical and virtual clusters.

7. "HDFS is fault tolerant. Is it true ? Justify your answer.

8. What is the purpose of heart beat in hadoop ?

9. List any four host security threats in public IaaS.

10. Identify the trust model based on a site's trust worthiness.

PART – B   (5×16=80 Marks)

11. a) i) Describe the infrastructure requirements for grid computing.

    ii) What are the issues in cluster design ? How can they be resolved ?

    (OR)

    b) i) Describe layered grid architecture. How does it map onto internet protocol architecture ?

    ii) Describe the architecture of a cluster with suitable illustrations.

12. a) "Data produced by a large Hadron Collider may exceed several petabyts". What type of grid service model(s) will you suggest for such an application ? Illustrate with diagrams.

(OR)

b) What is OGSA ? Explain open grid services architecture in detail with the functionalities of the components.

13. a) Describe service and deployment models of a cloud computing environment with illustrations. How do they fit in NIST cloud architecture ?

(OR)

b) What is virtualisation ? Describe para and full virtualisation architectures. Compare and contrast them.

14. a) Illustrate dataflow in HDFS during file read/write operation with suitable diagrams.

(OR)

b) What is GT4 ? Describe in detail the components of GT4 with a suitable diagram.

15. a) What is the purpose of GSI ? Describe the functionality of various layers in GSI.

(OR)

b) What is the purpose of IAM ? Describe its functional architecture with an illustration.